China as Number One?

China Understandings Today

Series Editors: Mary Gallagher and Emily Wilcox

China Understandings Today is dedicated to the study of contemporary China and seeks to present the latest and most innovative scholarship in social sciences and the humanities to the academic community as well as the general public. The series is sponsored by the Lieberthal-Rogel Center for Chinese Studies at the University of Michigan.

A complete list of titles in the series can be found at www.press.umich.edu.

China as Number One?

The Emerging Values of a Rising Power

Edited by
Yang Zhong and Ronald F. Inglehart

University of Michigan Press • *Ann Arbor*

Published in the United States of America by the
University of Michigan Press
Manufactured in the United States of America
Printed on acid-free paper
First published February 2024

A CIP catalog record for this book is available from the British Library.

Library of Congress Cataloging-in-Publication Data

Names: Zhong, Yang, 1960– editor. | Inglehart, Ronald, editor. | Michigan Publishing
   (University of Michigan), publisher.
Title: China as number one? : the emerging values of a rising power / edited by Yang
   Zhong and Ronald F. Inglehart.
Other titles: Emerging values of a rising power | China understandings today.
Identifiers: LCCN 2023030662 | ISBN 9780472076352 (hardcover) | ISBN
   9780472056354 (paperback) | ISBN 9780472903733 (ebook other)
Subjects: LCSH: Power (Social sciences)—China—21st century. | Public opinion—
   China—21st century. | China—Politics and government—2002– | China—Social
   conditions—2000– | BISAC: POLITICAL SCIENCE / World / Asian
Classification: LCC DS779.46 .C432 2024 | DDC 320.951—dc23/eng/20230909
LC record available at https://lccn.loc.gov/2023030662

DOI: https://doi.org/10.3998/mpub.12529012

Open access version made available with the support of The Lieberthal-Rogel Center for
Chinese Studies (LRCCS).

The University of Michigan Press's open access publishing program is made possible
thanks to additional funding from the University of Michigan Office of the Provost and
the generous support of contributing libraries.

Contents

Digital materials related to this title can be found on the Fulcrum platform via the following citable URL: https://doi.org/10.3998/mpub.12529012

List of Tables

List of Figures

Preface | In Memory of Ronald F. Inglehart

MARY E. GALLAGHER AND YANG ZHONG

Ronald F. Inglehart, the Amy and Alan Lowenstein Professor of Democracy, Democratization, and Human Rights at the University of Michigan, died on May 8, 2021. This edited volume is his last publication as he worked on the volume until the very end of his life. Inglehart championed the expansion of the World Values Survey (WVS) to China from the 1990s, but this volume marks his first major publication on the country. Ron's interest in China and its future exemplifies his intellectual curiosity and deep desire to understand the direction of the world's most populous country and its second largest economy.

Ron Inglehart was born in 1934 in Milwaukee, Wisconsin, educated at Northwestern University in his undergraduate years and at the University of Chicago for his doctorate. Ron then taught at the University of Michigan from 1966 to 2021, a tenure of fifty-five years! Ron was strongly attached to his roots in the upper Midwest of the United States, but he was also a citizen of the world, a peripatetic scholar interested in literally everywhere. He had friends, colleagues, and students from (nearly) every continent.

Ron's intellectual contributions are numerous. He had over four hundred peer-reviewed articles and fifteen authored or co-authored books, including this one. Ron was instrumental in founding the Eurobarometer surveys and was the founding president of the World Values Survey. In 2019, he was named as the most cited political scientist.[1] Nearly all are linked to his development of evolutionary modernization theory and the use of the World Values Survey as a cross-national survey tool to capture the political values and political cultures of people across the globe. From *The Silent Revolution* (1977) to *Cultural Evolution* (2018), Ron and his colleagues, such as Christian Welzel and Pippa Norris, built on his fundamental insight that generations brought up with economic and physical security are more likely to embrace "postmaterialist values" of openness, tolerance, and equality. However, Inglehart's theory is neither deterministic nor linear. He acknowledges that cultural and religious legacies, as well as global events, matter; value shift and cultural change are always bounded by specific cultural and historical contexts. In the last decade of his life, he wrote passionately about how growing economic inequality, cultural dislocation, and political polarization in the West could roll public opinion back toward materialist values. Ron was an optimist, but he was no Pollyanna.

Although Ron is most known for his contributions to understanding Western publics and public opinion, he worked tirelessly to expand the WVS to over one hundred societies and to build social science infrastructure and knowledge as widely as possible. During his long career, Inglehart was a visiting professor or scholar in France, Germany, the Netherlands, Switzerland, Japan, South Korea, Taiwan, Brazil, Nigeria, and New Zealand. In 2010, he helped found the Laboratory for Comparative Social Research (LCSR) in the Higher School of Economics in Moscow, Russia, which was later named in Inglehart's honor. His turn to China in his last volume is entirely appropriate, as China's impressive economic and social development over the past forty years make it a fertile environment for research on value and cultural change.

Mary knew Ron as a colleague for over twenty years in the political science department at the University of Michigan. Yang had read Ron's works on modernization value shifts and postmaterialism as a graduate student more than thirty-five years ago, but he only came to know Ron personally in 2016, when he invited Ron to give a talk at the School of International and Public Affairs at Shanghai Jiao Tong University. Little did he know that one day he would be working with him in co-editing Ron's last book on China. Before he met Ron, Yang did not realize that Ron was an avid observer of Chinese politics and followed what was happening in China closely even though most of Ron's works were focused on Europe. When Yang invited Ron to be a co-editor of this volume, Ron happily and enthusiastically agreed. On numerous occasions, Ron expressed his admiration for Deng Xiaoping and his courageous reform policies; he believed that China had the potential to be a strong competitor of the United States in the world if China continued to follow the path of Deng's policies. Ron initiated the draft of Chapter 1, came up with the first half of the title of the manuscript (*China as Number One?*), and was heavily involved in the writing of the conclusion chapter.

Ron's unexpected passing in May 2021 was in the midst of the Covid-19 pandemic, just as vaccines were becoming widely available and after a terrible year of lockdowns, health system collapses in many countries, and hundreds of thousands of deaths in the United States. Ron died knowing that the United States had performed poorly in protecting its citizens and that political polarization contributed to this public health failure. He also witnessed China's surprising turnaround in early 2020 that went from an initial cover-up of the virus's spread in Wuhan, to a draconian lockdown of much of central China, and then finally to a successful campaign to control the spread of the virus domestically. Ron could not have predicted the subsequent developments of the Chinese government's Zero Covid policy, which entails sporadic lockdowns, incessant testing, and mass surveillance of the population, and the Chinese government's decision to suddenly lift the Zero Covid case policy that led to massive affections and a large number of deaths in the winter of 2022. In any event, China's early success left a deep impression on Ron as he raced to finish the volume while his health deteriorated.

Even before the onset of the pandemic, Ron's recent writings indicate that he was deeply concerned about the state of democracy across the world, and most especially in the places that he knew best, the United States and Europe. He experienced Russia's growing anti-West sentiment, making it a more difficult place in which to do research, but he did not live to witness Putin's invasion of Ukraine in February 2022 and the devastating war that has followed, with tens of millions of Ukrainians displaced, thousands killed, and the relative peace and prosperity of the post–Cold War period in Europe irrevocably ended. While it is impossible to know with certainty how Ron would have interpreted these events, it is likely that he would also worry about the declining physical and territorial security felt by many in Ukraine and surrounding countries. As a scholar with an uncanny ability to articulate how sudden economic and geopolitical changes can generate substantial and speedy social change, Ron understood that democracy and attachment to the values that sustain democracy could shift quickly in response to changing global conditions. While we mourn Ron's passing and the now impossibility of running into him on campus or at a conference to ask for his insights, which he was always so happy to give, it is heartening to observe how the institutions that he created, such as the WVS, continue to inform and educate. In March 2022, Pippa Norris and Kseniya Kizilova used WVS data from Ukraine to analyze "What mobilises the Ukrainian resistance?"[2]

The chapters in this volume also attest to Ron's incredible academic career and his long-lasting legacies to the field, to his students, and to his many colleagues, friends, and co-authors the world over. China's trajectory is uncertain and the authors in this volume do not agree on its future path or its current situation. The relative openness of the early and mid-reform years has dissipated. The government of Xi Jinping is both more capable in its control over society and more ambitious to move China in a direction that looks less like convergence with the postmaterialist values of the West and many of its neighbors. Whatever China's path may be, which is both impossible to predict or to dictate, we hope that the WVS and social science research on Chinese public opinion will continue. Ron always championed the importance of this research not only for academics and scholars but also for policymakers and politicians. We can see Ron asking in his curious and generous way, "How can leaders rule well if they don't understand what the people desire and strive for?"

According to Marita, Ron's wife, Ron was still trying to edit the chapters of this book in the hospital when he was very sick. He told Marita that he believed the book would have a major scholarly impact when it was published. Both Mary and Yang feel privileged and proud to have known Ron as a person and a scholar and to be associated with the last work of Ronald Inglehart. This edited volume is dedicated to the loving memory of Ronald Inglehart, a scholarly giant and a good friend.

Notes

1. Hannah June Kim and Bernard Grofman, "The Political Science 400: With Citation Counts by Cohort, Gender, and Subfield," *PS: Political Science & Politics* 52, no. 2 (2019): 296–311, https://doi.org/10.1017/S1049096518001786.
2. "What Mobilises the Ukrainian Resistance?" World Values Survey, March 18, 2022, https://www.worldvaluessurvey.org/WVSNewsShow.jsp?ID=449.

Bibliography

Kim, Hannah June, and Bernard Grofman. "The Political Science 400: With Citation Counts by Cohort, Gender, and Subfield." *PS: Political Science & Politics* 52, no. 2 (2019): 296–311. doi:10.1017/S1049096518001786.

ONE | Introduction

RONALD F. INGLEHART AND YANG ZHONG

As the twenty-first century enters its third decade, China is poised to become a world power and possibly to replace the United States as the dominant power in the world in the foreseeable future. The most important world event between 2020 and 2022 is no doubt the Covid-19 pandemic. In the first phase of the pandemic, between 2020 and 2021, China had done what most other countries could not. After the initial weeks' confusion and denial at the beginning of the pandemic, China had moved decisively to bring the situation under control and become the only major economy that had returned to steady growth by the end of 2020. In contrast, the performance of the United States in dealing with the pandemic in the spring of 2020 was disappointingly less effective. There is no question that the Chinese government, by adopting extreme measures, had been more successful in controlling the spread of Covid-19 cases and Covid-related death than most countries in the world. By February 2022, the U.S. Covid-related death toll reached 921,984, while Covid-19 had killed 5,726 in China (even though this fatality number is questionable).[1]

Yet, the pandemic story is an unfolding and evolving one. The tables began to turn at the beginning of 2022. As the rest of the world decided to coexist with the virus and returned to more or less normal life, the Omicron variant crept up in China in March 2022. This led to lockdowns and partial lockdowns in forty-five cities, covering one third of the Chinese population and including Shanghai and Beijing, two of the most important megacities in China. The lockdown areas count for 40 percent of the Chinese annual GDP.[2] China's strict Covid control measures,

1

including lockdowns, mass testing, and restriction of movement, caused a huge amount of suffering, anxiety, frustration, and anger throughout the affected Chinese population—not to mention economic slowdowns.[3] People also began to question the effectiveness of the Chinese government's Zero Covid strategy. As a result, the Chinese government unexpectedly and suddenly gave up the Zero Covid policy in November 2022 without much preparation, which led to massive infections and a large number of deaths.

Nonetheless, its success in the first phase of the pandemic did give a lot of people the impression that China was in a stronger position than ever before to challenge the United States economically, politically, and diplomatically, and that China could serve as a model for other countries to follow. China's approach emphasizes a relentless drive for results and relies on an acquiescent public. In mastering the pandemic, the Chinese Communist authorities suppressed speech, individual freedom, and mobility, but its leaders felt vindicated. Other societies, like New Zealand and Taiwan, had also succeeded in containing the virus in the first phase of the pandemic without China's heavy-handed measures—but their impact on global opinion is somewhat limited due to the fact that they are dwarfed by China's population of 1.4 billion people.

This book explores the potential soft power of a rising China by examining the political and social values of Chinese citizens. What values do the Chinese people hold, and how are they evolving? How different are they from the prevailing values of other countries? In answering these questions, we will draw on the World Values Survey (WVS) database, which provides several waves of surveys that enable us to track changes and continuities in the political and social values of Chinese citizens and to interpret them in cross-national comparison. The findings from this edited volume will reveal whether a distinctive set of values has emerged that could enable China to become a leader and set an example for the rest of the world.

China's Lead in the World

When *Japan as Number One* was published forty years ago, it drew widespread attention.[4] Since the end of World War II, the United States had dominated the world economically, politically, and culturally, and seemed to be a model for other countries. However, after decades of spectacular economic growth, Japan had become the number-one automobile manufacturer and, with impressive social harmony, had very low crime rates, as well as—for a time—a higher per capita GDP than the

United States. Japan seemed to be an alternative model for the world. Ironically, Japan was about to experience decades of economic stagnation. By the start of the twenty-first century, Japan no longer looked like a world model—demonstrating the fragility of forecasting the future.

But China's potential to become number one has a broader base. Already the world's leading manufacturing power, China has had the world's largest economy (based on purchasing power parity estimates) since 2016 and is rapidly catching up with the United States technologically. Currently the world leader in such fields as artificial intelligence, solar energy, 5G, biotechnology, and quantum computing,[5] China recently surpassed the United States in the number of published academic research papers.[6] China is second to the United States in terms of total research and development (R&D) spending, accounting for 20 percent of the world's R&D expenditure.[7] China's scientific and technological advances during the past forty years has been encouraged by concerted government encouragement of scientific and technological innovation, as well as massive government funding of scientific activities and international scientific cooperation.

China has transformed its agriculture-based economy to a world industrial power in a few decades. The country has a comprehensive industrial system that enables it to produce everything from the most insignificant household goods to highly sophisticated items such as huge ships and telecommunication equipment. In fact, China, being the largest exporter in world trade, is the producer of so many consumer and industrial goods that it has significant control of world supply chains, as evidenced in the world supply chain crisis during the Covid-19 pandemic.[8] China has seven of the ten busiest ports in the world.[9] Much of China's industrial success has to do with its quick and massive infrastructural expansion. China has the most mileage of high-speed railways in the world. Moreover, China is expanding its infrastructure of connectivity with the rest of the world through its "One Belt and One Road" initiative.

In educational performance, China shows great long-term promise. Since 2000, the Organization for Economic Cooperation and Development (OECD) has conducted the Program for International Student Assessment (PISA), which measures fifteen-year-olds' ability to use their reading, mathematics, and science knowledge and skills to meet real-life challenges. Table 1.1 shows the latest available results. Students in four Chinese cities and provinces (Beijing, Shanghai, Jiangsu, and Zhejiang) took the PISA tests—and earned the world's top scores. These scores are only available for four areas that are among the best-educated

Table 1.1. Average Score on Mathematics, Science, and Reading (PISA 2018)

1	China (4 cities)	579
2	Singapore	556
3	Macao	542
4	Hong Kong	531
5	Estonia	525
6	Japan	520
7	S. Korea	520
8	Canada	517
9	Taiwan	517
10	Finland	516
11	Poland	513
12	Ireland	504
13	Slovenia	503
14	United Kingdom	503
15	New Zealand	502
16	Netherlands	502
17	Sweden	502
18	Denmark	501
19	Germany	500
20	Belgium	500
21	Australia	499
22	Switzerland	498
23	Norway	497
24	Czech Rep.	495
25	United States	495
26	France	494
27	Portugal	492
28	Austria	491
29	Latvia	487
30	Russia	481
31	Iceland	481
32	Lithuania	479
33	Hungary	479
34	Italy	477
35	Luxembourg	477
36	Belarus	472
37	Croatia	472
38	Slovakia	469
39	Israel	465

Table 1.1. (*Continued*)

40	Turkey	463
41	Ukraine	463
42	Malta	459
43	Greece	453
44	Serbia	442
45	Cyprus	438
46	Chile	438
47	United Arab Emirates	434
48	Malaysia	431
49	Romania	428
50	Bulgaria	427
51	Moldova	424
52	Uruguay	424
53	Brunei	423
54	Montenegro	422
55	Albania	420
56	Jordan	416
57	Mexico	416
58	Costa Rica	415
59	Qatar	413
60	Thailand	413
61	Colombia	405
62	Kazakhstan	402
58	Azerbaijan	402
64	Bosnia	402
65	Peru	401
66	Brazil	400
67	Macedonia	400
68	Argentina	395
69	Georgia	387
70	Saudi Arabia	386
71	Indonesia	382
72	Lebanon	377
73	Morocco	368
74	Panama	365
75	Kosovo	361
76	Philippines	350
77	Domin. Rep.	334

Source: http://factsmaps.com/pisa-2018-worldwide-ranking-average-score-of-mathematics-science-reading/.

regions of China; the country as a whole would almost certainly rank lower. But Confucian-influenced societies do exceptionally well on these tests, which suggests that even China as a whole might score relatively high: Students in China, Singapore, Macao, Hong Kong, Japan, South Korea, and Taiwan earned seven of the nine top scores on the PISA tests. All of these societies have Confucian-influenced cultural heritages and, as we will see, they have relatively similar cultural values today. For centuries, it was possible to attain power and prestige through diligent study for written examinations that enabled one to advance in Confucian bureaucracies. No other culture, with the possible exception of Judaism, placed as much emphasis on education, and it seems to have had a lasting impact: Students with a Confucian cultural heritage have showed outstanding academic performance throughout the world. The role of education has become so crucial to both economic and technological development that this enhances China's likelihood of becoming an influential world power.

Militarily, China is rapidly catching up with the United States. According to a 2020 report titled *Military and Security Developments Involving the People's Republic of China*, prepared by the Pentagon, China has reached military parity or exceeded the United States in areas such as naval ships (China already has the largest navy in the world), land-based conventional ballistic and cruise missiles, and integrated air defense systems.[10] China already has the world's largest military force, with 2.8 million personnel. According to this report, China has made significant strides in military readiness and nuclear deterrence. The People's Liberation Army (PLA) has a growing presence around the world, and China has two aircraft carriers and is planning to build eight more.

The Role of Culture

As mentioned earlier, China's successful control of the spread of its Covid-19 cases in a short period of time in 2020 was probably most impressive in the eyes of the rest of the world. The Chinese government's effective handling of this worldwide disaster seemed to have raised Chinese people's confidence in the Chinese Communist Party (CCP) and was a watershed event in improving the Party's legitimacy. What the Chinese government boasted most was the country's low Covid-related death rate, even though, conceivably, this data could be underreported. However, even if we were to assume that China's actual death toll was *five times* the reported rate, it would still mean that the United States had suffered fifty-four times as many deaths per capita as China. Covid-related death rates in Japan, South Korea, Taiwan, and Singapore were also very low compared with many other countries and had per capita death rates about one **fiftieth** as high as the U.S. rate.[11] The people of Confucian-influenced societies showed relatively high levels of trust in government and willingness to conform to recommended policies, which could contribute to their remarkably low death rates—though clearly this is only part of the story. For example, both Australia and New Zealand also responded effectively to the pandemic, with New Zealand showing an even lower per capita death rate than Japan, South Korea, or Singapore.

Table 1.2 shows China's initial success in minimizing the confirmed Covid-related deaths per 100,000 people compared to another 171 countries for which reliable data was available between the beginning of the pandemic and the end of 2020. This provides an indication of the relative success that given governments had in dealing with the pandemic; however, we also need to take into account the fact that some countries show low death rates simply because they are less developed, such as Burkina Faso, Benin, Papua New Guinea, and Tanzania, which had escaped contagion at that point simply because they had relatively little contact with the rest of the world. On the other hand, China, Taiwan, Hong Kong, South Korea, Japan, Australia, and New Zealand all had high rates of interaction with the rest of the world, but nevertheless managed to have strikingly low death rates—while the United States, Brazil, and Mexico not only had the world's highest absolute numbers of deaths, but also high per capita death rates.

What explains some countries' success and other countries' failure in controlling the spread of Covid-19 during the first phase of the pandemic in 2020? While leadership and policies are obvious factors, culture also seems to play an important role, with all of the Confucian-influenced societies, including China, Taiwan, Japan, South Korea, and Singapore (shown in bold face on Table 1.2), showing relatively low death rates in the initial phase of the pandemic presumably due to more effective virus control measures. A country's cultural heritage is only one of many factors shaping public confidence in the civil service, with its actual performance being at least equally important, but the people of Confucian-influenced societies tend to manifest relatively high levels of confidence in their civil service. Thus, the publics of China, Singapore, South Korea, Macau, Hong Kong, and Taiwan all express above-average levels of confidence in their country's civil service, with their median level falling in the top quintile among 111 countries. Japan's public—after decades of economic stagnation—rates their country's civil service in the third quartile, for performance does matter. During Japan's glory years, up to

Table 1.2. Coronavirus Deaths per 100K Population on December 29, 2020

Country	Deaths	Deaths/100K *
San Marino	57	169
Belgium	19,234	168
Slovenia	2,595	126
Italy	72,370	120
Bosnia, Herzeg.	3,942	119
North Macedonia	2,456	118
Peru	37,474	117
Montenegro	675	108
Andorra	83	108
Spain	50,122	107
United Kingdom	71,217	107
Czechia	11,152	105
Bulgaria	7,251	103
United States	**334,836**	**102**
Mexico	**122,855**	**97**
Argentina	42,868	96
France	63,235	94
Armenia	2,775	94
Hungary	9,161	94
Panama	3,892	93
Liechtenstein	35	92
Brazil	**191,570**	**91**
Croatia	3,739	91
Chile	16,443	88
Switzerland	7,362	86
Colombia	42,374	85
Moldova	2,909	82
Ecuador	13,994	82
Sweden	8,279	81
Bolivia	9,106	80
Luxembourg	487	80
Romania	15,334	79
Poland	27,147	71
Kosovo	1,317	71
Austria	5,931	67
Iran	54,814	67
Portugal	6,677	65

Table 1.2. (*Continued*)

Country	Deaths	Deaths/100K *
Georgia	2,418	65
Netherlands	11,135	65
Belize	236	62
South Africa	27,071	47
Lithuania	1,269	45
Ireland	2,205	45
Malta	215	44
Bahamas	170	44
Serbia	3,073	44
Greece	4,672	44
Costa Rica	2,144	43
Ukraine	18,555	42
Canada	15,169	41
Albania	1,164	41
Tunisia	4,518	39
Jordan	3,778	38
Russia	54,559	38
Germany	31,145	38
Israel	3,256	37
Slovakia	1,879	35
Iraq	12,791	33
Honduras	3,066	32
Paraguay	2,202	32
Oman	1,495	31
Latvia	578	30
West Bank, Gaza	1,332	29
Guatemala	4,773	28
Azerbaijan	2,538	26
Turkey	20,135	24
Domin. Republic	2,404	23
Kuwait	932	23
Bahrain	351	22
Libya	1,440	22
Kyrgyzstan	1,349	21
Guyana	164	21
Suriname	120	21
Denmark	1,204	21

(*Continued*)

Table 1.2. (*Continued*)

Country	Deaths	Deaths/100K *
Cabo Verde	112	21
Lebanon	1,409	21
El Salvador	1,313	20
Morocco	7,272	20
Saudi Arabia	6,196	18
Estonia	213	16
Kazakhstan	2,689	15
Eswatini	167	15
Belarus	1,394	15
Rep. of Congo	579	11
India	148,153	11
Jamaica	298	10
Finland	546	10
Cyprus	113	10
Maldives	48	9
Trinidad, Tobago	125	9
Qatar	244	9
Philippines	9,124	9
Norway	429	8
Sao Tome Principe	17	8
Indonesia	21,452	8
Iceland	28	8
Namibia	193	8
Monaco	3	8
Egypt	7,466	8
Mauritania	330	7
U. A. E.	660	7
Equatorial Guinea	86	7
Nepal	1,832	7
Algeria	2,737	6
Djibouti	61	6
Afghanistan	2,174	6
Gambia	123	5
Antigua Barbuda	5	5
Myanmar	2,618	5
Pakistan	9,992	5
Uruguay	160	5

Table 1.2. (*Continued*)

Country	Deaths	Deaths/100K *
Bangladesh	7,479	5
Syria	686	4
Australia	909	4
Venezuela	1,018	4
Sudan	1,468	4
Kenya	1,664	3
Gabon	64	3
Saint Lucia	5	3
Nicaragua	164	3
Japan	**3,152**	**2**
Senegal	390	2
Zimbabwe	354	2
Barbados	7	2
Lesotho	51	2
Guinea-Bissau	45	2
Zambia	384	2
Yemen	607	2
Haiti	236	2
Uzbekistan	613	2
Cameroon	448	2
Botswana	40	2
Ethiopia	1,912	2
Liberia	83	2
South Korea	**859**	**2**
Malaysia	455	1
Cen. African Rep.	63	1
Mali	256	1
Angola	403	1
Cuba	143	1
Ghana	333	1
Malawi	188	1
Madagascar	261	1
Sierra Leone	76	1
Tajikistan	90	1
Sri Lanka	194	1
Togo	68	1

(*Continued*)

Table 1.2. (*Continued*)

Country	Deaths	Deaths/100K *
Somalia	127	1
Comoros	7	1
Mauritius	10	1
Brunei	3	1
Chad	104	1
Nigeria	1,264	1
Guinea	80	1
Rwanda	75	1
Uganda	248	1
South Sudan	62	1
Mozambique	162	1
Côte d'Ivoire	137	1
Singapore	**29**	**1**
New Zealand	25	1
Niger	99	.44
Burkina Faso	78	.39
Benin	44	.38
China	**4,775**	**.34**
Dem. Rep. Congo	107	.13
Papua New Guinea	9	.10
Thailand	60	.09
Tanzania	21	-04
Vietnam	35	.04
Taiwan	**7**	**.03**

Source: Johns Hopkins Coronavirus Resource Center, https://coronavirus.jhu.edu/data/mortality.
* Rounded to nearest whole number except when that number would be zero

1990, its civil service, particularly the Ministry of International Trade and Industry (MITI), was widely credited with playing a key role in directing the country's success. Subsequent decades of relative stagnation seem to have tarnished that reputation. Nevertheless, the Confucian-influenced societies, including Japan, share a long-established cultural tradition of a merit-recruited Mandarin bureaucracy through which talented people, even from low-income backgrounds, could rise to positions of prestige and power by passing a series of examinations. This cultural heritage seems to make people relatively likely to comply with government directives. Thus, when the SARS pandemic broke out in 2003, the people of these societies readily complied with quarantines and wearing face masks in public—and when the Covid crisis subsequently erupted, many people in Hong Kong and Taiwan spontaneously began wearing masks without any government prodding. One downside should be pointed out, however: A compliant culture is not conducive to an environment in which leaders' choices, especially wrong decisions or mistakes, can be challenged and corrected, as evidenced by the Chinese government's seemingly irrational Zero Covid policy in 2022.

A large body of survey evidence indicates that China is part of a Confucian-influenced cultural zone, in which the various countries have relatively similar values. From 1981 to 2020, the World Values Survey (WVS) and European Values Study (EVS) have carried out hundreds of surveys in more than one hundred countries containing over 90 percent of the world's population.[12] These surveys cover the full range of cultural, economic, and political variation. Factor analysis of data from the forty-three countries covered in the 1990 WVS indicates that just two dimensions—a Traditional/Secular-rational values dimension and a Survival/Self-expression values dimension—account for over half of the cross-national variance in people's responses to scores of questions.[13] When this analysis was replicated with data from successive surveys, these same two dimensions again emerged—although the new surveys included dozens of additional countries.[14] Using these two dimensions, one can construct a cultural map on which the responses to many questions are boiled down to a mean score for each country, making it possible to place each country on a cultural map, and to examine broad patterns of cross-cultural variation on one compact figure.

Figure 1.1 shows where each of the forty-three countries surveyed in 2017–2019 fall on this global cultural map. It sums up the cross-national differences in people's views on a wide variety of topics, from religion to politics to sexual norms to attitudes toward work. As this figure indicates, the various Confucian-influenced countries have relatively similar locations—and this has been true in wave after wave of World Values Surveys.[15]

The vertical dimension of Figure 1.1 reflects the transition from agrarian to industrial society, which brings secularization, bureaucratization, urbanization, and rationalization; these changes are linked with a polarization between Traditional and Secular-rational values. Societies whose people have traditional religious values fall toward the bottom of Figure 1.1; those with Secular-rational values fall near the top. The people of traditional societies emphasize religion, consider large families

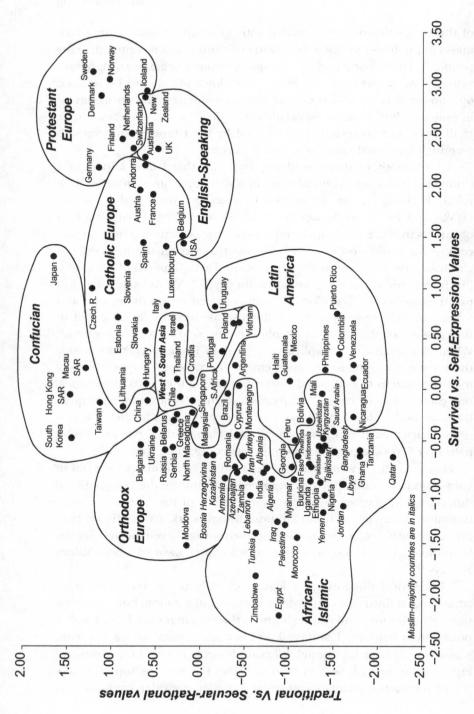

Figure 1.1. Global Cultural Map in 2017–2020

Source: Data from the 7th wave of the World Values Survey and European Values Study carried out between 2017-2020 (fieldwork was interrupted in

Table 1.3. Percent Saying God Is Very Important in Their Lives

Confucian-influenced	8
Protestant Europe	11
Catholic Europe	21
English-speaking	25
Orthodox	43
South Asia	53
Latin America	58
African/Islamic	74

desirable, and support showing more respect for authority; they also rank relatively low on achievement motivation and oppose divorce, abortion, and homosexuality. The people of other societies fall toward the opposite end of the spectrum on all of these orientations. There is a huge gap between the values of societies near the top of the map and those near the bottom: As Table 1.3 demonstrates, the percentage saying that God is very important in their lives ranges from 8 percent among the Confucian-influenced countries and only 3 percent in China (part of the Confucian zone but also shown separately) to 78 percent in the countries in the African-Islamic cultural zone.

Traditional values are negatively linked with a society's level of economic development, but positively linked with high fertility rates. Societies with Traditional values tend to emphasize maintaining the family and having many children, and it is not just a matter of lip service.

The transition from industrial society to knowledge society gives rise to another major dimension of cross-cultural variation on which a wide range of orientations are structured. The horizontal dimension of Figure 1.1 reflects the degree to which a society emphasizes Survival values and Materialist values (toward the left of the figure) or Self-expression values and Postmaterialist values (toward the right). Societies that emphasize Self-expression values and Postmaterialist values support gender equality and environmental protection and are far more tolerant of foreigners, members of the LGBTQIA+ community, and other outgroups compared to those that emphasize Survival values. This tolerance of diversity is linked with the fact that these countries tend to be democracies.

The peoples of the various cultural zones also show a wide range of values across the horizontal dimension. As Table 1.4 indicates, the people of the Confucian-influenced countries have the highest percentage of Materialist values found in any cultural zone, with China being

Table 1.4. Percent Having Materialist Values

Protestant Europe	15
English-speaking	20
Catholic Europe	24
Latin America	25
African/Islamic	38
South Asia	41
Orthodox	42
Confucian-influenced	44
China	(50)

slightly more materialist than the other Confucian-influenced countries. Although these countries are relatively prosperous today, this reflects the fact that for the past several decades, they have had the world's highest growth rates—and Materialist/Postmaterialist values largely reflect the degree of existential security experienced during one's preadult years. Consequently, there is a substantial time lag between the point at which a country reaches a high level of economic and physical security, and the point at which the adult population as a whole shows a high percentage of Postmaterialists. Protestant Europe and the English-speaking countries had already attained high levels of existential security by the 1970s, but China is still in the process of doing so. Nevertheless, as Table 1.5 shows, the Confucian-influenced countries (including China) show slightly higher levels of support for gender equality than the Orthodox or South Asian countries, and considerably higher levels than the African-Islamic countries. In keeping with the fact that China has a considerably lower income level than the other Confucian-influenced countries,

Table 1.5. Percent Saying Men Make Better Political Leaders than Women

Protestant Europe	14
English-speaking	17
Latin America	22
Catholic Europe	27
Confucian-influenced	48
China	(50)
Orthodox	52
South Asia	58
African/Islamic	70

the Chinese show somewhat more traditional values in Tables 1.5 and 1.6, but the difference is modest: In global perspective, the Confucian-influenced countries have relatively similar values.

As Table 1.6A indicates, Confucian-influenced societies—along with Protestant Europe—have relatively high levels of interpersonal trust, but as shown in Table 1.6B, they are relatively unwilling to engage in protest activities, such as signing a petition.

The main framework for this edited volume is modernization theory, especially evolutionary modernization theory. Evolutionary modernization theory holds that rising levels of existential security encourage a shift from Traditional values to Secular-rational values, and from Survival values to Self-expression values.[16] Accordingly, virtually all of the high-income countries rank high on both dimensions, falling into the upper-right region of the chart—while virtually all of the low and lower-middle-income countries rank low on both dimensions, falling into the lower-left region of the chart.

Table 1.6A. Percent Saying "Most People Can Be Trusted"

Protestant Europe	58
China	(64)
Confucian-influenced	48
English-speaking	43
Catholic Europe	28
Orthodox	19
African/Islamic	17
South Asia	14
Latin America	13

Table 1.6B. Percent Saying They Have Signed, or Might Sign, a Petition

English-speaking	93
Protestant Europe	86
Catholic Europe	71
Latin America	65
Confucian-influenced	59
China	(49)
Orthodox	44
South Asia	36
African/Islamic	30

But the evidence also supports the Weberian view that a society's cultural-religious heritage leaves a lasting imprint. Thus, the publics of the Confucian-influenced societies show relatively similar values across scores of questions—as do those of Protestant Europe, Catholic Europe, the Orthodox societies, the English-speaking countries, Latin America, and the African-Islamic zone. These clusters do not necessarily coincide with geographic proximity. Thus, the English-speaking zone extends from Great Britain to the United States to Australia, while the Latin American zone extends from Tijuana to Patagonia.

For those whose top priorities are gender equality, tolerance of outgroups, environmental protection, and democracy, the Nordic countries look like a desirable example to follow. But for the people of low-income countries, the impressive recent performances of the Confucian-influenced countries in economic growth and life expectancy may make China a more immediately attractive model.

As Table 1.7 indicates, the Nordic countries include six of the twelve top-ranking countries among the 189 countries included on the UN Human Development index. The Nordic countries also rank high on numerous other indicators of well-functioning societies, from low homicide rates and high economic equality to environmental protection and democracy. This largely reflects the fact that the Nordic peoples have had the good fortune to grow up under a combination of circumstances, including prosperity and high life expectancy, that produce a relatively strong sense of existential security. And one of the enduring realities of human behavior seems to be that secure people tend to behave better than desperate ones. The most prosperous Confucian-influenced societies—Hong Kong, Singapore, and Japan—also rank high on the Human Development index.[17] Countries with high Human Development scores tend to have much higher levels of gender equality, more tolerance of foreigners and ethnic minorities, higher levels of environmental protection, lower levels of corruption, and a higher likelihood of having democratic political institutions.

Though the Confucian-influenced countries have relatively similar basic cultural beliefs, they have widely differing political institutions, as Table 1.8 demonstrates. Freedom House uses expert ratings to evaluate the state of freedom in countries around the world. Each country is assigned between 0 and 4 points on a series of twenty-five indicators, including (1) Elections to executive, (2) Elections to legislature, (3) Full political rights for minorities, and (4) Freedom from pervasive corruption. These scores are used to rank countries from most free to least free.[18]

Table 1.7. UN Human Development Rankings in 2018

	Life Expectancy	Expected Years of Schooling	GDP/Capita (PPP $)
1 Norway	82.3	18.1	$68,059
2 Switzerland	83.6	16.2	59,375
3 Ireland	82.1	18.8	55,660
4 Germany	81.2	17.1	46,946
5 Hong Kong	84.7	16.5	60,221
6 Australia	83.3	22.1	44,097
7 Iceland	82.9	19.2	47,566
8 Sweden	82.7	18.8	47,958
9 Singapore	83.5	16.2	83,793
10 Netherlands	82.1	18.0	50,013
11 Denmark	80.8	19.1	48,836
12 Finland	81.7	19.3	41,779
13 Canada	82.3	16.1	43,602
14 New Zealand	82.1	18.8	35,108
15 United Kingdom	81.2	17.4	39,507
16 United States	78.9	16.3	56,140
17 Belgium	81.5	19.7	43,821
18 Liechtenstein	80.5	14.7	99,732
19 Japan	84.5	15.2	40,799
20 Austria	81.4	16.3	46,231
86 China	76.4	13.8	15,270
158 Nigeria	54.3	9.7	5,086

Source: United Nations, Human Development Report, 2019, http://hdr.undp.org/en.

Table 1.8 shows Freedom House's 2018 democracy rankings for the fifty highest-ranked countries plus a number of others. As it indicates, Nordic countries get the three highest rankings, with Finland, Norway, and Sweden rated as the world's most democratic countries. Among Confucian-influenced societies, Japan ranks 12th and Taiwan ranks 22nd, placing them above such long-established democracies as the United Kingdom and France, and far above the United States, which by 2018 had fallen to 33rd place, not far above South Korea, which ranked 40th. On the other hand, China ranked 145th and North Korea ranked 152nd out of 159 countries with populations over one million. The fact that both Japan and Taiwan now rank among the world's stable democracies

Table 1.8. Freedom House Democracy Rankings in 2018, Based on Combined Political Rights and Civil Liberties Scores

1 Finland	31 Greece
2 Norway	32 Latvia
3 Sweden	33 United States
4 Canada	34 Croatia
5 Netherlands	35 Mongolia
6 Australia	36 Argentina
7 New Zealand	37 Panama
8 Uruguay	38 Poland
9 Denmark	39 Ghana
10 Ireland	40 South Korea
11 Belgium	41 Trinidad
12 Japan	42 Romania
13 Portugal	43 Bulgaria
14 Switzerland	44 Benin
15 Chile	45 South Africa
16 Cyprus	46 Israel
17 Estonia	47 Jamaica
18 Germany	48 Brazil
19 Slovenia	49 India
20 Spain	50 Namibia
21 Austria	72 Indonesia
22 Taiwan	89 Singapore
23 United Kingdom	91 Nigeria
24 Costa Rica	102 Bangladesh
25 Czech Rep.	105 Pakistan
26 Lithuania	115 Turkey
27 France	129 Russia
28 Italy	145 China
29 Mauritius	152 North Korea
30 Slovakia	159 Syria

Source: Freedom House, *Freedom in the World, 2019,* 16. This page only shows countries with populations of one million or more.

undermines the claim that the values of Asian societies are incompatible with democracy. On the other hand, Singapore demonstrates that, despite the strong tendency for prosperity to be linked with democratic institutions, it is possible for an extremely prosperous society to function with an authoritarian government. And finally, the extremely low scores of China and North Korea demonstrate that less prosperous Confucian-influenced societies are compatible with extremely authoritarian institutions.

China's success in handling the pandemic reinforced its leaders' conviction that an authoritarian capacity to quickly mobilize people and resources gave China a decisive edge over other major powers like the United States. This is part of the story, but only part of it: A crucial element was the fact that for decades China adopted market-driven economic reforms and opening up. China's recent success was not inevitable. It had been badly governed for most of the past two centuries. And China's success did not happen because authoritarian governments are more effective than democracies. The Communist Party of the Soviet Union also had an authoritarian government that penetrated every sector of society, but under Leonid Brezhnev it fell further behind the West every year—not only in consumer goods, but in top-priority areas such as computers and intercontinental ballistic missiles. It got to the point that when Mikhail Gorbachev took power, he realized that the Communist Party had become a self-interested ruling class that was preventing much-needed reforms. This tendency is typical of authoritarian governments, which from Zimbabwe to Venezuela have been textbook examples of mismanagement—and China under Mao suffered disasters that cost millions of lives. China's recent success reflects the adoption of a distinctive version of authoritarian rule developed by Deng Xiaoping that incorporated some of democracy's key advantages, such as collegial rule for limited terms and political decentralization.

What China has accomplished since then is remarkable, but it doesn't necessarily reflect the superiority of authoritarian rule. China's recent economic miracle largely reflects Deng's policies of pragmatic market-oriented reforms and a regionally decentralized authoritarian system that made local experimentation possible and gave the Chinese people much freedom to pursue a better economic life. A large portion of credit for China's economic success should go to the Chinese people, who are hardworking and industrious, and who seized the opportunity to improve their economic circumstances. Deng's credit was that he transformed the Chinese economy from an ideologically driven system to a pragmatic one in which Deng and his colleagues experimented to see what worked. The results led them to move away from a state-run economy toward a market-driven economy, bringing annual growth rates of close to 10 percent for more than two decades—and rescuing hundreds of millions of Chinese citizens from desperate poverty.

Given its successes and relatively new international status, will China be successful in offering an attractive alternative set of values to compete with the United States and become the world's most influential power? Findings from this edited volume may provide some hints to answer this question. A key feature of this edited volume is that all the authors use World Values Survey data, which allow us not only to track the trends of social and political value changes and continuities inside China, but also to compare China with its neighbors and countries in other regions.[19] Our substantive chapters cover just about all the questions asked in World Value Surveys. If China is going to be a true world model, hardware such as economic might and military prowess will certainly not be enough. In other words, China must have sufficient soft power to be true challenger to the dominant position of the United States. According to Joseph Nye, who introduced the concept of soft power, the United States still has enough soft power to sustain American superpower status in the world.[20] The United States had won the Cold War without firing a shot, he argued. The collapse of the Soviet Union was largely due to its failed performance and unattractive official ideology.

The triumph of Western liberalism and the Third Wave of democratization in the 1990s led to Francis Fukuyama's claim that democracy was "the only game in town." But not long afterward, this liberal euphoria disappeared and democratic decline became evident, even in established Western democracies. It is uncertain how lasting this democratic backsliding will be, and it remains unclear whether a viable non-democratic alternative ideology has yet emerged.

This edited volume consists of eight chapters, which cover virtually all WVS questions in different waves of the WVS conducted in China over the past three decades. Wenfang Tang examines democratic or authoritarian political culture in the Chinese population in Chapter 2. Tang's analysis of how the Chinese people understand freedom, democracy, and human rights concludes that China has a democratic authoritarian political culture. He presents evidence that a majority of the Chinese people feel free and believe that they live in a democracy. But their understanding of democracy differs from the prevailing Western definition, which views the right to choose the country's leaders through elections that offer a choice between freely competing alternatives as an essential component of any democracy. Tang's view of democracy emphasizes social justice rather than competitive elections, and his evidence indicates that a majority of the Chinese public today prefer a strong leader who can ensure their economic well-being. As of 2018, they seemed to be satisfied with their country's level of democracy.

In Chapter 3, Lingnan He and Dali Yang explore the extent to which a participant political culture has emerged in China. Analyzing survey data covering the years 2007 to 2018, they find that online participation has taken shape and flourished over this period. However, they also find a decline in the percentage of people reporting that they are interested in politics, with growing numbers of people claiming that they are not. This holds true despite the fact that income and education—both of which are positively linked with political activism—have been rising rapidly during this period. Xi Jinping's contemporaneous rise to power may have had a dampening effect on this measure.

In Chapter 4, Yu Yan focuses on how growing feelings of security are reshaping the Chinese people's values, in particular, examining whether China's phenomenal economic growth is producing an intergenerational value shift toward postmaterialist values. In keeping with Inglehart's theory, Yan finds that the Chinese are less postmaterialist than the people of more affluent societies in both East Asia and the West, and that every Chinese age group holds values that are more materialistic than those of their counterparts in more developed countries. Nevertheless, survey data from 1995 to 2018 indicate that the younger generations are likelier than their elders to hold postmaterialist values, and that the Chinese public as a whole has become increasingly postmaterialist over time. But the rise of postmaterialism has weakened in recent years, suggesting the presence of a strong period effect that might be linked with the impact of Xi.

In Chapter 5, John James Kennedy examines changes and continuities in the social values of Chinese citizens over the past three decades. He finds that a growing share of the Chinese people are coming to hold such liberal values as the acceptance of homosexuality, divorce, and gender equality—though they are not yet as far advanced in this respect as their more prosperous Confucian-influenced neighbors in South Korea, Japan, Taiwan, and Hong Kong. Kennedy's analyses also show that younger people tend to hold more liberal social values than their elders, and that more educated and higher-income respondents have more liberal values than their less educated and less prosperous compatriots. This pattern is also observed in South Korea, Japan, Taiwan, and Hong Kong. Thus, as China experiences modernization and industrialization, it seems to be following trends similar to those found elsewhere in the world. But Kennedy also finds rising support for certain traditional values in the latest Chinese survey in 2018, leading him to suspect that Xi Jinping's increasing emphasis on traditional Chinese culture may contribute to this new conservative trend—which does not change the fact that younger people continue to hold stronger socially liberal and postmaterialist values than older people.

In Chapter 6, Alfred Wu, Eduardo Araral, and Biao Huang investigate public trust in contemporary China. Analyzing data from successive waves of surveys carried out from 1990 to 2018, the authors find that generalized interpersonal trust has increased over the past two decades. They also find that trust in strangers, people of another religion, and people of another nationality has increased during the last five years (though trust in the family showed a slight decline). The absolute percentage of Chinese saying most people can be trusted is significantly higher than in other Asian and Western societies. This is also true of the Chinese public's trust in government and governmental institutions. Moreover, the most recent (2018) WVS in China indicates that public confidence in political and public authorities has increased in recent years, perhaps due to better public services at the local level and the massive anti-corruption campaign of Xi Jinping's era.

In Chapter 7, Yang Zhong examines the Chinese public's level of religiosity and their attitudes toward science and technology. Evidence from surveys carried out since 1990 consistently indicates that China is one of the world's least religious countries, with an overwhelming majority of the public claiming to be non-religious. Nevertheless, starting from a very low base, religion has gained some ground. The latest WVS (2018) shows that 16 percent of the Chinese people hold religious beliefs, a substantial increase from the 5 percent found in 1990. During this period, the number of people claiming to be atheists dropped from 42 percent in 1990 to 34 percent in 2018. The citizens of both Hong Kong and Taiwan are more religious. On the other hand, survey evidence consistently demonstrates that an overwhelming majority of the Chinese people are strong supporters of science and technology, though a sizable segment of the Chinese population is worried that science may break down people's ideas of right and wrong. Nevertheless, when facing a potential conflict between religion and science, an overwhelming majority of mainland Chinese choose science. The people of Hong Kong and Taiwan are more critical of science and technology than those of mainland China, which may reflect intense Chinese official efforts to promote science and technology as key factors in enabling China to become a stronger country and a world power.

In Chapter 8 that concludes the book, Zhong and Inglehart summarize the major findings of the previous chapters and offer their observations and assessments of Chinese culture in the context of evolutionary modernization theory. They argue that the social, political, and economic values of the Chinese people are not drastically different from other countries, including China's neighbors. Most importantly, Chinese people's values are in line with the trajectory of a modernizing society impacted by crucial factors such as economic development level, education, and age. Zhong and Inglehart further argue that China still lacks a credible official ideology and an alternative set of social, political, and economic values and culture at the popular level to challenge the dominant soft power position of the United States. Due to its lack of soft power projection around the world, China still has some way to go to make itself a Number One power in the world in the foreseeable future.

Notes

1. Figures are cited from World Health Organization. See https://covid19.who.int/.

2. See https://www.wenxuecity.com/news/2022/05/02/11530809.html.

3. See Jessie Yeung, "180 Million People Impacted by China's Covid Lockdowns. Here's What You Need to Know," *CNN*, April 29, 2022, https://www.cnn.com/2022/04/28/china/china-covid-lockdown-explainer-intl-hnk/index.html.

4. Ezra Vogel, *Japan as Number One: Lessons for America* (Cambridge, MA: Harvard University Press, 1979).

5. Julian Baird Gewirtz, "China's Long March to Technological Supremacy: The Roots of Xi Jinping's Ambition to Catch Up and Surpass," *Foreign Affairs*, August 27, 2019, https://www.foreignaffairs.com/articles/china/2019-08-27/chinas-long-march-technological-supremacy.

6. Yanfei Li, "Understanding China's Technological Rise: The Three Factors Underlying China's Transformation into A Rising Technology Powerhouse," *The Diplomat*, August 3, 2018, https://thediplomat.com/2018/08/understanding-chinas-technological-rise/.

7. Reinhilde Veugelers, "China Is the World's New Science and Technology Powerhouse," *Bruegel*, August 30, 2017, https://www.bruegel.org/2017/08/china-is-the-worlds-new-science-and-technology-powerhouse/?utm_content=buffercd9dc&utm_medium=social&utm_source=twitter.com&utm_campaign=buffer+(bruegel).

8. Bonnie S. Glaser, "The Impact of China's Dominant Position in Global Supply Chains: A Conversation with Wang Tao," *CSIS*, September 8, 2020, https://www.csis.org/podcasts/chinapower/impact-chinas-dominant-position-global-supply-chains-conversation-wang-tao.

9. See Daniel Ren, "China Has Seven of the World's 10 Busiest Container Ports, Spurred by Booming Trade and a State Coffer That Invests in Public Works," *SCMP*, April 13, 2019, https://www.scmp.com/business/companies/article/3005945/china-has-six-worlds-10-busiest-container-ports-spurred-booming.

10. See *Military and Security Developments Involving the People's Republic of China: Annual Report to Congress* (Washington, DC: Office of the Secretary of Defense, 2020), 9, https://media.defense.gov/2020/Sep/01/2002488689/-1/-1/1/2020-DOD-CHINA-MILITARY-POWER-REPORT-FINAL.PDF.

11. "Mortality Analyses," Johns Hopkins Coronavirus Resource Center, December 28, 2020, https://coronavirus.jhu.edu/data/mortality.

12. The data, together with the questionnaires and fieldwork information, can be downloaded from the WVS website at http://www.worldvaluessurvey.org/.

13. For greater detail on how the two dimensions were constructed, see Ronald Inglehart, "Value Systems: The Subjective Aspect of Politics and Economics," in *Modernization and Postmodernization: Culture, Economic, and Political Change in 43 Societies* (Princeton: Princeton University Press, 1997).

14. Inglehart, "Value Systems"; Ronald Inglehart and Wayne Baker, "Modernization and Cultural Change and the Persistence of Traditional Values," *American Sociological Review* 65, no. 1 (2000): 19–51; Ronald Inglehart and Christian Welzel, *Modernization, Cultural Change, and Democracy: The Human Development Sequence* (New York: Cambridge University Press, 2005); Ronald Inglehart and Christian Welzel, "Changing Mass Priorities: The Link between Modernization and Democracy," *Perspectives on Politics* 8, no. 2 (2010): 551–67.

15. In most respects, Singapore is part of the Confucian-influenced cultural zone, but its position on this map is drawn down from the Secular-rational pole by the fact that 39 percent of its resident population is Christian, Muslim, or Hindu.

16. For a full presentation of evolutionary modernization theory, see Inglehart, *Modernization and Postmodernization*.

17. Taiwan is not ranked by UNDP.

18. For complete information on the methodology, see https://freedomhouse.org/report/freedom-world-2018/methodology.

19. All the WVS data and survey methodology (including survey design and questionnaires) can be found on WVS website at https://www.worldvaluessurvey.org/wvs.jsp.

20. Joseph Nye, *Bound To Lead: The Changing Nature of American Power* (New York: Basic Books, 1990).

Bibliography

Gewirtz, Julian Baird. "China's Long March to Technological Supremacy: The Roots of Xi Jinping's Ambition to 'Catch Up and Surpass.'" *Foreign Affairs*, August 27, 2019, https://www.foreignaffairs.com/articles/china/2019-08-27/chinas-long-march-technological-supremacy.

Inglehart, Ronald. "Value Systems: The Subjective Aspect of Politics and Economics." Chap. 1 in *Modernization and Postmodernization: Culture, Economic, and Political Change in 43 Societies.* Princeton: Princeton University Press, 1997.

Inglehart, Ronald, and Christian Welzel. "Changing Mass Priorities: The Link between Modernization and Democracy." *Perspectives on Politics* 8, no. 2 (2010): 551–67.

Inglehart, Ronald, and Christian Welzel. *Modernization, Cultural Change, and Democracy: The Human Development Sequence.* New York: Cambridge University Press, 2005.

Inglehart, Ronald, and Wayne Baker. "Modernization and Cultural Change and the Persistence of Traditional Values." *American Sociological Review* 65, no. 1 (2000): 19–51.

Li, Yanfei. "Understanding China's Technological Rise: The Three Factors Underlying China's Transformation into A Rising Technology Powerhouse." *The Diplomat,* August 3, 2018, https://thediplomat.com/2018/08/understanding-chinas-technological-rise/.

Nye, Joseph. *Bound To Lead: The Changing Nature of American Power.* New York: Basic Books, 1990.

Veugelers, Reinhilde. "China Is the World's New Science and Technology Powerhouse." *Bruegel,* August 30, 2017, https://www.bruegel.org/2017/08/china-is-the-worlds-new-science-and-technology-powerhouse/?utm_content=buffercd9dc&utm_medium=social&utm_source=twitter.com&utm_campaign=buffer+(bruegel).

TWO | Democratic Authoritarianism: A Study
of Chinese Political Orientations[1]

WENFANG TANG

Introduction

Freedom, democracy, and human rights are the cornerstones of a political system in the Western liberal world. This chapter will examine these concepts in the Chinese context. It will show how Chinese survey respondents view these ideas in relation to their own political system and how such perception differs from the way Western liberal elites (WLEs) portray China. The findings show that

1. Chinese citizens feel just as free or even freer than people in some liberal democratic societies;
2. the Chinese love democracy, perhaps just as much if not more than their Western liberal counterparts;
3. their understanding of democracy includes both political rights and social justice;
4. they are satisfied with their country's democracy;
5. they support government surveillance in public spaces but less so in private life; and
6. they prefer a strong leader with technical expertise to protect social justice.

The takeaway points of this study are that (1) assessment of democracy should be conducted by WLEs as well as by the public who live in their own society; (2) the majority of the Chinese public appears to enjoy plenty of freedom, democracy, and human rights; and (3) in China, there is a strong populist authoritarian tendency in which a strong leader can protect people's well-being in exchange for their political support.

Freedom

Western political scientists and social elites spend a lot of time every year assessing the level of democracy, freedom, and human rights in countries and regions around the world. One example of an organization engaged in this work is the widely popular and self-proclaimed authority Freedom House. Its "Board of Trustees is comprised of prominent business and labor leaders, former diplomats and senior government officials, scholars, and journalists" in the United States.[2] It publishes annual reports on its website, freedomhouse.org, ranking the levels of freedom in different countries and regions.

Under the leadership of its Board of Trustees, Freedom House's reports rely on a number of criteria to assess freedom, democracy, and human rights under the two general categories of political rights and civil liberty. Political rights consist of free and fair elections, multi-party competition and public participation in decision-making, and a representative, clean, and accountable government. Civil liberty is defined by freedom of expression and belief, associational and organizational rights, rule of law, personal autonomy, individual rights to travel and to own property, and social justice and minority rights.

Using the above criteria, the countries and regions that are ranked on top are overwhelmingly Western liberal societies (Figure 2.1a). Also as predicted, post-Communist and Communist societies such as Uzbekistan, Belarus, and China are ranked at the very bottom with zero or close to zero degrees of freedom, democracy, and human rights. These results are highly consistent with the Western liberal media's anti-Communist rhetoric. They come as no surprise if one takes a quick look at the above-mentioned composition of interests represented on Freedom House's Board of Trustees.

The criteria used for the Freedom House reports were developed by Western political and social elites. Freedom House is by no means the only organization that produces such reports. Another example of a similar Western liberal perspective is *Democracy Report 2021* by the V-Dem Institute, which gives China a very similar near-bottom score. In that report, China is ranked 174th out of 179 countries and regions for

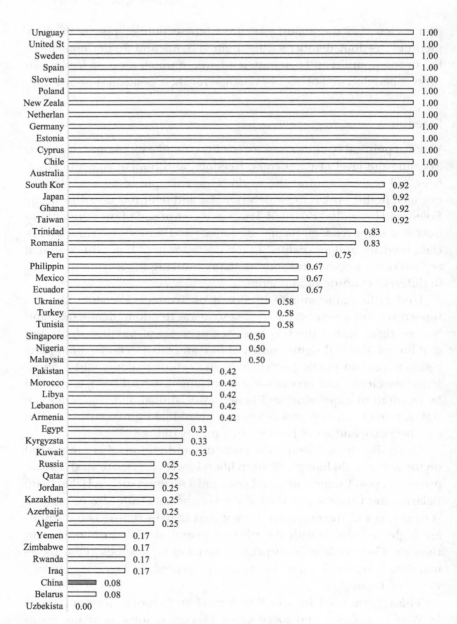

Uruguay	1.00
United St	1.00
Sweden	1.00
Spain	1.00
Slovenia	1.00
Poland	1.00
New Zeala	1.00
Netherlan	1.00
Germany	1.00
Estonia	1.00
Cyprus	1.00
Chile	1.00
Australia	1.00
South Kor	0.92
Japan	0.92
Ghana	0.92
Taiwan	0.92
Trinidad	0.83
Romania	0.83
Peru	0.75
Philippin	0.67
Mexico	0.67
Ecuador	0.67
Ukraine	0.58
Turkey	0.58
Tunisia	0.58
Singapore	0.50
Nigeria	0.50
Malaysia	0.50
Pakistan	0.42
Morocco	0.42
Libya	0.42
Lebanon	0.42
Armenia	0.42
Egypt	0.33
Kyrgyzsta	0.33
Kuwait	0.33
Russia	0.25
Qatar	0.25
Jordan	0.25
Kazakhsta	0.25
Azerbaija	0.25
Algeria	0.25
Yemen	0.17
Zimbabwe	0.17
Rwanda	0.17
Iraq	0.17
China	0.08
Belarus	0.08
Uzbekista	0.00

Figure 2.1a. Freedom in the World: FH Rankings 2012
Source: https://freedomhouse.org/report/freedom-world.

democracy. The countries ranked below China include Turkmenistan, Syria, Yemen, North Korea, and Eritrea. Though the V-Dem report and the Freedom House report do not use the same measures, the fact that their scores are highly correlated (see Chapter 8) suggests that their criteria are similar.[3]

One question that the Freedom House reports cannot answer is how ordinary people living in each society feel about these criteria. Fortunately, the sixth wave World Values Surveys included a question about people's *perceived* freedom:

> Some people feel they have completely free choice and control over their lives, while other people feel that what they do has no real effect on what happens to them. Please use this scale where 0 means "none at all" and 1 means "a great deal" to indicate how much freedom of choice and control you feel you have over the way your life turns out. (World Values Survey Wave 6)

When the respondents in the World Values Surveys were asked about how free they felt (Figure 2.1b), the results were interestingly inconsistent with the Freedom House rankings. The average value of Freedom House's "objective" scores in Figure 2.1a is .42 on a 0–1 scale, but people's subjective feeling of freedom was at a much higher level of .68 (Figure 2.1b). When the two sets of scores in Figures 2.1a and 2.1b are compared and weighted by each country's population, there is no statistically significant correlation[4] between "objective" and subjective freedom.

More importantly, the gap between different societies in the Freedom House measure is far greater than in the World Values Surveys. In other words, the Freedom House rankings seem to have exaggerated the gap between liberal and non-liberal societies. For example, China as a Communist country is given a near zero score in the Freedom House rankings. Yet the Chinese survey respondents reported an above-average level of perceived freedom comparable to its Asian neighbors in Taiwan, Japan, South Korea, and Singapore. Studies have shown that the Chinese government encourages the public to voice their opinions that may serve to adjust public policy.[5] For example, the National People's Congress and its local branches routinely hold public hearings before passing important policies related to income tax, environment regulations, and property tax, among many other issues.[6] This and other similar channels of voicing public opinion may have contributed to the Chinese people's feeling that they have freedom of expression.

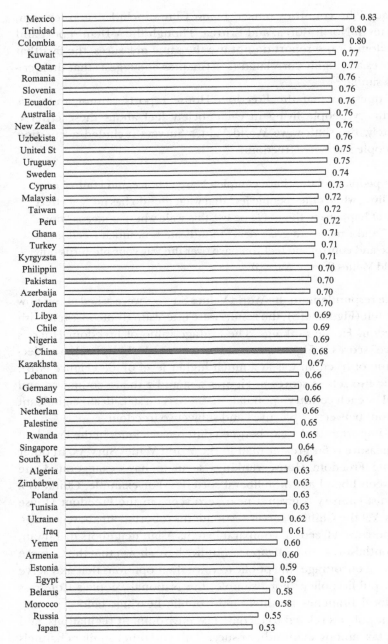

Mexico	0.83
Trinidad	0.80
Colombia	0.80
Kuwait	0.77
Qatar	0.77
Romania	0.76
Slovenia	0.76
Ecuador	0.76
Australia	0.76
New Zeala	0.76
Uzbekista	0.76
United St	0.75
Uruguay	0.75
Sweden	0.74
Cyprus	0.73
Malaysia	0.72
Taiwan	0.72
Peru	0.72
Ghana	0.71
Turkey	0.71
Kyrgyzsta	0.71
Philippin	0.70
Pakistan	0.70
Azerbaija	0.70
Jordan	0.70
Libya	0.69
Chile	0.69
Nigeria	0.69
China	0.68
Kazakhsta	0.67
Lebanon	0.66
Germany	0.66
Spain	0.66
Netherlan	0.66
Palestine	0.65
Rwanda	0.65
Singapore	0.64
South Kor	0.64
Algeria	0.63
Zimbabwe	0.63
Poland	0.63
Tunisia	0.63
Ukraine	0.62
Iraq	0.61
Yemen	0.60
Armenia	0.60
Estonia	0.59
Egypt	0.59
Belarus	0.58
Morocco	0.58
Russia	0.55
Japan	0.53

Figure 2.1b. Feeling Free
Source: 6th Wave World Values Surveys.

Some people in the liberal democratic world are often too quick to say that surveys are not reliable in authoritarian societies.[7] These people need to support their opinions with evidence, not just rely on their impressions, which could be heavily biased by the Western media. Others may think that Chinese citizens are brainwashed by their government's propaganda. That may be true, but their subjective feeling of freedom is valuable political capital for the legitimacy of the Chinese Communist Party and for political stability in any society. Freedom House's rankings are less meaningful if its version of freedom does not make people feel free.

Democracy

In the seventh wave of the World Values Survey in China, conducted in 2018, there is a set of questions related to people's preferred political system, including democracy, strong leader rule, military rule, expert rule, and religious rule. As shown in Figure 2.2, democracy was the top choice by an overwhelming majority of Chinese respondents (83 percent), followed by strong leader rule (54 percent), military rule (53 percent) and expert rule (52 percent). At the bottom was religious rule (24 percent), which is not surprising in an atheist society like China. Chinese respondents' preference for democracy was further reflected in another question in the same survey, where 85 percent of the respondents agreed that it is very important to live in a democratic country.[8]

The fact that democracy is the top choice of so many Chinese people may be surprising for many in the West, who customarily believe Communism and democracy cannot coexist, like water and oil. Others

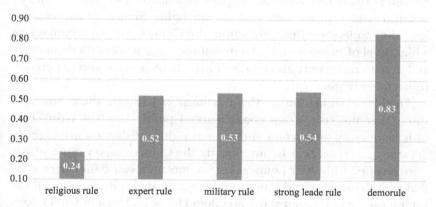

Figure 2.2. Preferred Political System in China
Source: World Values Survey China 2018.

may interpret such a result as democratic deprivation, meaning the Chinese people are deprived of democracy and that is why they want it so desperately.[9]

In fact, in the Chinese political vocabulary, *democracy* has never been a strange word.[10] On the official list of core socialist values developed under Xi Jinping, democracy is ranked second after prosperity, followed by civility, harmony, freedom, equality, justice, rule of law, patriotism, dedication, integrity, and friendship. In fact, these terms are posted publicly in many places in China. Living in this political culture, it is not surprising at all that so many Chinese people picked democracy as their preferred political system.

Other studies have shown that China as a non-democratic society carries a number of "democratic" characteristics, including accountability without democracy,[11] a growing middle class,[12] strong regime support,[13] civil society without democracy,[14] and a high rate of government responsiveness to public demand,[15] among many others.

It is one thing to show that people in China desire democracy; it is another to find out whether they think they have it in their own country. Studies like the Democracy Perception Index (DPI), conducted jointly by the Dalia Research Group and the Alliance of the Democracies, have shown that no government is living up to the democratic expectations of its citizens, and there is a gap called "democratic deficit" between people's expectation for democracy and how they actually experience it in their country.[16] Surprisingly, China is ranked in the top twenty countries with the smallest democratic deficit according to the DPI's survey results.

The seventh wave of the World Values Survey asked another set of questions related to Chinese people's satisfaction with their country's political system, democracy, and human rights. Similar to earlier studies,[17] the results show that satisfaction with China's political system was at a high level of 72 percent. In the meantime, satisfaction with democracy and human rights were also relatively high, at 68 percent and 72 percent, respectively (Figure 2.3).

Further examination of the relationship between these concepts shows that the correlation coefficients of political system satisfaction with democracy satisfaction and human rights satisfaction are high, at .63 and .41, respectively. In other words, the Chinese survey respondents were satisfied with their political system, mostly because they were satisfied with democracy and human rights within that system. Again, these findings seem to go against the Freedom House and V-Dem perceptions of China as having near-zero democracy and human rights.[18]

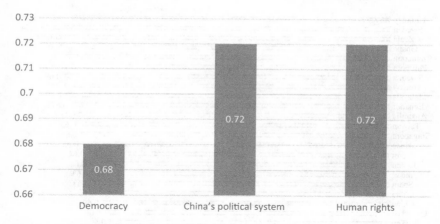

Figure 2.3. Political Satisfaction in China
Source: World Values Survey China 2018.

Further cross-country and cross-regional comparisons of satisfaction with democracy are possible using the sixth wave of the World Values Surveys (Figure 2.4). In these surveys, the maximum level of satisfaction with democracy is .74 on a 0–1 scale (Uruguay and Sweden), the minimum level is .32 (Armenia), and China is at .60, which is above the average score of .55. When compared with the Freedom House scores in Figure 2.1a, they do not show any statistically significant relationship with the scores in Figure 2.4 when weighted by each country's population.[19] In other words, there is no statistically significant relationship between the Freedom House's "objective" ranking of democracy and people's subjective satisfaction with democracy in their own societies.

Even if the Chinese survey respondents expressed their strong desire for and high degree of satisfaction with democracy, skeptics may still question the validity of these findings. For these skeptics, one unanswered question is the meaning of democracy in the Chinese context. The Chinese could define democracy very differently from the standard understanding in the West.

The meaning of democracy can be identified by a set of questions in the seventh World Values Survey in China. The respondents were asked to assess how essential each of a list of concepts was in their understanding of democracy, including political rights (competitive election and individual freedom), social justice (gender equality, unemployment protection, equal pay, taxing the rich), and rule by religious law.

While they considered religious law the least important for democracy (25 percent), the Chinese survey respondents considered political

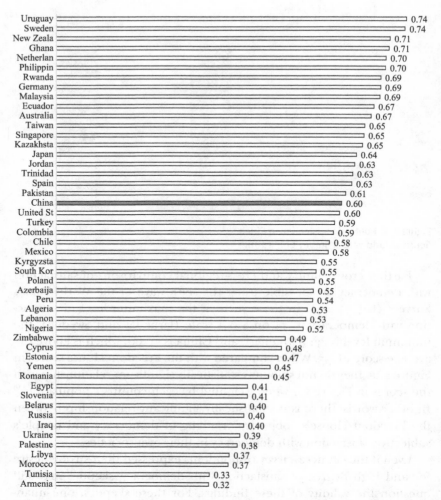

Figure 2.4. Satisfaction with Democracy in Selected Countries and Regions
Source: World Values Surveys Wave 6.

rights and social justice as each having equal importance. Eighty-five percent and 77 percent thought election and individual freedom were essential, and 89 percent, 81 percent, 77 percent, and 62 percent valued gender equality, unemployment protection (help jobless), income equality (equal pay), and taxing the rich as important for democracy (Figure 2.5). It seems that both political rights and social justice are the essential components in the Chinese perception of democracy.

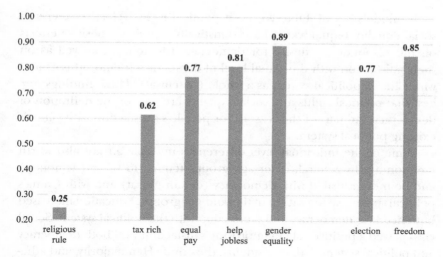

Figure 2.5. How Important Are These Items for Democracy?
Source: World Values Survey in China (2018).

So why are these elements, particularly elections and freedom, so important for the Chinese people when these elements do not exist in China in the eyes of the Western liberal elites? In the previous section, this study explained that Chinese survey respondents felt plenty of freedom in their everyday life and that the Freedom House ranking of freedom may be incomplete. One example of freedom of expression that the Freedom House reports missed is the fact that while the official media is indeed controlled by the Chinese government, citizens are allowed to express their opinions on social media, and such expressions frequently influence the government's decision-making.[20]

While it is true that China does not have multi-party direct elections, it does have indirect elections where lower-level delegates vote for the legislators in the next level up.[21] These elections are quite competitive among the candidates within the ruling Communist Party.[22] In this context, it is not surprising that the Chinese public consider freedom and election as necessary components of their political system.

To further confirm that political rights and social justice are essential in the Chinese understanding of democracy and in assessing the quality of China's political system, it is necessary to perform a multivariate analysis on the impact of these two elements in people's interpretation of democracy, while controlling for demographic and socioeconomic factors, including gender, age, education, social class, Party membership, urbanization, ethnicity, religiosity, media consumption, and geographic region.

In models 1–3 of Table 2.1, both political rights (electfreekey) and social equality (equalitykey) have statistically significant positive effects on the respondents' desire for democracy (demoimp), as well as on their satisfaction with the actual level of democracy (demorightsat) and with China's political system as a whole (systemsat). These findings suggest that political rights and social equality are part of the definition of democracy and part of the reasons for people's satisfaction with China's existing political system.

Some of the individual level differences in Table 2.1 are also worth mentioning. In general, older age groups tended to value (demoimp) and be more satisfied with democracy (demorightsat) and with China's political system (systemsat) than the younger groups. Education increased both need for democracy and satisfaction with the political system. Social class played a positive role in improving satisfaction with both democracy and political system. Urban residents, the ethnic Han majority, and atheists were less satisfied with China's political system than rural residents, ethnic minorities, and those who practice religion.

One of the more interesting findings concerns the role of media. While the official media (mediagov) expectedly helped increase people's

Table 2.1. Multivariate Analysis of Chinese Political Orientations (OLS Regression)

	demoimp	demorightsat	systemsat	govsurveillance	strongleader
	Model 1	Model 2	Model 3	Model 4	Model 5
electfreekey	0.208***	0.065***	0.086***	0.083**	-0.026
equalitykey	0.145***	0.057**	0.083**	0.128***	0.128***
Female	0.007	0.020***	0.008	-0.005	0.027***
age23–30	-0.026*	-0.054***	-0.031*	0.023	0.068***
age31–40	0.021	-0.054***	-0.012	0.011	0.068***
age41–50	0.032**	-0.042***	0.007	-0.027	0.055***
age51–60	0.030*	-0.023	0.035*	0.004	0.051**
age61–70	0.038**	0.006	0.059***	0.035	0.029
Education (yr)	0.005***	-0.001	0.002*	-0.003*	-0.001
Social class	-0.019	0.081***	0.096***	-0.033*	0.011
CCP	0.015	0.021	0.020	0.025	-0.024
Urban	-0.008	-0.007	-0.017*	0.011	-0.015
Han	-0.006	-0.009	-0.055***	-0.066***	0.067***
Atheist	-0.012	0.004	-0.021*	-0.003	-0.023
mediagov	0.056***	0.097***	0.089***	0.076***	-0.052**
mediasoc	0.041***	-0.029*	-0.032*	0.002	-0.037

Table 2.1. (*Continued*)

	demoimp Model 1	demorightsat Model 2	systemsat Model 3	govsurveillance Model 4	strongleader Model 5
Constant	0.460***	0.595***	0.563***	0.537***	0.484***
Observations	2,917	2,897	2,913	2,903	2,857
R-squared	0.143	0.090	0.085	0.057	0.058

Source: Seventh World Values Survey in China (2018).
Notes: * p<.10, ** p<.05, *** p<.01. Regions (provinces) are controlled but not shown. See Appendix for the summary statistics of the variables in this table. The variables in the tables are based on the following definitions:
demoimp: How important is it for R to live in a democratic country?;
demorightsat: factor index of R's satisfaction with China's level of democracy and with respect to human rights;
systemsat: R's overall satisfaction with the functioning of China's political system;
govsurveillance: factor index of R's support for surveillance in public space, in private email, and for collecting personal information without one's awareness;
strongleader: factor index of R's preferences for a strong leader not limited by fixed terms, and for expert rule;
electfreekey: factor index of support for free elections and for individual freedom;
equalitykey: factor index of support for gender equality, unemployment protection, equal pay, and taxing the rich;
mediagov: obtained social and political information through government media; and
mediasoc: obtained social and political information through social media.

desire for democracy and their satisfaction with democracy and with the political system, social media (mediasoc) decreased their satisfaction with democracy and with the political system. This is perhaps caused by the negative information that is more likely to be circulated on social media but censored in the official media.

Some studies have found the different meaning of democracy in China by showing the paternalistic relationship between the state and society.[23] The available evidence in the World Values Surveys does not seem to show any drastic difference from the standard Western definition of democracy, at least not in the definition of social democracy. The findings in this section suggest that political rights and social equality are closely associated with people's understanding of democracy in China, although elections and human rights may carry different meanings in China than in the Western liberal world.

Human Rights

Human rights is another concept frequently mentioned in the Western liberal democratic paradigm. In the sixth wave of World Values Surveys, there is a question regarding people's satisfaction with human rights in their respective societies (Figure 2.6). The highest level of human rights satisfaction is .91 (Qatar) and the lowest is .30 (Egypt). China's score is .67, which is above the average score of .55 among the selected countries and regions in Figure 2.6. When the perceived human rights satisfaction scores in Figure 2.6 are compared with the Freedom House rankings in Figure 2.1a, the correlation coefficient is -.32 (p<.05). The higher the "objective" democracy score by Freedom House, the lower the subjective satisfaction with human rights in a country or region. One explanation for the inconsistency between the two supposedly similar sets of scores is that people's understanding of human rights is different or even opposite from Freedom House's definition of the concept.

Unlike the liberal definition of human rights that emphasizes the individual's political rights, the Chinese concept of human rights prioritizes the right to survival over political rights, and the right of majority over the right of the minority (see also Chapter 1 in this volume). Such a definition of human rights provides the Chinese Communist Party with the legitimacy to focus on economic development before political decentralization, as well as the justification to suppress individual dissidents in the interest of the majority's economic well-being. More importantly, this means that Chinese survey respondents likely understand human rights as a broader concept that contains both economic and political rights.

As shown in Figure 2.6, the Chinese seem to accept and feel content with such a description of human rights. Another way to test the Chinese people's acceptance of their government's definition of human rights is to examine their attitude toward government surveillance, both of individual behavior in public spaces and in private life. There are three statements in the 2018 World Values Survey in China that measure this. The survey asks: "Do you think the government should have the right to do the following:

1. Keep people under video surveillance in public areas;
2. Monitor all emails and any other information exchanged on the internet;
3. Collect information about anyone living in China without their knowledge."

The first statement is more related to surveillance in public spaces, while the other two are more about surveillance in private life. The Chinese survey respondents were generally supportive of all the three measures.

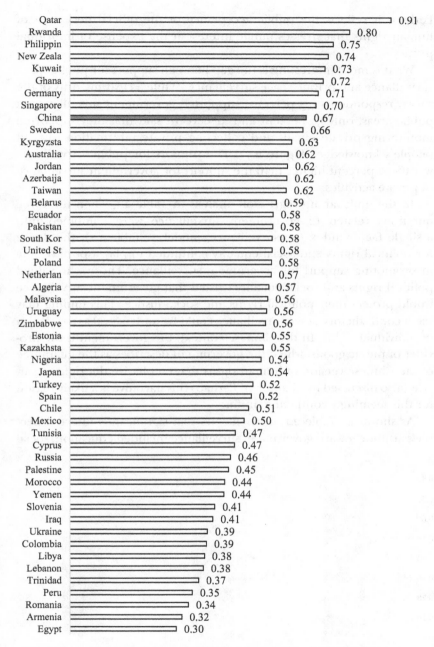

Figure 2.6. Satisfaction with Human Rights in Selected Countries and Regions
Source: World Values Surveys Wave 6.

Perhaps it reflects the public acceptance of the official definition of human rights that stresses public interest at the expense of individual privacy.

What is more interesting is the gap between support for public space surveillance and private space surveillance. While a clear majority of the survey respondents (73 percent) supported government surveillance in public areas, only 57 percent and 51 percent said that they supported monitoring private emails and collecting private information without people's knowledge (Figure 2.7). The support for public surveillance was 16–22 percent higher than the support for government surveillance of private activities.

In the multivariate regression analysis in Table 2.1, when the three questions related to government surveillance were combined into a single factor index (govsurveillance, model 4, Table 2.1), the desire for political rights and social equality continued to play a positive role in promoting support for government surveillance. Those who valued political rights and social equality trusted that government surveillance would protect their political rights and social justice. This finding may seem contradictory, since surveillance could be understood as a violation of individual rights. In the Chinese context, the government is the provider of public goods, which the government describes as the guarantee of the Chinese version of human rights that emphasize the right to survive (also discussed in Chapter 1). Perhaps this narrative is a likely reason for this seemingly conflicting finding.

As shown in Table 2.1, other factors that significantly affected people's attitude toward government surveillance included education, social

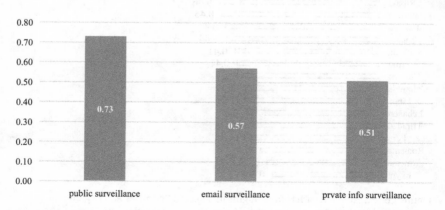

Figure 2.7. Support for Government Surveillance
Source: World Values Survey in China (2018).

class, ethnicity (han), and government media consumption (mediagov). The more educated, those in the upper classes, and the Han majority were more right-conscious and less likely to support government surveillance. Understandably, relying on the official media for social and political information helped promote support for government surveillance.

In short, the most interesting finding in this section is the clear distinction in people's understanding of public space versus private space, where their support for public monitoring is significantly stronger than for the monitoring of private life. The awareness of privacy may be somewhat surprising to those who expect Chinese citizens to whole-heartedly accept the official line of human rights that downplays the importance of individual privacy.

Democratic Authoritarianism

In the previous sections, this study has shown that the Chinese people hold a strong preference for democracy and freedom. This section will examine the tendency toward authoritarianism in the Chinese political orientation.

As the reader may remember from Figure 2.2, while the Chinese respondents demonstrated the strongest preference for democracy (83 percent), they were not turned off by a strong leader (54 percent), military rule (53 percent), or expert rule (52 percent). Further analysis shows that preferences for strong leader, military, and expert rule are positively correlated. For example, the correlation coefficient for strong leader and expert rule is r=.29, and r=.18 for strong leader and military rule.

When the Chinese preference for a strong leader is compared historically (Figure 2.8), it shows a steady increase from 37 percent in 2000 (fourth WVS), to 43 percent in 2008 (fifth WVS), to 46 percent in 2012 (sixth WVS), and finally to 53 percent in 2018 (seventh WVS). When the Chinese preference for a strong leader in 2018 is compared cross-societally, China ranks in the top eleven of the fifty-two countries and regions where data were available in the sixth World Values Surveys (Figure 2.8), suggesting a relatively strong authoritarian orientation in China.

When "strong leader" and "expert rule" are combined into a factor index in the multivariate analysis in model 5, Table 2.1 (strongleader), it generated some very interesting results. Desire for political rights had a weak and statistically insignificant negative effect on support for a strong

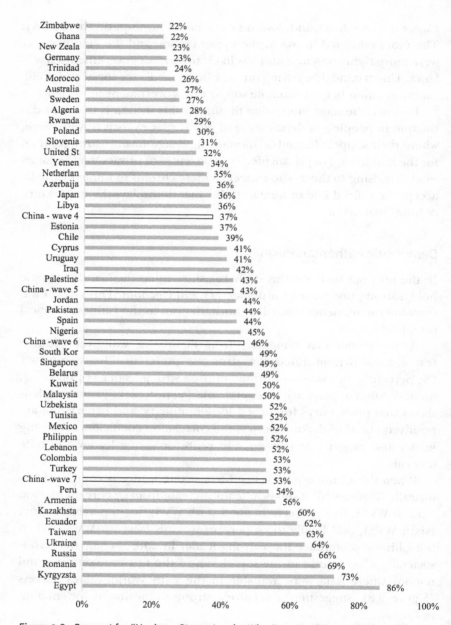

Figure 2.8. Support for "Having a Strong Leader Who Does Not Have to Bother with Parliament and Elections"
Sources: World Values Surveys Waves 4 (China only), 5 (China only), 6 (all countries/regions) and 7 (China only).

leader. Desire for social equality played a strong and statistically significant positive role in promoting strong leader support. In the minds of
the Chinese survey respondents, perhaps it was unclear if the strong
leader would provide them with more political rights, but they would for
sure provide more social equality.

The middle-aged groups were more supportive of a strong leader
than the youngest (16–22) and the oldest (70+) groups (Table 2.1).
These middle-aged groups were in their working ages and likely see the
benefits of having a strong leader who would promise them improved
social welfare benefits.[24] The Han majority was more supportive of
a strong leader than were the ethnic minorities, perhaps because the
strong leader represented the nationalistic tendency in the trade war
between China and the United States since Donald Trump became the
U.S. president in 2017.

Finally, as seen in Table 2.1, the official media did not meet the
expectation of promoting support for a strong leader. It actually
showed a negative effect on strong leader support. One possibility
may be the overexposure of Xi Jinping on the official media, causing
an averse public reaction. Similarly, Chinese Communist Party (CCP)
members were not enthusiastic about strong leader rule, with Party
membership having a negative and statistically insignificant effect. One
reason for the weak support among the Party members could be that
Xi Jinping, China's current strong leader, is a populist leader whose
style is to directly reach out to the Chinese society while bypassing
both Party members and the media. Another explanation is that Xi's
decision to remove his term limit from the Chinese Constitution in
early 2018 may have been met with reluctance among the Party members, although it was supported by the general public. In either case,
Chinese public opinion suggests a populist authoritarian tendency,[25]
where the strong leader often reaches out to the public directly during site visits to rural areas, factories, urban neighborhoods, and so
on, while circumventing Party members. As a result, the strong leader
enjoys strong public support.

Conclusion

This study has found that there is a strong desire for and a high level
of satisfaction with freedom, democracy, and human rights among the
Chinese public. They think China's political system is democratic, which
they define as satisfying people's political rights and social justice. In

the meantime, this study also found there is stronger support for government surveillance in public space than in private life. Finally, this study discovered that there is a lot of support for a populist authoritarian leader who can promote social equality for the ordinary people in China.

These findings point to at least three conclusions. First, they suggest that the Western liberal elites (WLEs) intentionally or unintentionally know very little about non-Western political cultures. Their perception of other political systems is vastly different from how people see their own political systems. When people's perceived freedom, democracy, and human rights are combined into a single index in selected countries and regions (Figure 2.9), these scores show no statistically significant relationship with the Freedom House rankings in Figure 2.1a when weighted by population.[26]

This finding calls for a need to include public opinion if organizations such as Freedom House want to make an honest and objective endeavor to understand the world.[27] This may not be possible, since these organizations have a strong ideological agenda to change how other countries and/or the world is run according to their values and beliefs. In this case, this study can still serve as a warning about the inaccuracy of certain Western-centric portraits of the world.

The second conclusion of this study is that concepts such as freedom, democracy, and human rights need to be more inclusive than how they are defined in the existing literature. Rather than showing that these concepts are missing in China, the findings in this study suggest that democracy, freedom, and human rights are common ideas in the Chinese political language. One should not simply disqualify China from being democratic just because it has a different political system than Western liberal democracies. Democracy is similarly defined in the Chinese mind as requiring elections and freedom.[28] Only by taking a closer look at the meanings of election and freedom one can see how differently these concepts are understood in the Chinese context. WLEs may argue that these definitions cannot be used to describe elections and freedom, but that will be a highly subjective and ideological decision with limited credibility.

The third and final conclusion is that the Chinese political attitude has a populist authoritarian nature. Chinese public opinion seems to strongly support a populist version of democracy, going against a Western-style institutional version. They demand a technically capable strong leader who can provide social justice and protection of social welfare, a point that echoes the Confucian political culture elaborated on

New Zeala	0.73
Rwanda	0.73
Philippin	0.72
Ghana	0.71
Sweden	0.71
Germany	0.69
Uruguay	0.67
Singapore	0.67
Australia	0.66
Ecuador	0.65
Taiwan	0.65
Netherlan	0.65
China	0.65
Malaysia	0.64
Jordan	0.64
United St	0.61
Kazakhsta	0.61
Pakistan	0.61
Kyrgyzsta	0.61
Azerbaija	0.60
Japan	0.59
Spain	0.58
Mexico	0.58
Turkey	0.58
South Kor	0.57
Poland	0.57
Chile	0.57
Algeria	0.57
Nigeria	0.56
Trinidad	0.55
Colombia	0.54
Zimbabwe	0.54
Estonia	0.52
Cyprus	0.51
Belarus	0.50
Peru	0.49
Lebanon	0.49
Yemen	0.47
Slovenia	0.46
Palestine	0.45
Romania	0.45
Russia	0.44
Morocco	0.44
Tunisia	0.44
Iraq	0.43
Ukraine	0.42
Libya	0.42
Egypt	0.39
Armenia	0.36

Figure 2.9. Support for Combined Index of Freedom, Democracy, and Human Rights in Selected Countries and Regions
Source: 6th Wave World Values Surveys.

in the introductory chapter.[29] Before the WLEs tell us what the world should be, it is important to develop an accurate understanding of what the world is.

Notes

1. The authors wish to thank Eva Jialei Zhou for her research assistance.
2. See "Board & Leadership," https://freedomhouse.org/about-us/board-leadership.
3. See https://www.v-dem.net/media/filer_public/74/8c/748c68ad-f224-4cd7-87f9-8794add5c6of/dr_2021_updated.pdf.
4. The correlation coefficient is .27 (p<.10) without weighting, but .16 (p=.2633) with weighting.
5. *Economist*, "The 1.4bn-People Question: Apparatchiks and Academics Alike Struggle to Take China's Pulse. Pollsters Have to Use Roundabout Ways to Find Out What People Are Thinking," October 24, 2020, https://www.economist.com/china/2020/10/24/apparatchiks-and-academics-alike-struggle-to-take-chinas-pulse; Jidong Chen and Yiqing Xu, "Why Do Authoritarian Regimes Allow Citizens to Voice Opinions Publicly?" *The Journal of Politics* 79, no. 3 (2017): 792–803.
6. See, for example, http://www.npc.gov.cn/npc/c199/200508/a5c12fb1d b934d65984a4bf407e341d7.shtml.
7. Dieter Fuchs, "The Political Culture Paradigm," in *Oxford Handbook of Political Behavior*, ed. Russell J. Dalton and Hans-Dieter Klingemann (Oxford Handbooks Online, 2007), 161–84; Richard Rose, "Perspectives on Political Behavior in Time and Space," in *Oxford Handbook of Political Behavior*, ed. Russell J. Dalton and Hans-Dieter Klingemann (Oxford Handbooks Online, 2007), 283–304.
8. Weighted.
9. R. Truex, "Populist Authoritarianism: Chinese Political Culture and Regime Sustainability by Wenfang Tang, Oxford University Press," a book review in *Perspectives on Politics* 15, no. 2 (2016): 617–18.
10. Yun-han Chu, Larry Diamond, Andrew J. Nathan, and Doh Chull Shin, eds., *How East Asians View Democracy* (New York: Columbia University Press, 2008).
11. Lily Tsai, *Accountability Without Democracy: Solidarity Groups and Public Goods Provision in Rural China* (New York: Cambridge University Press, 2007).
12. Jie Chen and Bruce Dickson, *Allies of the State: China's Private Entrepreneurs and Democratic Change* (Cambridge, MA: Harvard University Press, 2010).
13. Jie Chen, *Popular Political Support in Urban China* (Redwood City: Stanford University Press, 2014).
14. Bruce J. Dickson, *The Party and the People: Chinese Politics in the 21st Century* (Princeton: Princeton University Press, 2021).
15. Wenfang Tang, "The 'Surprise' of Authoritarian Resilience in China," *American Affairs* II, no. 1 (2018): 101–17.
16. Fred Deveaux, *Democracy Perception Index–2020* (Dalia Research & the Alliance of Democracies, 2020), https://www.allianceofdemocracies.org/initiatives/the-copenhagen-democracy-summit/dpi-2020; J. Peder Zane, "Democracy and the Challenges Imposed by Freedom," *The New York Times*, September 14, 2015.

17. Qing Yang and Wenfang Tang, "Exploring the Sources of Institutional Trust in China: Culture, Mobilization, or Performance?" *Asian Politics & Policy* 2, no. 3 (2010): 415–36; Yingnan Joseph Zhou, Wenfang Tang, and Xuchuan Lei, "Social Desirability of Dissent: An IAT Experiment with Chinese University Students," *Journal of Chinese Political Science* 25 (2020): 113–38.

18. Tang, "The 'Surprise' of Authoritarian Resilience."

19. R=.15, p=.3283

20. Gary King, Jennifer Pan, and Margaret E. Roberts, "How Censorship in China Allows Government Criticism but Silences Collective Expression," *American Political Science Review* 107, no. 2 (2013): 326–43.

21. National People's Congress, "Constitution of the People's Republic of China (Adopted at the Fifth Session of the Fifth National People's Congress on December 4, 1982)," https://www.elegislation.gov.hk/hk/A1%21en.assist.pdf.

22. Yongnian Zheng, *The Chinese Communist Party as Organizational Emperor: Culture, Reproduction, and Transformation* (New York: Routledge, 2009).

23. Jie Lu and Tianjian Shi, "The Battle of Ideas and Discourses before Democratic Transition: Different Democratic Conceptions in Authoritarian China," *International Political Science Review* 36, no. 1 (2015): 20–41.

24. Frederick Solt, Yue Hu, Kevan Hudson, Jungmin Song, and Dong "Erico" Yu, "Economic Inequality and Class Consciousness," *The Journal of Politics* 79, no. 3 (2017): 1079–83.

25. Wenfang Tang, *Populist Authoritarianism: Chinese Political Culture and Regime Sustainability* (New York: Oxford University Press, 2016).

26. R=-.09, p=.5281, weighted by 2012 population.

27. Some WLEs are more cool-minded. For these people, China is a threat to the Western system precisely because the Chinese government is capable of rallying public support (Brooks 2019).

28. Yun-han Chu, Larry Diamond, Andrew J. Nathan, and Doh Chull Shin, *How East Asians View Democracy* (New York: Columbia University Press, 2008).

29. Also see Ronald Inglehart, "Postmaterialist Values and the Shift from Survival to Self-Expression Values," in *Oxford Handbook of Political Behavior*, ed. Russell J. Dalton and Hans-Dieter Klingemann (New York: Oxford University Press, 2007).

Bibliography

Brooks, David. "How China Brings Us Together." *The New York Times*, February 14, 2019.

Chen, Jidong, and Yiqing Xu. "Why Do Authoritarian Regimes Allow Citizens to Voice Opinions Publicly?" *The Journal of Politics* 79, no. 3 (2017): 792–803.

Chen, Jie, and Bruce Dickson. *Allies of the State: China's Private Entrepreneurs and Democratic Change*. Cambridge, MA: Harvard University Press, 2010.

Chu, Yun-han, Larry Diamond, Andrew J. Nathan, and Doh Chull Shin, eds. *How East Asians View Democracy*. New York: Columbia University Press, 2008.

Deveaux, Fred. *Democracy Perception Index–2020*. Dalia Research & the Alliance of Democracies, https://www.allianceofdemocracies.org/initiatives/the-copenhagen-democracy-summit/dpi-2020/, 2020.

Dickson, Bruce J. *The Party and the People: Chinese Politics in the 21st Century*. Princeton: Princeton University Press, 2021.

The Economist. "The 1.4bn-People Question: Apparatchiks and Academics Alike Struggle to Take China's Pulse." October 22, 2020, https://www.economist.com/china/2020/10/24/apparatchiks-and-academics-alike-struggle-to-take-chinas-pulse.

Fuchs, Dieter. "The Political Culture Paradigm." In *Oxford Handbook of Political Behavior*, edited by Russell J. Dalton and Hans-Dieter Klingemann, 161–84. Oxford Handbooks Online, 2007.

Inglehart, Ronald. "Postmaterialist Values and the Shift from Survival to Self-Expression Values." In *Oxford Handbook of Political Behavior*, edited by Russell J. Dalton and Hans-Dieter Klingemann, 223–39. New York: Oxford University Press, 2007.

King, Gary, Jennifer Pan, and Molly, E. Roberts. "How Censorship in China Allows Government Criticism but Silences Collective Expression." *American Political Science Review* 107, no. 2 (2014): 326–43.

Lu, Jie, and Tianjian Shi. "The Battle of Ideas and Discourses before Democratic Transition: Different Democratic Conceptions in Authoritarian China." *International Political Science Review* 36, no. 1 (2015): 20–41.

National People's Congress. "Constitution of the People's Republic of China (Adopted at the Fifth Session of the Fifth National People's Congress on December 4, 1982)." https://www.elegislation.gov.hk/hk/A1%21en.assist.pdf.

Rose, Richard. "Perspectives on Political Behavior in Time and Space." In *Oxford Handbook of Political Behavior*, edited by Russell J. Dalton and Hans-Dieter Klingemann, 283–304. Oxford Handbooks Online, 2007.

Solt, Frederick, Yue Hu, Kevan Hudson, Jungmin Song, and Dong "Erico" Yu. "Economic Inequality and Class Consciousness." *The Journal of Politics* 79, no. 3 (2017): 1079–83.

Tang, Wenfang. *Populist Authoritarianism: Chinese Political Culture and Regime Sustainability*. New York: Oxford University Press, 2016.

Tang, Wenfang. "The 'Surprise' of Authoritarian Resilience in China." *American Affairs* II, no. 1 (2018).

Truex, Rory. Review of *Populist Authoritarianism: Chinese Political Culture and Regime Sustainability*, by Wenfang Tang. *Perspectives on Politics* 15, no. 2 (2017): 617–18.

Tsai, Lily. *Accountability Without Democracy: Solidarity Groups and Public Goods Provision in Rural China*. New York: Cambridge University Press, 2007.

Yang, Qing, and Wenfang Tang. "Exploring the Sources of Institutional Trust in China: Culture, Mobilization, or Performance?" *Asian Politics & Policy* 2, no. 3 (2010): 415–36.

Zane, J. Peder. "Democracy and the Challenges Imposed by Freedom." *The New York Times*, September 14, 2015.

Zheng, Yongnian. *The Chinese Communist Party as Organizational Emperor: Culture, Reproduction, and Transformation*. New York: Routledge, 2009.

Zhou, Yingnan Joseph, Wenfang Tang, and Xuchuan Lei. "Social Desirability of Dissent: An IAT Experiment with Chinese University Students." *Journal of Chinese Political Science* 25, no. 4 (August 2019).

Appendix Summary Statistics

Variable	Obs	Mean	Std. Dev.	Min	Max
demoimp	3,013	.863628	.185059	0	1
electfreekey	2,964	.815447	.1947479	0	1
equalitykey	2,967	.8055372	.162474	0	1
demorightsat	2,985	.7070152	.1915891	0	1
systemsat	3,001	.7283128	.2174793	0	1
strongleader	2,936	.5257174	.2700958	0	1
govsurveil~e	3,003	.5859616	.2681293	0	1
female	3,036	.5490777	.4976675	0	1
agroup1	3,036	.0816864	.2739315	0	1
agroup2	3,036	.1261528	.3320762	0	1
agroup3	3,036	.1959816	.3970198	0	1
agroup4	3,036	.2318841	.4221049	0	1
agroup5	3,036	.1818182	.3857581	0	1
agroup6	3,036	.1824769	.3863007	0	1
edyr	3,036	10.08531	4.415746	0	21
class	3,006	1.293081	.7969985	0	3
ccp	3,036	.0958498	.2944336	0	1
urban	3,036	.4041502	.4908077	0	1
han	3,036	.9463109	.2254402	0	1
atheist	3,036	.8577075	.3494074	0	1
mediagov	3,036	.4009387	.2270535	0	1
mediasoc	3,036	.5089139	.3095417	0	1
Shanghai	3,036	.0194335	.1380655	0	1
Yunnan	3,036	.0204216	.1414608	0	1
Inner Mongolia	3,036	.0197628	.1392073	0	1
Beijing	3,036	.0197628	.1392073	0	1
Jilin	3,036	.020751	.1425731	0	1
Sichuan	3,036	.0503953	.2187952	0	1
Tianjin	3,036	.0204216	.1414608	0	1
Ningxia	3,036	.0191041	.1369134	0	1
Anhui	3,036	.0405138	.1971935	0	1
Shandong	3,036	.1083663	.3108936	0	1
Shanxi	3,036	.0362319	.1868974	0	1
Guangdong	3,036	.083004	.2759336	0	1
Guangxi	3,036	.0408432	.1979595	0	1
Jiangsu	3,036	.0365613	.1877129	0	1

Variable	Obs	Mean	Std. Dev.	Min	Max
Jiangxi	3,036	.0167984	.1285367	0	1
Hebei	3,036	.0125165	.111193	0	1
Henan	3,036	.1399868	.3470305	0	1
Zhejiang	3,036	.0385375	.1925217	0	1
Hainan	3,036	.0200922	.1403389	0	1
Hubei	3,036	.0408432	.1979595	0	1
Hunan	3,036	.0217391	.1458545	0	1
Gansu	3,036	.0210804	.143676	0	1
Fujian	3,036	.0378788	.1909345	0	1
Guizhou	3,036	.0200922	.1403389	0	1
Liaoning	3,036	.020751	.1425731	0	1
Chongqing	3,036	.0115283	.1067669	0	1
Shanxi	3,036	.0204216	.1414608	0	1
Qinghai	3,036	.020751	.1425731	0	1
Heilongjiang	3,036	.0214097	.1447697	0	1

Source: Seventh World Values Survey in China (2018).

THREE | Political Participation in China: Social Surveys as Windows to Chinese Political Attitudes and Behavior

LINGNAN HE AND DALI L. YANG

Introduction

This chapter explores political participation in China through survey research. When we discuss political participation, we refer to citizens' activities affecting politics. And just as the scope and scale of politics have expanded over time, the conception of political participation has also undergone significant change in political science.[1] In this chapter, we make use of the three most recent waves of the World Values Survey (WVS) to assess people's attitudes and reported political participatory behavior in China over the past two decades.

Research on modern China has long been fascinated with how the vast upheavals associated with the Chinese revolutions since the late nineteenth century have offered enormous opportunities as well as traps for individuals of diverse backgrounds and motivations to participate. Studies of political participation during the Mao era focused, by necessity heavily, on the numerous Maoist movements and campaigns.[2] In contrast, because of the diversification of Chinese socioeconomic and, to a more limited extent, political life, and because of the availability of new forms of research technologies (such as survey research and online data), studies of political participation in the post-Mao era have increasingly given attention to a broad range of phenomena associated with comparative politics, including voting, campaign activities, appeals, adversarial activities, cronyism, resistance, and boycotts.[3]

Survey research had a slow start in the post-Mao era because of costs and operational challenges, and it has played an important role in improving our understanding of political participation since the 1990s. Wenfang Tang draws on data from the 1986–1987 World Bank–Chinese Academy of Social Sciences joint survey to examine employee participation in management decision-making in Chinese local industrial firms.[4] In the early 1990s, a collaborative survey project undertaken by the University of Michigan and Peking University enabled scholars to study political participation in the Chinese countryside.[5] In 1990, with the support of a National Science Foundation grant, Andrew Nathan and Tianjian Shi cooperated with the Research Center on Contemporary China (RCCC) of Peking University to carry out the first "scientifically valid national sample survey done in China on political behavior and attitudes."[6] The survey assessed around fifty political-culture variables, allowing researchers to investigate the relationship between public belief and democratization, among others. Since 1997, Bruce Dickson has collaborated with the RCCC to conduct a series of surveys on Chinese officials and capitalists.[7] By studying their views on current policies as well as political and social beliefs, Dickson and his co-authors have written some of the most informative studies of Chinese entrepreneurs and sought to assess whether Chinese private entrepreneurs could be proponents of democratic political change as democratization theory predicts. In parallel, in her exploration of the relationship between economic liberalism and political freedom, Kellee Tsai combined a nationwide survey of private entrepreneurs (funded by the National Science Foundation) and hundreds of field interviews.[8] Among her findings was her widely noted conclusion that Chinese private entrepreneurs did not pose a threat to the regime. Other important survey research has explored citizens' voting preferences across rural and urban areas. Jie Chen and Yang Zhong, using a survey fielded in the Beijing area in 1995, found that those with stronger attachment to democratic values are less willing to vote in semicompetitive elections.[9] The same authors reached similar conclusion on village elections.[10]

In spite of the political constraints on conducting opinion surveys, particularly the limitations on the questions that could be asked in China, extant survey-based research has produced valuable information on and insights into the political attitudes and selected political behavior, including various aspects of political participation, in China.

Nonetheless, because of the relatively small number of surveys carried out in China, researchers using survey data have found it challenging to assess the long-term trends of Chinese political participation and other forms of political behavior.

Meanwhile, since first connecting to the internet in 1987, China's online world has blossomed in spite of pervasive censorship and the blocking of major websites and services offered by Facebook, Google, and Twitter by Chinese cyber regulators.[11] In 2020, the number of internet users in China surpassed 900 million.[12] As the internet has facilitated communications and connections, it has also enabled various forms of activism, from the formal to the illicit, to get organized online. Not surprisingly, China scholars have also increasingly paid attention to online participation.[13]

Besides providing new ways to participate in politics, the internet has also enabled researchers to conduct surveys online, allowing them to partially overcome some of the drawbacks and constraints of fielding national surveys.[14] For instance, the "Chinese Political Compass" (CPC),[15] initiated by a group of students at Peking University in 2017, is modeled on the UK platform *The Political Compass* to rate political ideology on a spectrum. The survey website has been collecting entries with city-level IP information in China, allowing data analysts to measure multiple dimensions of political ideology among the Chinese participants.[16] As the repertoire of actions constituting political participation has expanded, the need to examine the impact of the internet on political participation has grown, and interestingly, some of that need can be satisfied using surveys, including those conducted online.

The World Values Survey (WVS) includes questions that allow us to assess certain aspects of political participation. With the growing importance of online activities, WVS 7 introduced unique questions about the use of the internet for political information and participation. In this chapter, we make use of the three most recent waves of the WVS to assess people's attitudes and reported political participatory behavior in China over the past two decades. The summary statistics for the three waves of surveys, conducted in 2007, 2012/13, and 2018, respectively, are shown in Table 3.1.

The timing of the three waves of surveys needs to be kept in mind as we try to make sense of the empirical measurements of a variable across the different waves. For instance, 2007 was the year before the Beijing Summer Olympics, and the People's Republic of China was only a few years into the World Trade Organization. China as a country was eager to win the acceptance of the rest of the world, while the Chinese public

Table 3.1. Summary Statistics for Socioeconomic Variables (Chinese Respondents)

Survey Wave	N	Variable	Mean
WVS 7 (2018)	2,352	Age	45.4
		Female	0.54
		Government Employee	0.21
		Education Level (highest attained; see Appendix)	0.78
		CCP member	0.1
		Income Level (reported total income last year: 1 = under 5,000 yuan, 16 = more than 300,000 yuan)	9
		Urban hukou	0.39
WVS 6 (2012–2013)	11,219	Age	44.43
		Female	0.52
		Government Employee	0.17
		Education Level (highest attained)	1.38
		CCP member	0.21
		Income Level (reported income decile)	4.92
WVS 5 (2007)	1,991	Age	44.72
		Female	0.54
		Government Employee	0.15
		Education Level (highest attained)	0.95
		CCP member	0.13
		Income Level (reported income decile)	4.67

was beginning to rally around the national flag in eager anticipation of the Beijing Summer Olympics in 2008.[17] Looking at 2012/13, this was a time of high Chinese national pride in the aftermath of China's vigorous economic performance during and after the Great Recession in the rest of the world; it was also a time of leadership transition from Hu Jintao to Xi Jinping. Finally, by 2018, Xi had substantially consolidated his political dominance of the Chinese political system, and most of the Chinese elite and public had learned of the need to sing praises of Xi's leadership while the United States–China trade war was still in its early stages. Table 3.1 shows the composition of each of the three surveys, broken down by age, gender, government employment, education, income, CCP membership, and urban/rural location.

Political participation is often situational, and there is great diversity in its types and forms, as well as the implications of each.[18] The WVS covers a wide range of questions that allow us to disaggregate some of the forms of political participation. We present the patterns of different types of participation among Chinese citizens, and empirically interrogate the distinct incentives behind different dimensions of participation. Our results suggest that Chinese citizens engage in various forms of political participation to seek redress as well as to hold government officials accountable, to a limited extent. Moreover, we examine the socioeconomic features associated with patterns of political participation. Among the various factors we consider, age, education level, CCP membership, and occupation are strongly correlated with certain forms of political participation.

A major strength of the WVS is its coverage of multiple countries. Whereas China stands out in terms of population size, spatial scale, and rapidity of change over the period we cover, it is nonetheless informative to compare the findings on China with those for other societies even when we recognize the limitations of such an exercise. For ease of implementation, we have chosen to make two kinds of comparisons. The first is to compare mainland China with Hong Kong, Taiwan, and South Korea, societies that share a history of Confucian influence. The second is to compare China with the United States, the world's two largest economies with contrasting political and legal systems. We find that respondents from the East Asian societies tend to be similarly reserved in participation, while the U.S. respondents are generally more engaged in politics. However, the level of participatory difference varies depending on the specific forms of participation.

Political Interest and Forms of Political Participation

In this section, we present the self-reported interest (levels) in politics and the pattern of political participation as revealed through data from WVS 5, 6, and 7. Before we do so, however, we recognize that such self-reporting is subject to various forms of cognitive and psychological biases, especially when it comes to controversial forms of participation like protest activism. As Pippa Norris points out, surveys are usually stronger at tapping attitudes and values rather than actual behavior, and they are generally more reliable at reporting routine actions like attending church rather than occasional acts.[19] The problem might be aggravated in the Chinese sociopolitical context, where it is more likely that respondents will tend to underreport certain actions that are seen as socially or politically controversial or even dangerous. As a result, we not only include the results of the percentage of respondents who claim they "have done" a certain action, but we also include other categories like "might do," or even missing values and declining to answer.[20]

Given the enormous changes China has undergone in recent decades, we are strongly interested in documenting these changes across time. Unfortunately, for a variety of reasons, notably political sensitivity, the key questions concerning political participation have been included in the WVS China surveys only sporadically. In particular, they were not included in WVS 3 (1995) and WVS 4 (2001), and only partially in WVS 5 (2007). As a result, we comment on differences across survey waves when the original data allow us to do so, but we are significantly constrained in discussing long-term trends. In all tables that follow, the percentages are rounded to the nearest percent.

Interest in Politics

Even though political interest tracks the predisposition to get involved in politics rather than the behavioral involvement itself, research has found that political interest tends to be a strong predictor of many forms of political engagement.[21] We therefore start with a presentation of the empirical findings on political interest.

Table 3.2 summarizes the level of political interest among survey respondents across the three WVS waves (5–7). What immediately stands out from the table is the sharp decline in the percentage of respondents who say they are very interested in politics, from 28 percent in 2007, the year prior to the Beijing Summer Olympics, to only 11 percent in 2018, the year Xi Jinping's predominance in Chinese politics reached new heights following the abolition of term limits for the "State Chairmanship" (presidency) in the Chinese Constitution. Overall, it appears larger percentages of the Chinese population have become turned off from politics each year. Prima facie, this change is related to the rise of Xi's strongman rule and the climate of fear that the Party rank and file has had to endure.[22]

Table 3.2. Interest in Politics

	How interested would you say you are in politics?				
	Very	Somewhat	Not very	Not at all	N
WVS 7 (2018)	11%	41%	37%	11%	3033
WVS 6 (2012)	11%	35%	33%	21%	1219
WVS 5 (2007)	28%	36%	23%	13%	1991

Meanwhile, there has also been a significant increase in the percentage of survey respondents who say they are either "not very" or "not at all" interested in politics. It rose from 36 to 48 percent between 2007 and 2018, albeit the combined total reached as high as 54 percent in 2012/13. Nonetheless, those who say they are not at all interested in politics rose from 13 percent in 2007 to 21 percent in 2012/13 but has fallen to a low of 11 percent in 2018. After all, whether for the Party rank and file or the school pupil, there is no escaping the ubiquity of political documents and slogans, not to mention the phone app Xuexi Qiangguo (which formally debuted on January 1, 2019, after WVS 7 had been completed) for studying Xi Jinping's thoughts.

Protest Activism

Samuel H. Barnes et al. categorize political participation into three dimensions: protest activism (attend a lawful demonstration, join in boycotts, join an unofficial strike, sign a petition, occupy buildings or factories), civic activism (belong to organizations), and voter turnout (vote in elections).[23] Such a categorization underscores the vast chasm separating the systems of politics in China and liberal democracies. Article 1 of the Constitution of the People's Republic of China states clearly: "The socialist system is the fundamental system of the People's Republic of China. Leadership by the Communist Party of China is the defining feature of socialism with Chinese characteristics. It is prohibited for any organization or individual to damage the socialist system."

Because the Chinese Communist Party brooks no opposition and is determined to crash any anti-regime activities, the room for collective action has been limited even in years of relative openness.[24] Table 3.3 displays the percentage of respondents who claim that they have participated in various forms of protest activism. It is no surprise that the percentage of WVS respondents who indicate having participated in protest activities is low and, tellingly, some of the questions were not even asked for WVS 7.

Among the forms of protest activities, the rate of signing a petition (having done/might do) is noticeably higher than other types of protest activism, with 2018 (52 percent) being the highest across the three waves. Very few respondents report that they have ever joined in boycotts, attended peaceful demonstrations, or joined strikes. It should be kept in mind that some of the petitioning or peaceful demonstrations as reported may well have been patriotic and regime-supporting.[25] In

Table 3.3. Protest Activism

For each one, whether you have actually done any of these things, whether you might do it, or would never, under any circumstances, do it.

	Have done (%)	Might do (%)
WVS 7 (2018)		
Sign a petition	7	45
Join in boycotts	3	36
Attend peaceful demonstrations	1	32
Join strikes	2	25
WVS 6 (2012)		
Sign a petition	29	22
Join in boycotts	7	24
Attend peaceful demonstrations	10	30
Join strikes	7	23
Other act of protest	4	26
WVS 5 (2007)		
Sign a petition	6	44
Join in boycotts	3	41

contrast, those respondents who participated in anti-government activities may have underreported their involvement.

We need to be cautious about interpreting self-reported engagement in contentious forms of participation in the Chinese context. First of all, participants in the more radical activities often practiced in liberal democracies might face very high costs under authoritarian rule. China is under one-party rule, and the crackdown on protestors in 1989 and thereafter make people hesitate when they think of engaging in activities that may challenge the authorities. While the regulatory state in Western democracies has evolved in response to public demands within the framework of democratic accountability, Chinese regulatory institutions have developed in a political environment "characterized by weak laws and inadequate legal institutions, the continuing dominance of the Communist Party, and a strong preoccupation with stability maintenance."[26] Hence, even when the national law appears to guarantee people's rights to some political participation, that guarantee may exist on paper only, and those who seek to enjoy these rights encounter major obstacles and bear significant political costs in their quest.

Second, radical forms of political participation are often situational. In other words, demonstrations and unofficial strikes are often triggered in reaction to specific events and particular circumstances, depending on the opportunities generated by particular issues, specific events, and the role of leaders, rather than reflecting the distinctive social or attitudinal profile of citizens.[27] As a result, there are significant limitations to the study of protest propensity through surveys in dictatorial political environments.

Third, as Ronald Inglehart has noted, the process that brings more "favorable existential conditions" tends to shift a society's belief system from a more closed to a more open outlook, and its values from those of survival to those of self-expression.[28] Following more than three decades of improvement in living standards, Chinese respondents are among the most optimistic in the world.[29] While the Chinese political system has become more austere in recent years under Xi Jinping, there is nonetheless an indication of growing societal toleration of values and behaviors that were considered taboo at the start of the post-Mao era. When asked the question whether "children should give up their own will to realize their parents' wishes," the younger cohorts in China are increasingly saying no.[30] In a way, the efforts of General Secretary Xi Jinping to tighten political control are in response to the value changes that have occurred in China.

Voting in Elections for Local People's Congresses

Within the system of "people's democratic dictatorship" under the leadership of the Chinese Communist Party, Article 97 of the Chinese Constitution provides for direct elections of "deputies to the people's congresses of counties, cities not divided into districts, municipal districts, townships, ethnic townships and towns." The competitiveness of these elections is severely limited.[31] Local Party organizations and leadership have come up with and adopted various controlling strategies and tactics to select the candidates as well as to manage and manipulate the election processes.[32] Most delegates, as Kevin J. O'Brien notes, are chosen by the authorities and are thus agents of the regime; even the remonstrators, ostensibly critics of policies, are "quasi-insiders."[33] Nonetheless, Melanie Manion shows that many delegates have played an important role representing their constituencies and in so doing have helped bolster the legitimacy of the Chinese political system.[34]

In such a political framework for local elections, many members of the electorate, even regime supporters, would be turned off by such heavy-handed tactics. Waves six and seven of the WVS include a question about voting in elections for delegates of local people's congresses,

Table 3.4. Local People's Congress Elections

How frequently did you vote in the local congress elections during the past several years?		
	% Always	% Sometimes	% Never
WVS 7	10	19	71
WVS 6	30	24	47

and we tally the frequencies in Table 3.4. Strikingly, only 10 percent of respondents in 2018 (WVS 7) indicated that they had always cast votes in local people's congress elections during the past few years, a decline of 20 percentage points from 2012 (WVS 6). Meanwhile, 71 percent of the respondents answered that they had never voted in these elections in the past several years, up 24 percent from 2012.

Online and Other Forms of Political Activism/Participation

Table 3.5 presents the data on various forms of social and political actions or activism from the WVS. Nearly two-thirds (87 percent) of respondents say they have donated or might donate to a group or campaign, while 45 percent have contacted or might contact government officials, 38 percent have encouraged or will encourage others to vote, and 16 percent have encouraged or will encourage others to take actions about political issues. In interpreting these figures, we need to keep in mind the Chinese political context. Even though the question asked on the Chinese questionnaire in China is the same wording used in liberal democracies, Chinese respondents may well interpret the question differently than their counterparts in other countries. This is clearly the case for "donating to a group or campaign": The Chinese public would tend to interpret this question as referring to philanthropic donations, such as donating to earthquake relief (e.g., the 2008 Wenchuan Earthquake in Sichuan) or to help pupils in underdeveloped areas. Such donations are acts of civic participation, but they are definitely not contributions to political groups or campaigns that are even remotely against the ruling

Table 3.5. Types of Participation

	Have done/might do (%)
Donating to a group or campaign	87
Contacting a government official	45
Encouraging others to take action on political issues	16
Encouraging others to vote	38

regime and should generally be interpreted as pro-regime. In the case of the Sichuan Earthquake, for instance, civically engaged citizens had to toe a careful political line and avoid raising sensitive political questions about the deaths of students from the collapse of thousands of shoddily-built school buildings.[35] Once we recognize the sociopolitical context for "donations" in China, particularly the collectivist pressures for making contributions to official causes, then the high percentage of WVS respondents who answered that they had donated to a group or campaign in China makes sense.

At the same time, the low percentages of respondents who have engaged in other types of political activities are no surprise. What is interesting is that the percentage of people who "might" engage in such behaviors is substantially higher than commonly recognized, a phenomenon the late Tianjian Shi brought attention to in his pioneering research.[36] While there is a need to probe into the calculus of political stakes respondents use in answering this question, it is an interesting indication that the percentage of respondents answering "might do" is much lower on the question of "encouraging others to take action on political issues." The mention of "political issues" appears to have raised respondents' sensitivity antenna.

The growth of digitalization has changed the way people connect with each other, share information across geographical and language barriers, and organize political activities, including campaigns and protests.[37] As noted earlier, the number of internet users in China surpassed 900 million in 2020 and now reaches into its most remote areas.[38] An absolute majority of these are also mobile internet users. As online access has expanded vastly, new forms of participation have emerged online, particularly among the young cohorts of the population. Coping with an increasingly elaborate regime of censorship, netizens in China may nonetheless petition, interact with local officials, and discuss political issues. Online channels for political participation have often become more influential than their offline counterparts; for example, the traditional form of contacting Party and government offices by letter has atrophied.

In 2018, WVS 7 introduced new questions about whether Chinese respondents have engaged in certain forms of political participation using the internet. The survey responses to these questions are tallied in Table 3.6. Keep in mind that in China the mention of words like "politics" or "political" is sensitive for many people. Also note that the question is asked of all respondents, not just internet users. Table 3.6 shows

Table 3.6. Online Political Participation

Type	Have done/might do (%)
Seeking information about politics and political events	51
Signing an election petition	30
Encouraging other people to take some form of political action	15
Organizing political activities, events, protests	13

that about 51 percent of respondents indicated that they have searched or might search for information about politics and political events. What is remarkable is that nearly half of the respondents answered that they "would never" use the internet to search for information about politics and political events. Since we know that virtually all mobile internet users are bombarded with news and other information, often delivered to them by AI technology, this answer appears to us to be likely underreported, as respondents probably chose to either shy away from "politics" or adopt a narrow definition of what they think is "political."

On petitions, encouraging others to take political action, and organizing political activities, events, and protests, the percentages of respondents who answered "have done" or "might do" are much lower, at 30, 15, and 13 percent, respectively. What is interesting here is the much higher percentage of people who say they might engage in such activities, a strong indication of the potential of using the internet to overcome obstacles to collective action and bring like-minded people together. For the same reason, the Party propaganda-censorship regime has become a pervasive presence online, and one of its major missions is to forestall collective action and help maintain social stability.[39]

Online political activism in China does not equate to being against the ruling system. On the one hand, the authorities throughout China have populated the internet comments pages and chat rooms with pro-regime voices, from government staff members to the fifty-cent army. On the other, amid rising sentiments of national pride and nationalism, there have emerged groups of online users, such as the "voluntary fifty-cent army" and "little pinkies," that take pride in supporting China online and in attacking those they see as "Han betrayers" or traitors.[40] Thus the Party-state has tamed the online space within China and created as well as benefited from an online public sphere that is regime-defending. Indeed, as the previous chapter notes, within the confined political space dominated by the Chinese Party-state, Chinese citizens have largely indicated their support for the concept of a socialist democracy with Chinese characteristics and, when asked, readily express their satisfaction with the state of democracy in China.

One of the latest such phenomena is known as "fan activism," which refers to fan-driven efforts to address civic issues through engagement with and strategic deployment of popular culture content.[41] Participants in such activism at first sought to change corporate practices.[42] In 2019, however, a large number of youth online users from China, nicknamed "fangirls" for their zeal and organizing methods, used VPNs to access Facebook, Twitter, and Instagram, and flooded portions of these networks with nationalist comments and "slogans and memes shaming brands" to defend China from Hong Kong protestors and foreign critics.[43] As the influence of the "fangirls" grew, even Party-state organizations such as the Chinese Communist Youth League appropriated elements of this popular and participatory culture in their efforts to reach a broader audience. In an ironic twist, despite their nationalist displays, the power and appeal of the "fan circles" have prompted authorities to curb their online presence.

Socioeconomic Factors and Political Participation

In this section, we examine how various socioeconomic factors map to a variety of political behaviors. Figures 3.1 to 3.5 summarize the socioeconomic factors and individual characteristics associated with each type of political participation. The plots display the magnitude and confidence intervals of the multinomial ordinal logistic regression coefficients in different models. First, in general, CCP members are more politically engaged compared with non-Party respondents (Figures 3.1 to 3.5).

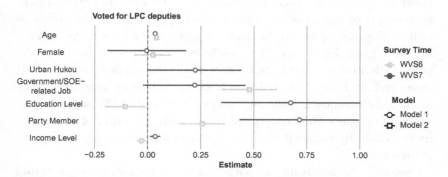

Figure 3.1. Demographic Breakdown of Vote for Local People's Congress Deputies

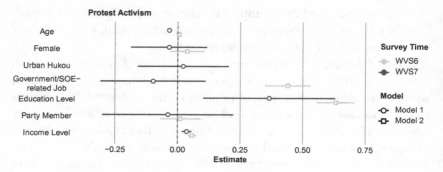

Figure 3.2. Demographic Breakdown of Protest Activism

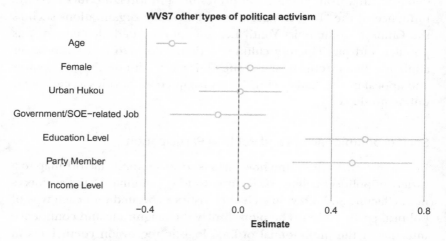

Figure 3.3. Demographic Breakdown of Other Types of Political Participation (WVS 7)

Specifically, CCP members are more likely to vote in LPC elections (Figure 3.1) or participate in other forms of political activities online or offline (Figures 3.3 to 3.5), but they are not more willing to risk offending the regime (Figure 3.2). The results are not surprising because compared with other social groups, CCP members tend to be more politically aware and are better able to link politicians' actions to policy and developmental outcomes. In contrast, except for voting in LPC elections, government or state-owned enterprise (SOE) employees do not seem to be more politically engaged compared with people without government-related jobs.

Second, the literature on participation in democracies has found that education drives a wide range of civic actions.[44] Specifically, higher

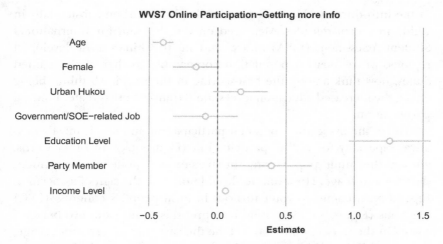

Figure 3.4. Demographic Breakdown of Online Participation (WVS 7)

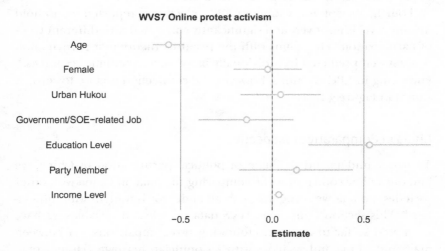

Figure 3.5. Demographic Breakdown of Other Online Activism (WVS 7)

education is associated with higher socioeconomic status, which increases citizens' material and ideational ability to follow politics,[45] and better educated citizens may place a higher premium on self-expression and individual voice.[46] In China, education level is also positively correlated with the likelihood of political participation, especially when it comes to online participation (Figures 3.4 and 3.5). As Inglehart and Zhong note in the introductory chapter, education levels have risen substantially in China in recent decades. Measured on the Program for International Student Assessment (PISA) index, students in China's most developed regions, which boast a population comparable to that of the United States, now rank among the best-scoring in the world. All things being equal, the increased education level should translate into greater political participation.

Third, the association between participation and age is mostly negative, especially for online participation (Figure 3.5). In other words, among the adult population, the passion for political engagement decreases with age. However, we should note that the sign of association flips when it comes to voter turnout in local people's congress (LPC) elections (Figure 3.1). We could interpret this result from two perspectives: On the one hand, it may well be the case that as respondents age, there is a higher likelihood that they engage in certain activities. On the other hand, it is also possible that voting is a relatively conventional type of participation that older people are more familiar with.

Fourth, except for voting in LPC elections, reported household income level is positively and significantly correlated with different types of participation. This aligns with the resource theory that participation is often well predicted by individually based socioeconomic resources.[47] For voting in LPC elections, however, the connection is close to zero, as shown in Figure 3.1.

China in Comparative Perspective

To better understand the state of political participation in China, we join our fellow contributors by comparing the data on China with other societies, even as we recognize such an endeavor is fraught with difficulties.[48] This section utilizes the WVS data on selected variables we have examined so far to make the following two comparisons: (1) between mainland China and societies with a Confucian heritage (Hong Kong, Taiwan, South Korea); and (2) between mainland China and the United States. Clearly these five societies differ greatly in scale, level of economic development, type of political regime, and degree of organization, and are not amenable to easy comparisons. Our goal is to use the comparisons to stimulate reflections on China and on these other societies, and perhaps even to provoke further research. For those who wish to delve into the topic further, we provide the full results of our data explorations in the Appendix.

We first compare the East Asian societies. In their earlier research based on the East Asia Barometer (EAB) surveys, Chu et al. found that a large share of the respondents in East Asian societies expressed reservations about political participation. In all of the regions they studied except Mongolia, "fewer than 18 percent of the respondents felt that they were capable of both understanding and participating in politics."[49]

Using the WVS Wave 7 (2018) data, we find, for the four East Asian societies—Hong Kong, mainland China, Taiwan, and South Korea—some similarities as well as major differences in political attitudes and participation. Despite the regime differences, they exhibit similar patterns in "interest in politics," with mainland China having a higher percentage of respondents in the "interested" or "very interested" categories (Figure 3.6). We also find it fascinating that the four societies score similarly on "contacting a government official" whereas mainland China stands out for the high percentage of respondents who made donations.

People's attitudes toward different forms of political participation vary significantly in these societies, and the patterns beg further inquiry. For "contacting a government official," "encouraging others to take political action," and various forms of online participation, mainland China and Taiwan tend to be closer together and score lower than Hong Kong and South Korea (Figures 3.7 and 3.8). The major exception is in

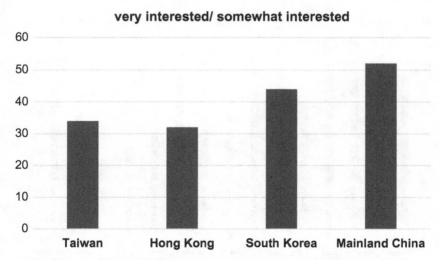

Figure 3.6. Interest in Politics (%) in Taiwan, Hong Kong, South Korea, and Mainland China

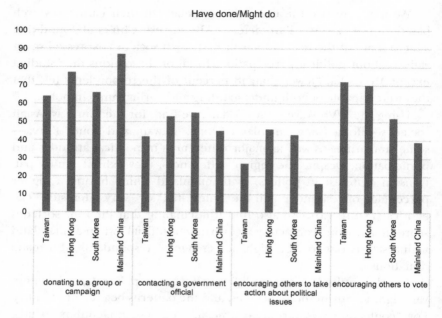

Figure 3.7. Other Types of Participation (%) in Taiwan, Hong Kong, South Korea, and Mainland China

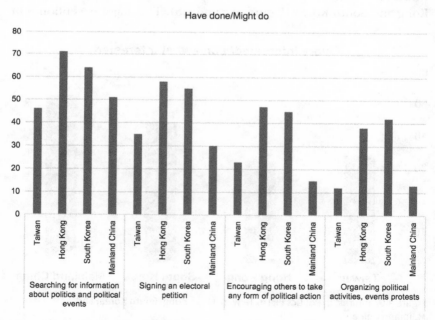

Figure 3.8. Online Participation (%) in Taiwan, Hong Kong, South Korea, and Mainland China

the category "encouraging others to vote," where Taiwan, with its robust democracy, scores the highest, while mainland China, not surprisingly, scores the lowest.

When we compare (Mainland) China and the United States in 2018, the contrasts between the two societies immediately stand out (Figures 3.9 and 3.10). Americans show higher interest in politics overall. Most importantly, as measured in the levels of actual or potential protest activism in Figure 3.10, Americans are far more likely to have participated or consider participating in some form of political action, from signing a petition to joining in demonstrations, boycotts, and strikes, than Chinese respondents. These differences are not surprising in view of the contrasting political systems of the two countries. The massive protests that occurred in the United States in 2020 are thus reflective of the wellspring of popular propensities to engage in protests.

What is especially interesting, however, is that significant percentages of Chinese respondents, about half as many as Americans, also indicate an inclination to engage in protests. China's leadership has instituted an elaborate maintenance system to promote stability and contain petitions and protests.[50] However, as many scholars have noted, China has experienced many protests in the past, and the preferences revealed here suggest that protests will continue to be part of China's political scene in the future.[51]

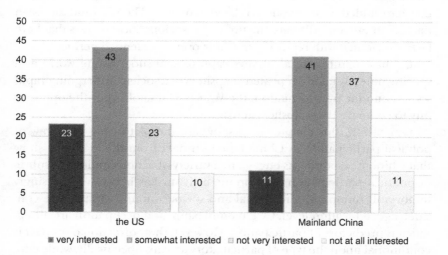

Figure 3.9. Interest in Politics (%) in the United States and Mainland China

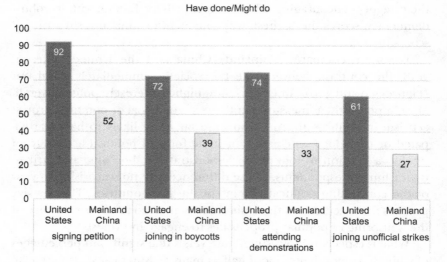

Figure 3.10. Protest Activism (%) in the United States and Mainland China

Conclusion

Of the major nationally representative surveys anchored in academic settings in China, the China General Social Surveys (CGSS) and China Family
Panel Studies (CFPS) have tended to be more socially oriented even as
they have added some questions related to politics. The WVS and the Asian
Barometer Survey (ABS) are the two major sociopolitical surveys that have
been distributed with regularity in China over an extended period.

By their nature, social surveys capture snapshots of the world at a
specific time. By taking repeated snapshots of a society undergoing rapid
socioeconomic transformation, the WVS in China offers us the opportunity to compare the snapshots across time.

Our task in this chapter is to showcase the picture we can draw of
political participation in China based on data from the WVS. We show
that Chinese respondents engage in a variety of actions under the rubric
of political participation, and online activism has become increasingly
important. Among the individual and socioeconomic variables we consider, age, education level, CCP membership, and occupation are all significant predictors of participation. However, their direction of impact is
conditional upon the type of participatory activity. Specifically, while education level and income are generally positively correlated with different

types of political activism, the relationship between political membership and participation varies across different types of participation.

In chapter 1, Inglehart and Zhong suggest that countries under
Confucian influence share similar values on various social-cultural
dimensions. The realm of political participation, however, may be a
major exception. While mainland China stands out for its authoritarian
rule and leaves little room for robust societal participation in national
governance, recent political development in South Korea, Taiwan, and
Hong Kong underscores that people in these societies are not politically
acquiescent by nature or culture. As a result, the categorical differen-
tiation between Confucian and non-Confucian societies may now be of
limited utility in helping us understand the variations in political activism across Asia. In the spirit of this volume, we have included the WVS
Wave 7 data from the United States, Taiwan, Hong Kong, South Korea,
and mainland China to compare the level of political interest and participation in these societies, thus putting mainland China in comparative
context. In East Asia, mainland China and Taiwan tend to be similar on a
number of indicators in spite of their contrasting political systems. In the
case of China vs. the United States, it is not surprising that these societies
offer significant contrasts in political interest and activism. Nonetheless,
the revealed propensity for activism in China reminds us of China's rich
history of protest and points to the potential for greater activism in the
future, especially if the Chinese preoccupation with stability maintenance is ever relaxed.

The multidimensional nature of political participation makes its
conceptualization, measurement, and interpretation challenging. In
interpreting the survey results on political participation in China, we
must be aware of limits on the questions that could be asked, challenges
in sampling, and constraints on administering the surveys across time
and space—factors that the editors have discussed and put in context.
Our findings also point to the need to be attentive to the context when
designing survey questions and interpreting survey results.

Notes

1. For a review, see Jan W. van Deth, "A Conceptual Map of Political
Participation," *Acta Politica* 49, no. 3 (2014): 349–67.
2. James R. Townsend, *Political Participation in Communist China* (Berkeley:
University of California Press, 1967); John P. Burns, *Political Participation in Rural
China* (Berkeley: University of California Press, 1988).

3. Tianjian Shi, *Political Participation in Beijing* (Cambridge, MA: Harvard University Press, 1997).

4. Wenfang Tang, "Workplace Participation in Chinese Local Industries," *American Journal of Political Science* 37, no. 3 (1993): 920–40.

5. Melanie Manion, "The Electoral Connection in the Chinese Countryside," *American Political Science Review* 90, no. 4 (1996): 736–48; M. Kent Jennings, "Political Participation in the Chinese Countryside," *American Political Science Review* 91, no. 2 (1997): 361–72; M. Kent Jennings, "Gender and Political Participation in the Chinese Countryside," *The Journal of Politics* 60, no. 4 (1998): 954–73.

6. Andrew Nathan and Tianjian Shi, "Cultural Requisites for Democracy in China: Some Findings from a Nationwide Survey," *Daedalus* 122, no. 2 (1993): 95–123.

7. Bruce J. Dickson, *Wealth into Power: The Communist Party's Embrace of China's Private Sector* (Cambridge: Cambridge University Press, 2008); Bruce J. Dickson, *Red Capitalists in China: The Party, Private Entrepreneurs, and Prospects for Political Change* (Cambridge: Cambridge University Press, 2003).

8. Kellee S. Tsai, *Capitalism without Democracy: The Private Sector in Contemporary China* (Ithaca: Cornell University Press, 2007).

9. Jie Chen and Yang Zhong, "Why Do People Vote in Semicompetitive Elections in China?" *The Journal of Politics* 64, no. 1 (2002): 178–97.

10. Yang Zhong and Jie Chen, "To Vote or Not to Vote: An Analysis of Peasants' Participation in Chinese Village Elections," *Comparative Political Studies* 35, no. 6 (2002): 686–712.

11. James Griffiths, *The Great Firewall of China: How to Build and Control an Alternative Version of the Internet* (London: Zed Books Ltd, 2019).

12. *Sixth Tone*, "China's Internet Users Reach 904 Million," April 29, 2020, https://www.sixthtone.com/news/1005584.

13. The amount and range of such research has grown enormously. A sampling of the different types of research include: Rongbin Han, *Contesting Cyberspace in China: Online Expression and Authoritarian Resilience* (New York: Columbia University Press, 2018); Guobin Yang, *The Power of the Internet in China: Citizen Activism Online* (New York: Columbia University Press, 2009); Junyan Jiang, Tianguang Meng, and Qing Zhang, "From Internet to Social Safety Net: The Policy Consequences of Online Participation in China," *Governance* 32, no. 3 (2019): 531–46.

14. Mick P. Couper, "Web Surveys: A Review of Issues and Approaches," *The Public Opinion Quarterly* 64, no. 4 (2000): 464–94.

15. "中国政治坐标测试 (Chinese Political Compass Assessment)," Peking University BBS, accessed on October 1, 2020, http://zuobiao.me/.

16. Danqing Xiao and Tu Lan, "Mapping Ideological Opinions in China Using Online Survey," *Annals of GIS* 23, no. 2 (2017): 79–91; Jennifer Pan and Yiqing Xu, "China's Ideological Spectrum," *The Journal of Politics* 80, no. 1 (2018): 254–73.

17. Holger Preuss and Christian Alfs, "Signaling through the 2008 Beijing Olympics—Using Mega Sport Events to Change the Perception and Image of the Host," *European Sport Management Quarterly* 11, no. 1 (2011): 55–71.

18. Pippa Norris, *Democratic Phoenix: Reinventing Political Activism* (Cambridge: Cambridge University Press, 2002).

19. Norris, *Democratic Phoenix.*

20. In regression analysis, we adopted different coding schemes for different types of participation. For the first dimension, whether one voted or not in the national election, we code the dependent variable, voter turnout, as a dummy. For the other dimensions, including participation in protest and etc., we do not code each variable into dummy because fewer people claim they have done so. We suspect that people may not be willing to admit that they have participated in certain activities due to political concerns.

21. Markus Prior and Lori D. Bougher, "'Like They've Never, Ever Seen in This Country'? Political Interest and Voter Engagement in 2016," *Public Opinion Quarterly* 82, no. S1 (2018): 822–42; Markus Prior, *Hooked: How Politics Captures People's Interest* (Cambridge: Cambridge University Press, 2018).

22. Minxin Pei, "China in 2017: Back to Strongman Rule," *Asian Survey* 58, no. 1 (2018): 21–32.

23. Samuel H. Barnes, Klaus R. Allerbeck, Barbara G. Farah, Felix J. Heunks, Ronald F. Inglehart, M. Kent Jennings, Hans Dieter Klingemann, Alan Marsh, and Leopold Rosenmayr, *Political Action: Mass Participation in Five Western Democracies* (Beverly Hills: Sage, 1979).

24. Diana Fu, "Disguised Collective Action in China," *Comparative Political Studies* 50, no. 4 (2017): 499–527; Dali Yang, "China's Troubled Quest for Order: Leadership, Organization and the Contradictions of the Stability Maintenance Regime," *Journal of Contemporary China* 26, no. 103 (2017): 35–53.

25. Jessica Chen Weiss, *Powerful Patriots: Nationalist Protest in China's Foreign Relations* (Oxford: Oxford University Press, 2014).

26. Dali L. Yang, "China's Illiberal Regulatory State in Comparative Perspective," *Chinese Political Science Review* 2, no. 1 (2017): 114–33.

27. Norris, *Democratic Phoenix.*

28. Ronald Inglehart, "Postmodernization Erodes Respect for Authority, but Increases Support for Democracy," in *Critical Citizens: Global Support for Democratic Government,* ed. Pippa Norris (Oxford: Oxford University Press, 1999), 236–56; Ronald Inglehart, *Modernization and Postmodernization: Culture, Economic, and Political Change in 43 Societies* (Princeton: Princeton University Press, 1997); Paul R. Abramson and Ronald Inglehart, "Generational Replacement and the Future of Post-Materialist Values," *The Journal of Politics* 49, no. 1 (1987): 231–41.

29. Pew Research Center, "GDP Growth and Optimism about Children's Future," October 8, 2014, https://www.pewresearch.org/global/2014/10/09/emerging-and-developing-economies-much-more-optimistic-than-rich-countries-about-the-future/inequality-21/.

30. Lijun Chen et al., "Youth Values and Attitudes," chap. 8 in *Child and Youth Well-Being in China* (New York: Routledge, 2018), 77–89.

31. Tianjin Shi, "Voting and Nonvoting in China: Voting Behavior in Plebiscitary and Limited-Choice Elections," *The Journal of Politics* 61, no. 4 (1999): 1115–39; Chen and Zhong, "Why Do People Vote in Semicompetitive Elections?"

32. Zhongyuan Wang, "Playing by the Rules: How Local Authorities Engineer Victory in Direct Congressional Elections in China," *Journal of Contemporary China* 26, no. 108 (2017): 870–85.

33. Kevin J. O'Brien, "Agents and Remonstrators: Role Accumulation by Chinese People's Congress Deputies," *The China Quarterly* 138 (1994): 359–80.

34. Melanie Manion, *Information for Autocrats: Representation in Chinese Local Congresses* (Cambridge: Cambridge University Press, 2015).

35. Bin Xu, *The Politics of Compassion: The Sichuan Earthquake and Civic Engagement in China* (Redwood City: Stanford University Press, 2017).

36. Tianjin Shi, *Political Participation in Beijing* (Cambridge, MA: Harvard University Press, 1997).

37. Russell J. Dalton, *The Good Citizen: How a Younger Generation Is Reshaping American Politics* (London: CQ Press, 2015); W. Lance Bennett, *Civic Life Online* (Cambridge, MA: The MIT Press, 2007); Yannis Theocharis, "Cuts, Tweets, Solidarity and Mobilisation: How the Internet Shaped the Student Occupations," *Parliamentary Affairs* 65, no. 1 (2012): 162–94.

38. China Internet Network Information Center, "The 45th China Statistical Report on Internet Development," 2020, https://www2.cnnic.net.cn/IDR/ReportDownloads/202012/P020201201530023411644.pdf.

39. Gary King, Jennifer Pan, and Margaret E. Roberts, "How Censorship in China Allows Government Criticism but Silences Collective Expression," *American Political Science Review* 107, no. 2 (2013): 326–43.

40. Rongbin Han, "Defending the Authoritarian Regime Online: China's 'Voluntary Fifty-Cent Army,'" *The China Quarterly* 224 (2015): 1006–25.

41. Henry Jenkins, "'Cultural Acupuncture': Fan Activism and the Harry Potter Alliance," in *Popular Media Cultures: Fans, Audiences and Paratexts,* ed. Lincoln Geraghty (London: Palgrave Macmillan, 2015), 206–29.

42. Jenkins, "Cultural Acupuncture."

43. Zheping Huang, "'Fangirls' Defend China from Hong Kong Protesters and the World," *Bloomberg*, December 9, 2019, https://www.bloomberg.com/news/articles/2019-12-09/-fangirls-defend-china-from-hong-kong-protesters-and-the-world; Lauren Teixeira, "China Is Sending Keyboard Warriors over the Firewall," *Foreign Policy*, August 26, 2019, https://foreignpolicy.com/2019/08/26/china-is-sending-keyboard-warriors-over-the-firewall/.

44. Norris, *Democratic Phoenix*; Sidney Verba and Gabriel Almond, *The Civic Culture: Political Attitudes and Democracy in Five Nations* (Princeton: Princeton University Press, 1963); Ronald La Due Lake and Robert Huckfeldt, "Social Capital, Social Networks, and Political Participation," *Political Psychology* 193 (1998): 567–84.

45. Kevin Croke, Guy Grossman, Horacio A. Larreguy, and John Marshall, "Deliberate Disengagement: How Education Can Decrease Political Participation in Electoral Authoritarian Regimes," *American Political Science Review* 110, no. 3 (2016): 579–600.

46. Ronald Inglehart and Christian Welzel, *Modernization, Cultural Change, and Democracy: The Human Development Sequence* (New York: Cambridge University Press, 2005).

47. Sidney Verba, Kay Lehman Schlozman, Henry Brady, and Norman H. Nie, "Citizen Activity: Who Participates? What Do They Say?" *American Political Science Review* 87, no. 2 (1993): 303–18; Jan E. Leighley and Jonathan Nagler, "Individual and Systemic Influences on Turnout: Who Votes? 1984," *The Journal of Politics* 54, no. 3 (1992): 718–40.

48. Giovanni Sartori, "Comparing and Miscomparing," *Journal of Theoretical Politics* 3, no. 3 (1991): 243–57.
49. Yun-han Chu, Larry Diamond, Andrew J. Nathan, and Doh Chull Shin, eds., *How East Asians View Democracy* (New York: Columbia University Press, 2008).
50. Dali L. Yang, "China's Troubled Quest for Order."
51. Eeresa Wright, *Popular Protest in China* (Cambridge, UK: Polity, 2018).

Bibliography

Abramson, Paul R., and Ronald Inglehart. "Generational Replacement and the Future of Post-Materialist Values." *The Journal of Politics* 49, no. 1 (1987): 231–41.

Almond, Gabriel Abraham, and Sidney Verba. *The Civic Culture: Political Attitudes and Democracy in Five Nations.* Princeton: Princeton University Press, 2015.

Bachman, David. Review of *Wealth into Power: The Communist Party's Embrace of China's Private Sector,* by Bruce J. Dickson. *Perspectives on Politics* 8, no. 2 (2010): 633–35.

Barnes, Samuel Henry, and Max Kaase. *Political Action: Mass Participation in Five Western Democracies.* Beverly Hills, Calif.: Sage Publications, 1979.

Chen, Jie, and Yang Zhong. "Why Do People Vote in Semicompetitive Elections in China?" *The Journal of Politics* 64, no. 1 (2002): 178–97.

Chen, Lijun, Qiang Ren, Dali L. Yang, and Di Zhou. *Child and Youth Well-Being in China.* New York: Routledge, 2018.

Chu, Yun-han, Larry Diamond, Andrew J. Nathan, and Doh Chull Shin, eds. *How East Asians View Democracy.* New York: Columbia University Press, 2018.

Couper, Mick P. "Web Surveys: A Review of Issues and Approaches." *The Public Opinion Quarterly* 64, no. 4 (2000): 464–94.

Croke, Kevin, Guy Grossman, Horacio A. Larreguy, and John Marshall. "Deliberate Disengagement: How Education Can Decrease Political Participation in Electoral Authoritarian Regimes." *American Political Science Review* 110, no. 3 (2016): 579–600.

Dalton, Russell J. *The Good Citizen: How a Younger Generation Is Reshaping American Politics.* Washington, DC: CQ Press, 2015.

Dickson, Bruce J. *Red Capitalists in China: The Party, Private Entrepreneurs, and Prospects for Political Change.* Cambridge: Cambridge University Press, 2003.

Fu, Diana. "Disguised Collective Action in China." *Comparative Political Studies* 50, no. 4 (2017): 499–527.

Griffiths, James. *The Great Firewall of China: How to Build and Control an Alternative Version of the Internet.* London: Bloomsbury Publishing, 2021.

Han, Rongbin. "Defending the Authoritarian Regime Online: China's 'Voluntary Fifty-Cent Army.'" *The China Quarterly* 224 (2015): 1006–25.

Inglehart, Ronald. "Postmodernization Erodes Respect for Authority, but Increases Support for Democracy." In *Critical Citizens: Global Support for Democratic Governance,* edited by Pippa Norris, 236–56. Oxford: Oxford University Press, 1999.

Jenkins, Henry. "'Cultural Acupuncture': Fan Activism and the Harry Potter Alliance." In *Popular Media Cultures*, edited by Lincoln Geraghty, 65–74. London: Palgrave Macmillan, 2015.

Jennings, M. Kent. "Gender and Political Participation in the Chinese Countryside." *The Journal of Politics* 60, no. 4 (1998): 954–73.

Jennings, M. Kent. "Political Participation in the Chinese Countryside." *American Political Science Review* 91, no. 2 (1997): 361–72.

Kennedy, Scott. Review of *Capitalism Without Democracy: The Private Sector in Contemporary China*, by Kellee S. Tsai. *Perspectives on Politics* 6, no. 2 (2008): 414–15.

King, Gary, Jennifer Pan, and Margaret E. Roberts. "How Censorship in China Allows Government Criticism but Silences Collective Expression." *American Political Science Review* 107, no. 2 (2013): 326–43.

La Due Lake, Ronald, and Robert Huckfeldt. "Social Capital, Social Networks, and Political Participation." *Political Psychology* 19, no. 3 (1998): 567–84.

Leighley, Jan E., and Jonathan Nagler. "Individual and Systemic Influences on Turnout: Who Votes? 1984." *The Journal of Politics* 54, no. 3 (1992): 718–40.

Manion, Melanie. "The Electoral Connection in the Chinese Countryside." *American Political Science Review* 90, no. 4 (1996): 736–48.

Manion, Melanie. *Information for Autocrats: Representation in Chinese Local Congresses.* Cambridge: Cambridge University Press, 2015.

Nathan, Andrew J., and Tianjian Shi. "Cultural Requisites for Democracy in China: Findings from a Survey." *Daedalus* 122, no. 2 (1993): 95–123.

Norris, Pippa. *Democratic Phoenix: Reinventing Political Activism.* Cambridge: Cambridge University Press, 2002.

O'Brien, Kevin J. "Agents and Remonstrators: Role Accumulation by Chinese People's Congress Deputies." *The China Quarterly* 138 (1994): 359–80.

Pan, Jennifer, and Yiqing Xu. "China's Ideological Spectrum." *The Journal of Politics* 80, no. 1 (2018): 254–73.

Pei, Minxin. "China in 2017: Back to Strongman Rule." *Asian Survey* 58, no. 1 (2018): 21–32.

Preuss, Holger, and Christian Alfs. "Signaling through the 2008 Beijing Olympics—Using Mega Sport Events to Change the Perception and Image of the Host." *European Sport Management Quarterly* 11, no. 1 (2011): 55–71.

Prior, Markus. *Hooked: How Politics Captures People's Interest.* Cambridge: Cambridge University Press, 2018.

Prior, Markus, and Lori D. Bougher. "'Like They've Never, Ever Seen in This Country'? Political Interest and Voter Engagement in 2016." *Public Opinion Quarterly* 82, no. S1 (2018): 822–42.

Sartori, Giovanni. "Comparing and Miscomparing." *Journal of Theoretical Politics* 3, no. 3 (1991): 243–57.

Shi, Tianjian. *Political Participation in Beijing.* Cambridge, MA: Harvard University Press, 1997.

Shi, Tianjian. "Voting and Nonvoting in China: Voting Behavior in Plebiscitary and Limited-Choice Elections." *The Journal of Politics* 61, no. 4 (1999): 1115–39.

Tang, Wen Fang. "Workplace Participation in Chinese Local Industries." *American Journal of Political Science* 37, no. 3 (1993): 920–40.

Theocharis, Yannis. "Cuts, Tweets, Solidarity and Mobilisation: How the Internet Shaped the Student Occupations." *Parliamentary Affairs* 65, no. 1 (2012): 162–94.

Townsend, James Roger. *Mass Political Participation in Communist China.* Berkeley: University of California Press, 1965.

Van Deth, Jan W. "A Conceptual Map of Political Participation." *Acta Politica* 49, no. 3 (2014): 349–67.

Verba, Sidney, Kay Lehman Schlozman, Henry Brady, and Norman H. Nie. "Citizen Activity: Who Participates? What Do They Say?" *American Political Science Review* 87, no. 2 (1993): 303–18.

Wang, Zhongyuan. "Playing by the Rules: How Local Authorities Engineer Victory in Direct Congressional Elections in China." *Journal of Contemporary China* 26, no. 108 (2017): 870–85.

Weiss, Jessica Chen. *Powerful Patriots: Nationalist Protest in China's Foreign Relations.* Oxford: Oxford University Press, 2014.

Welzel, Christian, Ronald Inglehart, and Franziska Deutsch. "Social Capital, Voluntary Associations and Collective Action: Which Aspects of Social Capital Have the Greatest 'Civic' Payoff?" *Journal of Civil Society* 1, no. 2 (2005): 121–46.

Wright, Teresa. *Popular Protest in China.* Hoboken: John Wiley & Sons, 2018.

Xiao, Danqing, and Tu Lan. "Mapping Ideological Opinions in China Using Online Survey." *Annals of GIS* 23, no. 2 (2017): 79–91.

Xu, Bin. *The Politics of Compassion: The Sichuan Earthquake and Civic Engagement in China.* Redwood City: Stanford University Press, 2017.

Yang, Dali L. "China's Illiberal Regulatory State in Comparative Perspective." *Chinese Political Science Review* 2, no. 1 (2017): 114–33.

Yang, Dali L. "China's Troubled Quest for Order: Leadership, Organization and the Contradictions of the Stability Maintenance Regime." *Journal of Contemporary China* 26, no. 103 (2017): 35–53.

Zhong, Yang, and Jie Chen. "To Vote or Not to Vote: An Analysis of Peasants' Participation in Chinese Village Elections." *Comparative Political Studies* 35, no. 6 (2002): 686–712.

Appendix 1. Sample Size in WVS 7

	N
U.S.	2596
Taiwan	1223
Hong Kong	2075
South Korea	1245

Appendix 2. Interest in Politics

Interest in politics (%)	very interested	somewhat interested	not very interested	not at all interested
United States	23	43	23	10
Taiwan	4	30	39	27
Hong Kong	3	29	46	22
South Korea	2	42	49	7
Mainland China	11	41	37	11

Appendix 3. Protest Activism

Protest Activism (%)		Have done	Might do	Would never do
Signing petition	United States	62	30	8
	Taiwan	20	40	41
	Hong Kong	21	44	35
	South Korea	18	47	35
	Mainland China	7	45	48
Joining in boycotts	United States	24	49	28
	Taiwan	9	39	51
	Hong Kong	10	40	51
	South Korea	5	47	48
	Mainland China	3	36	61
Attending demonstrations	United States	20	55	26
	Taiwan	7	41	52
	Hong Kong	20	41	39
	South Korea	10	49	41
	Mainland China	1	32	67
Joining unofficial strikes	United States	8	53	39
	Taiwan	1	34	65
	Hong Kong	3	42	54
	South Korea	2	45	53
	Mainland China	2	25	73

Appendix 4. Social Activism

Social activism (%)		Have done	Might do	Would never do
Donating to a group or campaign	Unite States	45	34	20
	Taiwan	43	21	36
	Hong Kong	38	38	23
	South Korea	16	50	34
	Mainland China	66	21	13
Contacting a government official	United States	41	43	16
	Taiwan	16	27	58
	Hong Kong	11	42	47
	South Korea	11	44	45
	Mainland China	8	37	55
Encouraging others to take action about political issues	United States			
	Taiwan	5	21	73
	Hong Kong	10	36	54
	South Korea	3	40	57
	Mainland China	1	15	84
Encouraging others to vote	United States	65	25	10
	Taiwan	38	34	28
	Hong Kong	31	39	30
	South Korea	7	45	48
	Mainland China	8	31	62

Appendix 5. Online Participation

Online participation (%)		Have done	Might do	Would never do
Searching information about politics and political events	United States	61	27	12
	Taiwan	25	21	54
	Hong Kong	33	38	28
	South Korea	19	45	36
	Mainland China	27	24	49
Signing an election petition	United States	49	36	15
	Taiwan	13	22	65
	Hong Kong	21	37	42
	South Korea	7	48	45
	Mainland China	4	26	71

Online participation (%)		Have done	Might do	Would never do
Encouraging other people to take any form of political action	United states	37	40	23
	Taiwan	6	17	77
	Hong Kong	12	35	53
	South Korea	3	42	55
	Mainland China	1	14	85
Organizing political activities, events, protests	United States	7	44	48
	Taiwan	1	11	88
	Hong Kong	7	31	61
	South Korea	2	40	58
	Mainland China	1	12	87

FOUR

Postmaterialism in China: Generational
Differences and Cross-National
Comparisons

YU YAN

Introduction

This chapter examines the trajectory of postmaterialist values in Chinese
society cross-nationally and temporally. More than four decades ago,
Ronald Inglehart first proposed the postmaterialist values theory, emphasizing the impact of economic development on bringing high levels of
existential security, cultural change, and political change.[1] Inglehart
argues that economic prosperity makes survival less precarious, bringing
higher levels of existential security. As a new generation grows up taking
survival for granted, people gradually shift their values: from materialist
values that prioritize economic and physical security above all, to postmaterialist values that prioritize individual autonomy, self-expression,
and quality of life.[2] As Inglehart states, this value change is a "revolution"
with far-reaching impacts.[3] For example, in the political realm, postmaterialist values may provide momentum for democratization and promote political participation, while in the societal realm, they may lead to
diminishing respect for authority and demands for a more equal social
structure.[4]

Over the past few decades, China has experienced dramatic economic and social changes. According to the International Monetary
Fund (IMF), between 1978 and 2018 China's GDP per capita has grown

by almost 32 times, from 309.35 US dollars to over 10 thousand US dollars.[5] According to Inglehart's postmaterialism theory,[6] in a society with prolonged and extraordinary economic development, younger generations would shift their value priorities from materialist to postmaterialist. This value shift has a wide range of consequences, as postmaterialism is a comprehensive set of values involving politics, economics, family norms, and religious beliefs. Although this postmaterialist values theory was originally based on evidence from advanced industrial societies in the West,[7] it has been revised as a universal framework and has been applied to other regions. So far, there has been extensive scholarly attention on the theory's conceptual construct, theoretical arguments, and empirical evidence.

In addition to this theoretical background, value changes have been noted in public discussion in China, where it is often claimed that younger generations, such as the 1990 generation or the 2000 generation, are shifting away from traditional culture, which prioritizes the collective good, to more individualistic values, which prioritize personal fulfillment. If this observation is true, it seems that China is at an early stage of the shift toward postmaterialism. Although value changes in China may not be the same as those in advanced industrial societies, this observation suggests that they are occurring nonetheless.

Against this theoretical and empirical background, this chapter investigates whether and how postmaterialist values have changed in Chinese society. Inglehart's work on value shift from materialism to postmaterialism has attracted considerable attention to this topic, and its application to China has also grown in studies, most of which confirm the rise of postmaterialism there. This study contributes to the scholarship by examining a more comprehensive dataset including five waves of the World Values Survey (hereafter WVS) data on China collected between 1995 and 2018. Similar to previous studies, this chapter explores whether Chinese people have shifted their value orientation away from materialism and toward postmaterialism. This chapter also places China in a comparative context with other countries, including its East Asian neighbors and three advanced industrial societies in the West.

Statistical analyses have shown that Chinese society has become more postmaterialist as the economy continues to grow. Younger generations are more likely to hold postmaterialist values, like individual autonomy and self-expression, than older cohorts. However, the rise of postmaterialism has slowed down and even declined in recent years. In particular, youngsters who were born after 1982 have moved toward materialism as shown in recent surveys, even though they are still more postmaterialist than their elders.

Compared to more prosperous societies in East Asia and the West, China is less postmaterialist. Almost every generation in China prefers materialist values, such as promoting economic growth, fighting rising prices, and strengthening national defense, more heavily than their counterparts in more developed countries. However, reflecting the fact that intergenerational value change involves multi-decade time lags, intergenerational value differences in China are not as large as those found in countries with less rapid recent growth rates, such as South Korea and Germany, both of which experienced rapid growth several decades ago.

Previous studies on China have largely relied on cross-sectional data.[8] This practice, probably due to data availability, is problematic even though it allows comparisons between age cohorts. A careful examination of the postmaterialism theory requires time-series data and cross-national data. This chapter provides a more comprehensive examination of value changes in China by analyzing five waves of the WVS data from 1995 to 2018. Although sophisticated statistical techniques are not used here, the analyses presented in later sections provide some ideas for further research.

This chapter is arranged as follows: The first section provides an overview of the long-lasting debate on postmaterialism and a review of previous studies on China. The second section reviews studies on Chinese political culture in an era of impressive economic and social transformation. The third section explores how social values have changed over time and across generations from 1995 to 2018 in China. The fourth section examines China from a comparative perspective with more affluent societies in East Asia and the West. Following that, the chapter's final section presents a discussion and issues that deserve further attention.

The Postmaterialist Values Theory and the Ongoing Debate

Regarding how postmaterialist values emerge, there are two hypotheses in Inglehart's theory. First, a scarcity hypothesis connects individuals' priorities to what is in short supply. In an economically affluent society with a well-established social welfare system, individuals are less likely to need to worry about survival and thus shift their emphasis to autonomy, self-expression, gender equality, and other postmaterialist values. If people live in less developed countries with weaker social welfare protection, the constant concern for survival and the corresponding feelings of insecurity constrain their motivation and strength to pursue anything beyond economic and physical security.

According to Inglehart's second hypothesis, a society's value priorities change primarily through intergenerational population replacement. The socialization hypothesis emphasizes the long-lasting influence of one's preadult experience on one's value orientation as an adult.[9] Individuals whose preadult lives were shaped by economic scarcity would still prioritize materialist values when they reach adulthood, even though the society they live in has become more economically developed. Due to generational time lag, the shift from materialist to postmaterialist values occurs as younger generations gradually replace older cohorts.

Two theoretical issues related to Inglehart's theory deserve further elaboration. First, existential security encompasses more than just economic development or prosperity. Economic development does indeed make survival less precarious, but existential security also depends on the absence of wars, on the safety net provided by social welfare institutions, and on physical protection from violence and disease.[10] Thus, economic growth, although often used in empirical studies, is by itself not a sufficient indicator of existential security.[11] Although we can assume that relatively high rates of economic growth will lead to a rise in postmaterialism,[12] the shift toward high levels of postmaterialist values requires sustained high levels of economic prosperity. Rapid economic growth, even a double-digit growth rate, may move a nation only to the middle-income group. It may even unpleasantly undermine existential security when accompanied by increasing unemployment, declining wages, and shrinking welfare benefits.[13] Something more than economic growth or economic security is required to cultivate postmaterialist values: individuals' subjective sense of existential security. According to Inglehart, people's subjective sense of security is the theoretically crucial factor rather than such objective measures of socioeconomic development as GDP per capita. Increasing existential security first enhances people's subjective assessment of their socioeconomic conditions, which further shapes their value priorities. The existing literature, however, sometimes overlooks this point.

The second theoretical issue concerns whether and when individuals' values crystallize. After more than forty years of theoretical and empirical debates on Inglehart's postmaterialism, there are at least three perspectives. Inglehart initially proposed that formative social-ization experiences (e.g., existential security and the subjective assess-ment during the period of one's maturation) produce a long-lasting impact on individuals' value orientation.[14] According to this view, the shift in the direction of postmaterialist values largely occurs across gen-erations. This is what Inglehart calls birth cohort effects or long-term cohort effects.[15] But one must also take period effects or short-term fluc-tuations into account, because people also have a short-term reaction to current socioeconomic conditions.[16] Economic downturns with rising unemployment and inflation make all birth cohorts less postmaterialist, while economic prosperity has the opposite influence. As Inglehart and his associates clarify theoretically and demonstrate empirically, period effects or short-term fluctuations have from the start been an inherent part of the postmaterialism theory. Another perspective emphasizes the impact of individuals' sociodemographic characteristics, such as educa-tion and age. This perspective challenges the notion that people's values crystallize at any time point. Values can and do change over the course of one's life. Some scholars argue that generational differences in post-materialism result from rising levels of education because based on the current measures of postmaterialist values,[17] items like protecting free-dom of speech and giving people more say in government are very likely to be appreciated by people with more education. Another perspective emphasizes life-cycle effects, arguing that as individuals grow older, their material needs become more salient, which in turn pushes them to pri-oritize materialist values.[18]

A voluminous literature has been devoted to empirically testing the validity of the postmaterialist values theory. It is hardly possible to sum-marize all the extant studies here. To better understand the theoretical underpinnings and empirical evidence of the postmaterialism thesis, the author recommends readers explore Inglehart's work[19] and the debates between him and other scholars. Paul Abramson also provides a nice summary of the critiques and counter-critiques of the postmaterialism theory.[20] This paper adds empirical evidence from China to the ongoing debate.

Several predictions of value change can be drawn from Inglehart's theories and his conversations with other scholars. These predictions involve generational differences in all societies and cross-national com-parisons. As previously mentioned, this chapter specifically focuses on generational differences in China and how China compares with some other nations and regions.

First, given China's phenomenal economic and social transformation, younger generations have become more inclined to embrace post-materialist values than older cohorts.

Second, levels of economic development are positively associated with the popularity of postmaterialist values. China is less postmaterialist than other industrialized countries because it is still less economically developed.

Third, high economic growth rates are related to larger differences between the values of younger and elder generations. Generational gaps are larger in China than in other advanced industrial countries.

Economic Development and Political Culture in China

As the most populous country, China has impressed the world with its remarkable economic and social transformations, including rapid economic growth, massive urbanization, and increasing globalization. These changes have been widely witnessed and documented since Deng Xiaoping kicked off China's reforms at the 1978 Central Economic Work Conference. The growth of China's national wealth since 1978 has been extraordinary, as shown in Figure 4.1. Between 1995 and 2018,[21] GNI per capita has grown by more than five times, from 2,522 to 16,121 USD.

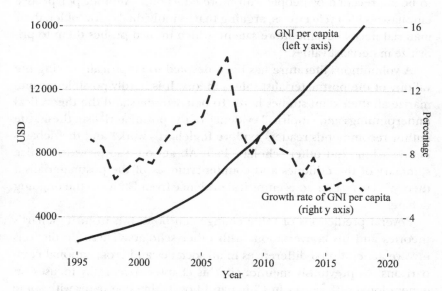

Figure 4.1. GNI per Capita and Growth Rate in China, 1995–2018
Source: GNI per capita from the World Bank Open data (https://data.worldbank.org/indicator/NY.GNP.PCAP.CD?name_desc=false); GNI growth rate is calculated by the author.

During the same period, the average growth rate for GNI per capita is 8.42 USD, with its peak at 14.10 USD in 2007. In 1978, only around 18 percent of Chinese people lived in cities.[22] In 2019, the percentage reached 60 percent.[23]

China's remarkable economic progress and social changes make it an interesting case for examining value changes. As Inglehart states, low-income countries with relatively high rates of economic growth will experience larger differences between the values of young and old cohorts, even though people holding the postmaterialist values will still be a minority.[24] In the context of rapid economic growth since the 1990s, China is a great case for testing this hypothesis. It is expected that younger generations will be less likely to be concerned about survival and thus more likely than their elders to hold postmaterialist values.

A small number of existing studies that explicitly examine postmaterialism in China have basically confirmed that younger generations are more postmaterialist than older cohorts in mainland China and Hong Kong.[25] Generational differences are larger in China than in the United States.[26] Individual-level education, income, and subjective class identification are found to be influential in shaping postmaterialist values. However, there is inconclusive evidence on formative experiences as measured by family class status.[27]

If postmaterialism has emerged, what does this mean for political development in China? It has long been argued that traditional Chinese political culture has contributed to the stability and legitimacy of Communist rule.[28] Traditional political culture in China, heavily influenced by Confucianism, features several characteristics: collective-oriented, respect for authority in a hierarchic power structure, and favoring harmony over conflict.[29] Collective interests are prioritized over personal interests when they clash. Ordinary citizens commonly show respect to and follow government officials, but expect them to satisfy their demands in return. However, this reciprocal relationship does not mean popular participation is an essential part of political life in China. Reciprocity is expected to exist under the ruling of elites, leaving little room for the public to take part in politics. Under these value orientations, it is widely found that traditional political culture has contributed to high levels of political trust in and political support for the Communist regime.[30]

The rise of postmaterialism is challenging the Chinese traditional political culture. In the political realm, postmaterialism brings a growing emphasis on individual autonomy and self-expression, declining respect for authority, and increasing demands for political participation.[31] As being quite a departure from the essence of the traditional Chinese political culture, these changes are perceived to be conducive to democratization in the most populous country in the world. Recent studies have indeed found rising support for democratic values, including freedom of expression and direct elections, among Chinese citizens.[32] As the Chinese public becomes increasingly postmaterialist, their demands for more freedom and more influence in government will generate more pressure on the Chinese government. Although any kind of large-scale political reform in China is unlikely in the foreseeable future, a cultural shift toward a more open and democratic political system may pose inevitable challenges for the Chinese government. However, the prospect of democratization should not be viewed too positively. It is clear that misinformation and indoctrination through education and official media have been influential in shaping people's perceptions of and preferences for democracy in China.[33]

Temporal Changes and Generational Differences in Postmaterialism

This section examines how postmaterialism has evolved across generations in China. Analyses of the WVS data on China over the past five waves from 1995 to 2018 show how China as a society has moved on the continuum of materialism and postmaterialism. This section also explores generational patterns, testing whether younger cohorts are moving in the direction of postmaterialism. It demonstrates that Chinese society, as expected, has become more postmaterialist overall, but this cultural shift has weakened in recent years. This weakening trend is present in all generations, but most pronounced in the youngest generation, those born after 1982.

Six waves of WVS have been conducted in China, from 1990 to 2018. This study makes use of the last five waves of data, that is, Waves 3 to 7, collected in 1995, 2001, 2007, 2013, and 2018. The wave collected in 1990 is not included due to its heavy oversampling of urban and educated respondents. In total, there are 9,827 observations, of which 1,500 were collected in 1995, 1,000 in 2001, 1,991 in 2007, 2,300 in 2013, and 3,036 in 2018.[34]

Postmaterialism is indicated by the composite index provided in the WVS dataset. This index has a scale from 0 to 5. It is based on six survey questions, in which twelve items are given as survey options.[35] These twelve items are: (1) Maintaining order in the nation; (2) Giving people more say in important government decisions; (3) Fighting rising prices; (4) Protecting freedom of speech; (5) A high level of economic growth; (6) Making sure that this country has strong defense forces; (7) Seeing that people have more say about how things are done at their jobs and in their communities; (8) Trying to make our cities and countryside more beautiful; (9) A stable economy; (10) The fight against crime; (11) Progress toward a less impersonal and more humane society; and (12) Progress toward a society where ideas count more than money.

Items 2, 4, 7, 11, and 12 are designed to measure postmaterialist values.[36] As the postmaterialism index ranges from 0 to 5, 0 means none of these five items is chosen, while 5 means all five items are given high priority. Intermediate scores reflect the number of postmaterialist items a respondent picks. This index is treated as a continuous variable in the following analyses, making the results easier to interpret.

Figure 4.2 shows how postmaterialism has evolved in China throughout the past three decades. The overall trend is that from 1995 to 2018, China has become more postmaterialist. But although a shift toward postmaterialism has emerged, this tendency has weakened since 2013, when the postmaterialism index reached a peak value of 1.39. In 2018, the number declined to 1.32, indicating the shift toward postmaterialism has seemingly slowed down or even reversed.

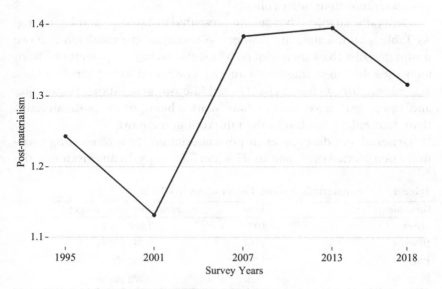

Figure 4.2. Temporal Variation in Postmaterialism in China

This chapter examines the values of four Chinese generations: those born before 1949, those born from 1950 to 1964, those born from 1965 to 1981, and those born after 1982. These four groups are defined on the basis of distinctive collective experiences. The oldest generation was born before the Chinese Communist Party (CCP hereafter) rose to power in 1949. The second oldest generation consists of those who were born in the early years of the Communist regime. They experienced the consolidation of the new regime, and they also lived through the economic and social turmoil of the Great Leap Forward (1958–1962) and the Cultural Revolution (1966–1976). The third generation includes individuals born from 1965 to 1981. Although the oldest members of this cohort experienced the chaotic Cultural Revolution when they were toddlers, the socialization period of this generation was characterized by a shift from class conflict to economic development under the pragmatic top leaders of the CCP. Not only did people from this generation begin to focus on economic growth, but they also enjoyed a relaxed political environment, particularly in the late 1980s. The youngest generation refers to those born after 1982 under the one-child policy. Although the policy was put into effect in 1979, it was implemented nationwide after 1982. Since China's economy began to take off rapidly starting in the 1990s, individuals born since then are more likely to have grown up under relatively secure conditions, and they are expected to be more postmaterialist than older cohorts.

Generational value changes are presented in Table 4.1 and Figure 4.3. As Table 4.1 indicates, the younger generations are consistently more postmaterialist than their elders. Thus, the youngest generation, born after 1982, has an average value of 1.53, compared to 1.17 for the oldest generation born before 1949. The middle two generations (1950–1964 and 1965–1981) have intermediate scores, being more postmaterialist than their elders, but less so than the youngest cohort.

Generational differences in postmaterialism show interesting variation when plotted over time, as shown in Figure 4.3. In any given year the

Table 4.1. Postmaterialism across Generations in China

Generations	Mean	Frequency (Percentage)
–1949	1.17	1,389 (14%)
1950–64	1.20	3,147 (32%)
1965–81	1.35	3,569 (36%)
1982–	1.53	1,722 (18%)

* The youngest respondents were born in 2000

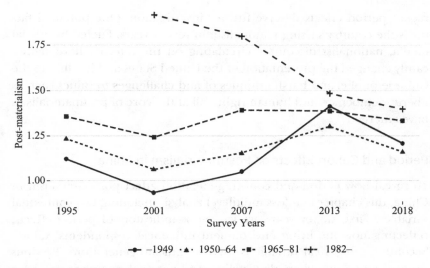

Figure 4.3. Postmaterialism of Chinese Generations over Time

younger generations are more postmaterialist than the older cohorts, except for the 1949 generation in 2013.[37] The largest generational gap occurs in 2001, between the youngest (1982) generation and the other three cohorts. In that year, the 1982 generation had been included in the survey sample for the first time, displaying the strongest support for post-materialism. Despite this, 2001 marked the lowest point of postmaterial-ist values in China as a whole because the other three elder generations all moved toward materialism that year.

Generational differences do exist, but not all generations have become more materialist in recent years, making the gaps between them much smaller. In particular, in 2013 the youngest generation showed a dramatic decline in postmaterialism. This weakening trend in postma-terialism is also present, but to a lesser extent, in the other generations during this period. It could be argued that as time passes, the aging of the youngest generation pushes them away from postmaterialism. But, theoretically, such a life-cycle effect is not part of the postmaterialist val-ues theory proposed by Inglehart. Age matters, as found in empirical studies, but Inglehart argues for the long-lasting effects of one's preadult experience in value priorities when individuals reach their adulthood. Moreover, if age has such a large effect, it does not seem to impose the same degree of influence on older generations. Given the decline of postmaterialism present in China as a society and across all generations, recent period effects deserve further investigation. One potential factor is the country's rising nationalism in recent years. Fueled by official media, nationalist discourses circulating on the internet have significantly changed the presentation of the United States and its allies to the Chinese public, and harsh critiques of and challenges to values such as liberty, democracy, and human rights, all at the core of postmaterialism, have emerged.[38]

Period and Cohort Effects on Postmaterialism in China

To reveal how period and cohort/generation affect postmaterialism in China, this chapter employs multilevel analysis including two contextual variables. First, survey years are viewed as indicators of period effects, reflecting how the living environment influences respondents' values. Second, a categorical variable is used to indicate generations. Previous studies, especially when they make cross-national comparisons, have coded every ten years as a generation.[39] Since this study focuses on the Chinese story, the coding of each generation ought to be more relevant to the history of Chinese society. Inspired by previous studies on value differences,[40] four generations are identified based on their birth years: before 1949, 1950–1964, 1965–1981, and after 1982. As described in the previous section, each generation has had distinctive socialization experiences. Although the coding of this variable is based on birth year, the generation variable has a different connotation. Unlike individual experience measured by birth year, generation measures the collective memory and experiences that individuals from the same generation share with each other. That is why generation is used as a contextual-level variable to estimate the influence of cohort effects.

Several individual-level variables are also used as controls: age, gender, education, and self-reported social class status. As mentioned above, age and education are found to play an important role in shaping postmaterialist values. As individuals grow older, their material needs become more salient, which in turn pushes them to prioritize materialist values.[41] Education matters because in the current measures of postmaterialist values, people with higher levels of education are likely to care more about items like protecting freedom of speech and giving people more say in government.

Because individuals are nested within higher-level units, this study employs cross-classified multilevel modeling.[42] What makes the analyses here different from some previous studies is that there are two higher-level units: survey years and generations. Individuals are grouped into a certain generation category to indicate cohort effects, and they are also nested within survey years when they experience similar socioeconomic development with others. Thus, cross-classified multilevel modeling is adopted to simultaneously estimate the influence of contextual variables.

Results of cross-classified multilevel models are reported in Table 4.2. Intraclass correlation (hereafter ICC) is reported to show the magnitudes of cohort effects and period effects. Larger values of ICC indicate a greater impact of clustering (that is, generations and survey years in this chapter). Indicated by very small values of ICC, statistical results show very limited influence of period effects. In contrast, cohort effects are

Table 4.2. Cross-Classified Multilevel Modeling

	Postmaterialism
Age	-0.01*** (0.001)
Male	0.03 (0.02)
Primary School	0.10 (0.09)
Middle School	0.18** (0.09)
High School	0.21** (0.09)
Higher Education	0.46*** (0.10)
Working Class	-0.11 (0.14)
Lower Middle Class	-0.15 (0.12)
Upper Middle Class	-0.10 (0.07)
Upper Class	-0.01 (0.04)
Constant	1.27*** (0.12)
Log Likelihood	-11895.52
ICC	
Generations	0.22
Survey Years	0.05
Observations	7918

Note: *p<0.1, **p<0.01, ***p<0.01

found to be much more important with much larger values of ICC. Thus, it shows that cohort effects are much more significant than period effects in shaping China's postmaterialism.

As for individual characteristics, age and education are found to be influential. Age is consistently negatively associated with postmaterialism, indicating that as individuals get older, their values become less postmaterialist. Although this age effect does not necessarily indicate the rise of materialism, it reminds us that values are more fluid than Inglehart's theory expects. Even though socialization greatly shapes individuals' values, they may still change their attitudes and beliefs as time passes. Although underrated by Inglehart, a significant life-cycle effect is present in value change.

Education becomes the most influential factor in shaping social values. The general pattern is that as people become more educated, they move toward postmaterialist values. This pattern is present in those who finished middle school, high school, and higher education. The positive influence of higher education is most remarkable.[43] Compared to those without education, those receiving higher education is 0.46 higher in postmaterialist index.

China in Comparative Perspective

This section compares China and eight advanced industrial societies: five from East Asia and three from the West. Hong Kong, Japan, Singapore, South Korea, and Taiwan are chosen because they share similarities in Confucianism, collective-oriented cultures, and respect for authority,[44] and they are also grouped into the same cultural zone in Inglehart's works. They differ from one another on levels of economic development and welfare provision. Germany, Sweden, and the United States are selected not only because they are more prosperous than China, but also because they represent different types of welfare regimes in the Western world.[45] This section uses the same measures of economic development and postmaterialism to draw comparisons between China and these countries, using data from the five waves of the WVS carried out from 1995 to 2018.

Major economic gaps exist between China and the advanced industrial countries, as shown in Table 4.3 and Figures 4.4 and 4.5. Economic growth in China has been phenomenal since 1995, with its GNI growth rates averaging 8.42 percent (shown in Table 4.3). It is also notable that over this same period, China has grown much faster than the high-income

Table 4.3. Average GNI per Capita and Growth Rate between 1995 and 2018

Country	GNI per capita*	GNI per capita growth rate (%)
China	7,787	8.42****
Taiwan**	18,241	3.36
South Korea	26,699	3.80
Japan	36,185***	1.04
Germany	39,836	1.49
Sweden	41,094	2.20
Hong Kong	44,137	2.68
United States	48,943	1.59
Singapore	63,130	2.84

* 2011 international dollars adjusted for purchasing power parity.
** Taiwan data come from Taiwan National Statistics, nominal values.
*** Data cover years from 1995 to 2017, due to missingness in 2018.
**** Data cover years from 1996 to 2017, due to missingness in 1995.

countries. The average growth rates for the East Asian countries range from 1.04 percent (Japan) to 3.80 percent (South Korea), and the numbers for the three Western countries are between 1.49 percent (Germany) and 2.20 percent (Sweden). China's economic growth is at least three times faster than that of the Western countries. This leads us to expect the value differences between younger and elder generations in China to

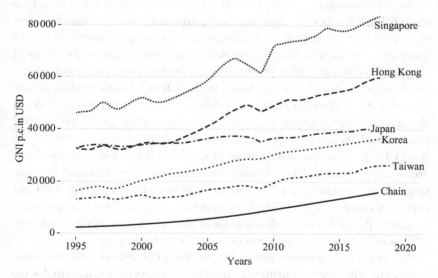

Figure 4.4. Gross National Income per Capita in East Asia
Source: The World Bank Open data (https://data.worldbank.org/indicator/NY.GNP.PCAP.
CD?name_desc=false).

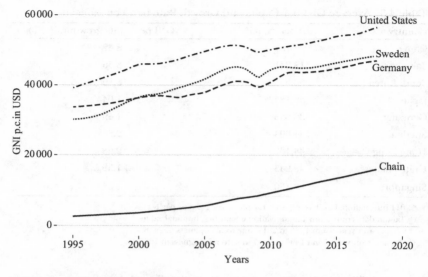

Figure 4.5. Gross National Income per Capita in China and the West
Source: The World Bank Open data (https://data.worldbank.org/indicator/NY.GNP.PCAP.
CD?name_desc=false).

be larger than those in East Asian countries and even larger than those
in Western societies.

Rapid economic growth, however, does not immediately bring prolonged high levels of prosperity. As Figures 4.4 and 4.5 show, between
1995 and 2018, this chapter's comparison cases have always been far
more affluent than China. In East Asia, Singapore is currently the most
prosperous country with a per capita GNI in 2011 purchasing power parity of $63,130—roughly seven times higher than China's, and wealthier
than the three Western countries examined here. Hong Kong ranks as
the second most prosperous case in East Asia, while Japan takes third
place. South Korea and Taiwan are also more economically developed
than China, although less so than Japan. The three Western countries
are more prosperous than China's neighbors in East Asia and are also
more similar to each other. The United States, with an average GNI per
capita of close to $49,000 dollars between 1995 and 2018, is 5.3 times
wealthier than China. Sweden and Germany are close to each other, with
GNI per capita around $40,000 over the same time span.

We expect postmaterialism to be positively correlated with economic
prosperity. However, according to Inglehart's concept of existential security, welfare institutions are also an important part of the story. Although
data on welfare expenditures in some East Asian societies are unreliable,

it is still worthwhile to discuss the potential influence of welfare institutions. It is widely acknowledged that social-democratic regimes such as Sweden's are more generous than conservative-corporatist welfare regimes represented by Germany, which in turn are more generous than liberal democratic regimes exemplified by the United States.[46] China and its East Asian neighbors have been categorized as developmental welfare regimes,[47] which are similar to or less generous than liberal democratic regimes.[48] Combining the evidence of economic prosperity and welfare generosity, China is expected to have the lowest levels of postmaterialism compared to the other eight cases. Between East Asia and the West, East Asia should be less postmaterialist than Germany, Sweden, and the United States, because it is generally less wealthy and its welfare provision is less generous.

Results reported in Table 4.4 show noticeable gaps between China and its neighbors in East Asia. As discussed in the previous section, the postmaterialism index ranges from 0 to 5, with 5 indicating the highest level of postmaterialism. With the smallest average value, China is the least postmaterialist country in this region. In contrast, Hong Kong and Japan have higher average numbers of postmaterialism across all generations (2.16 and 2.18, respectively, in Table 4.4). Singapore, as the most affluent society in East Asia, is not the most postmaterialist society among all the East Asian cases. In fact, Singapore has a slightly weaker postmaterialist orientation than expected, suggesting that factors other than economic prosperity may influence social values as well. However, this does not deny the significance of economic affluence, as the general overall pattern in East Asia follows what is expected from Inglehart's arguments. Taiwan is found to be much more similar to China than other nations. This may not be surprising given that Taiwan is only slightly economically wealthier than China, as Figure 4.4 shows. But its considerably low level of postmaterialism still raises questions about whether context-specific factors are hindering the shift away from materialism.

Table 4.4. The Distribution of Materialist and Postmaterialist Values in East Asia

Country/Region	Weighted Mean	Sample Size
China	1.31	9,827
Taiwan	1.48	4,468
South Korea	2.00	6,094
Singapore	2.05	3,484
Hong Kong	2.16	4,327
Japan	2.18	7,308

Generational differences between China and its neighboring countries in East Asia are presented in Table 4.5, which contains the weighted mean values of postmaterialism for each generation. The average values of all generations in China and its neighbors confirm the expectations of postmaterialist values theory. Cross-nationally, each generation in China is more inclined toward materialism than its counterparts in East Asia, albeit the differences are smaller between mainland China and Taiwan. For example, for millennials,[49] identified as those born after 1986 in this paper, the average value in China is 1.53 as compared to above 2 in the other countries studied here. On the other hand, generational differences follow the pattern argued by Inglehart: Younger generations are likelier to hold postmaterialist values than older cohorts. This pattern is present in all East Asian societies. Taiwan stands out as an interesting case. It also witnesses a generational shift toward postmaterialism, but gaps between the youngest generation and the elder ones are the largest in Taiwan. This significant shift toward postmaterialism in Taiwan contrasts with mainland China, where the changes have been more gradual.

Given China's remarkable economic and social transformation, one might expect to find that generational value differences in China would be particularly large—except for the fact that China has attained high levels of existential security very recently. The bottom row of Table 4.5 reports the largest gap between any two generations within society. To obtain this index, the highest value among all the generations is subtracted from the lowest value. With a value of 0.37, China shows larger generation differences only compared with Japan (0.25) and Singapore (0.35). Generational changes in Hong Kong, South Korea, and Taiwan are even more pronounced with their values around 1. Younger generations in these three societies, especially the youngest ones who were born after 1986, are very different from elder generations.

Table 4.5. Postmaterialism across Generations in East Asia

Generations	China	Hong Kong	Japan	Singapore	South Korea	Taiwan
Before 1945	1.16	1.78	2.08	1.81	1.38	1.14
1946–1955	1.17	1.80	2.20	1.88	1.83	1.36
1956–1965	1.22	1.96	2.18	1.97	1.94	1.39
1966–1975	1.33	2.06	2.26	2.08	2.15	1.44
1976–1985	1.46	2.23	2.23	2.17	2.29	1.62
After 1986	1.53	2.73	2.33	2.16	2.42	2.05
Largest Gap	0.37	0.95	0.25	0.35	1.04	0.91

Note: The youngest respondent is born in 2001.

Table 4.6. The Distribution of Materialist and Postmaterialist Values in China and the West

Country	Weighted Mean	Percentage of Postmaterialism index = 0	Percentage of Postmaterialism index >=3	Sample Size
China	1.31	23.7	13.0	9,827
United States	2.19	7.7	38.3	8,819
Sweden	2.71	2.2	55.5	4,233
Germany	2.75	2.7	58.6	7,764

Value differences between China and three Western countries are presented in Table 4.6. With a mean of 1.31, China is significantly less postmaterialist than Germany (2.75), Sweden (2.71), and the United States (2.19). This finding confirms the expectation that China is the least postmaterialist society presented here due to its lower level of economic prosperity compared to advanced industrial societies. In China, people who prioritize materialism only comprise 24 percent of the population, which is much higher than the other three countries. Percentages of respondents holding the same values are much smaller in the Western cases, particularly in Germany and Sweden. As bigger numbers indicate higher levels of postmaterialism, more than 55 percent of respondents in Sweden and Germany score three points or higher. The proportion in the United States is close to 40 percent. In sharp contrast, the percentage in China is 13 percent.

Generational differences between China and the Western countries are presented in Table 4.7. For every generational group, China scores lower than Germany, Sweden, and the United States. The average values of these countries support this observation. However, the results do

Table 4.7. Postmaterialism across Generations in China and the West

Generations	China	Germany	Sweden	United States
Before 1945	1.16	2.36	2.52	2.06
1946–1955	1.17	2.79	2.86	2.11
1956–1965	1.22	2.88	2.79	2.09
1966–1975	1.33	2.95	2.61	2.24
1976–1985	1.46	2.81	2.91	2.26
After 1986	1.53	3.00	2.68	2.48
Largest Gap	0.37	0.64	0.39	0.42

Note: The youngest respondent is born in 2001.

not support this chapter's hypothesis that generational value differences should be the largest in China. It shows that the generational gap in China is smaller (0.37) than that in Germany (0.64), Sweden (0.39), and the United States (0.42). This finding deviates from the author's expectation that China should show the largest generational gaps due to its rapid economic development.

Conclusion

Ever since Inglehart proposed the postmaterialism theory, considerable empirical evidence has demonstrated the gradual but significant value changes in economically prosperous societies. This study contributes to this ongoing research by providing a more comprehensive examination of China through studying temporal variation, generational changes, and cross-national comparisons. As the Chinese economy took off starting in 1978, millions of people have been lifted out of poverty. As the postmaterialist values theory predicts, rising economic and social conditions would lead to the rise of postmaterialist values emphasizing individual autonomy, self-expression, and quality of life. Analyses of the WVS data generally confirm this trend, discovering that younger generations have become more postmaterialist than older cohorts.

But the rise of postmaterialism weakened between 2013 and 2018. This trend is present in all generations, particularly in the youngest 1982 generation. When this generation first entered the surveys in 2001, they were significantly more postmaterialist than older cohorts. But they have noticeably moved toward materialism in the past decade, making generational value gaps much smaller than before. Previous studies have largely overlooked this temporal trend, which makes the prospect for postmaterialism less promising.

Cross-national comparisons also tend to confirm the postmaterialism theory. Due to notable economic gaps between China and other industrialized countries in East Asia and the West, there are significant differences in value orientations between Chinese respondents and those in the other countries and regions. Not only is the Chinese society as a whole less postmaterialist than more prosperous countries, but also nearly all generations in China are more materialist than their peers in more affluent societies. These findings support the postmaterialism theory. But despite its high rates of economic growth, China is not the country where value differences between younger and elder generations are the largest. Countries with much lower recent growth rates, like South

Korea and Germany, have experienced larger intergenerational value changes that can be traced to the high growth rates they experienced several decades ago.

Several issues deserve further investigation. First, what Inglehart identifies as the theoretically crucial factor—subjective evaluations of existential security—has been seriously understudied or taken for granted in most previous studies. Only when individuals believe that survival is no longer a pressing issue do they start to embrace postmaterialist values emphasizing autonomy, gender equality, and self-expression. It is often assumed that individuals will feel more secure about their survival when they become wealthier, but existential security also depends on social welfare institutions, the absence of wars, and physical safety from violence and disease.[50] Thus, economic growth, although very often used in empirical studies, by itself is not a sufficient indicator of existential security.[51] However, it is challenging to empirically examine the effects of subjective evaluations of existential security.

Analyses show that some contextual factors may also shape value changes in China. The author suspects at least two issues worth further research: economic inequality and social media. Economically, China has achieved impressive progress. However, this fast-growing wealth has not been distributed evenly. According to the official National Statistical Bureau, China's Gini coefficient was 0.465 in 2016,[52] which is much higher than the threshold of severe income inequality (0.4) set by the United Nations. One study conducted by Southwest University of Finance and Economics in China, for example, puts China's Gini coefficient at 0.61 for 2010.[53] These estimates indicate that China has become one of the most unequal societies in the world. It has been widely acknowledged that economic inequality affects various aspects of our societies: politics, economics, family, and personal health.[54] Rising economic inequality indicates the benefits of economic development are heavily skewed toward the most prosperous groups of individuals, leaving the others behind. Even with prolonged economic growth, large segments of the population still face challenges to make ends meet. These individuals cannot take survival and security for granted. Future studies may provide more evidence showing the effects of widening economic gaps.

The recent rise of social media is unprecedented in China, as well as in the world overall. Online platforms, such as Weibo and WeChat, have become essential parts of daily life. They serve as the most important channels through which individuals obtain information and express their opinions and emotions. These online platforms are far from free of government intervention, especially under the current administration. Their increasing popularity is accompanied by rising influence from the Chinese government. It is clear that the Chinese government shapes people's thoughts via media.[55] But how the government affects cultural values and public opinion via social media has not yet been fully studied. Given the recent increase in nationalist discourse on social media, it is probable that the value shift toward postmaterialism has slowed down or even reversed.

Notes

1. Ronald Inglehart, *The Silent Revolution: Changing Values and Political Styles among Western Publics* (Princeton: Princeton University Press, 1977).

2. Inglehart, *Silent Revolution*; Ronald Inglehart, *Modernization and Postmodernization: Cultural, Economic, and Political Change in 43 Societies* (Princeton: Princeton University Press, 1997).

3. Inglehart, *Silent Revolution*.

4. Inglehart, *Modernization and Postmodernization*.

5. GDP per capita data come from IMF website, accessed February 17, 2020, https://www.imf.org/external/datamapper/NGDPDPC@WEO/CHN?zoom=CHN&highlight=CHN<.

6. Inglehart, *Silent Revolution*; Inglehart, *Modernization and Postmodernization*.

7. Ronald Inglehart, *Culture Shift in Advanced Industrial Society* (Princeton: Princeton University Press, 1990).

8. Zhaoxi Josie Liu, "Media Use and Postmaterialist Values in China and the US: A Comparative Study," *Chinese Journal of Communication* 5, no. 4 (2012): 383–98; Kwok-Fai Ting and Catherine CH Chiu, "Materialistic Values in Hong Kong and Guangzhou: A Comparative Analysis of Two Chinese Societies," *Sociological Spectrum* 20, no. 1 (2000): 15–40; Tony Huiquan Zhang, Robert Brym, and Robert Andersen, "Liberalism and Postmaterialism in China: The Role of Social Class and Inequality," *Chinese Sociological Review* 49, no. 1 (2017): 65–87.

9. Inglehart, *Culture Shift*, 57; Raymond M. Duch and Michaell A. Taylor, "Postmaterialism and the Economic Condition," *American Journal of Political Science* 37, no. 3 (1993): 747–79; Russell J. Dalton, "Was There a Revolution? A Note on Generational Versus Life Cycle Explanations of Value Differences," *Comparative Political Studies* 9, no. 4 (1977): 459–74.

10. Inglehart, *Silent Revolution*; Inglehart, *Modernization and Postmodernization*; Ronald Inglehart, "Changing Values among Western Publics from 1970 to 2006," *West European Politics* 31, no. 1–2 (2008): 130–46.

11. Ronald Inglehart, "After Postmaterialism: An Essay on China, Russia and the United States: A Comment," *Canadian Journal of Sociology* 41, no. 2 (2016): 213–22.

12. Paul R. Abramson and Ronald Inglehart, "Generational Replacement and Value Change in Eight West European Societies," *British Journal of Political Science* 22, no. 2 (1992): 183–228.

13. Clair Brown, Barry J. Eichengreen, and Michael Reich, *Labor in the Era of Globalization* (Cambridge: Cambridge University Press, 2009); David R. Cameron, "The Expansion of the Public Economy: A Comparative Analysis," *American Political Science Review* 72, no. 4 (1978): 1243–61; Jeff Dominitz and Charles F. Manski, "Using Expectations Data to Study Subjective Income Expectations," *Journal of the American Statistical Association* 92, no. 439 (1997): 855–67; Gøsta Esping-Andersen, Duncan Gallie, Anton Hemerijck, and John Myles, *Why We Need a New Welfare State* (Oxford: Oxford University Press, 2002); Jérôme Gautié and John Schmitt, *Low-Wage Work in the Wealthy World* (New York: Russell Sage Foundation, 2010); Neil Gilbert, *Transformation of the Welfare State: The Silent Surrender of Public Responsibility* (Oxford: Oxford University Press, 2002); Jude Hays, Sean Ehrlich, and Clint Peinhardt, *Globalization in the Study of Comparative and International Political Economy* (Mimeo, 2002); Steffen Mau, Jan Mewes, and Nadine M. Schöneck, "What Determines Subjective Socio-Economic Insecurity? Context and Class in Comparative Perspective," *Socio-Economic Review* 10, no. 4 (2012): 655–82; Dani Rodrik, "Why Do More Open Economies Have Bigger Governments?" *Journal of Political Economy* 106, no. 5 (1998): 997–1032; Kenneth Scheve and Matthew J. Slaughter, "Economic Insecurity and the Globalization of Production," *American Journal of Political Science* 48, no. 4 (2004): 662–74.

14. Inglehart, *Silent Revolution*; Inglehart, *Modernization and Postmodernization*.

15. Paul R. Abramson and Ronald Inglehart, "Education, Security, and Postmaterialism: A Comment on Duch and Taylor's 'Postmaterialism and the Economic Condition,'" *American Journal of Political Science* 38, no. 3 (1994): 797–814; Ronald Inglehart and Pippa Norris, "Trump and the Xenophobic Populist Parties: The Silent Revolution in Reverse," *Perspectives on Politics* 15, no. 2 (2017): 443–54.

16. Abramson and Inglehart, "Generational Replacement and Value Change"; Harold D. Clarke and Nitish Dutt, "Measuring Value Change in Western Industrialized Societies: The Impact of Unemployment," *American Political Science Review* 85, no. 3 (1991): 905–20; Raymond M. Duch and Michaell A. Taylor, "Postmaterialism and the Economic Condition," *American Journal of Political Science* 37, no. 3 (1993): 747–79; Ronald Inglehart, "Aggregate Stability and Individual-Level Flux in Mass Belief Systems: The Level of Analysis Paradox," *American Political Science Review* 79, no. 1 (1985): 97–116; Inglehart, *Culture Shift*; Inglehart and Norris, "Trump and the Xenophobic Populist Parties."

17. There are two ways to calculate postmaterialism: four-item measure and twelve-item measure. Details are provided in the Appendix.

18. Russell J. Dalton, "Was There a Revolution? A Note on Generational Versus Life Cycle Explanations of Value Differences," *Comparative Political Studies* 9, no. 4 (1977): 459–74.

19. Inglehart, *Silent Revolution*; Inglehart, *Culture Shift*; Inglehart, *Modernization and Postmodernization*; Inglehart, "Changing Values."

20. Paul R. Abramson, "Critiques and Counter-Critiques of the Postmaterialism Thesis: Thirty-Four Years of Debates," *Center for the Study of Democracy*, 2011, https://escholarship.org/uc/item/3f72v9q4.

21. GNI data analyzed here are collected from the World Development Indicators database in 2020. These data cover years from 1995 to 2018, being consistent with the WVS data.

22. Wen-Chin Wu, Yu-Tzung Chang, and Hsin-Hsin Pan, "Does China's Middle Class Prefer (Liberal) Democracy?" *Democratization* 24, no. 2 (2017): 347–66.

23. National Bureau of Statistics of China, "Statistical Communiqué of the People's Republic of China on the 2019 National Economic and Social Development," February 28, 2020, http://www.stats.gov.cn/english/PressRelease/202002/t20200228_1728917.html.

24. Inglehart, *Modernization and Postmodernization.*

25. Liu, "Media Use and Postmaterialist Values in China"; Ting and Chiu, "Materialistic Values in Hong Kong and Guangzhou"; Zhang, Brym, and Andersen, "Liberalism and Postmaterialism in China"; Ka-Ying Wong and Po-San Wan, "New Evidence of the Postmaterialist Shift: The Experience of Hong Kong," *Social Indicators Research* 92, no. 3 (2009): 497–515.

26. Liu, "Media Use and Postmaterialist Values in China."

27. Ting and Chiu, "Materialistic Values in Hong Kong and Guangzhou"; Wong and Wan, "New Evidence of the Postmaterialist Shift."

28. Tianjian Shi, "Cultural Values and Political Trust: A Comparison of the People's Republic of China and Taiwan," *Comparative Politics* 33, no. 4 (2001): 401–19; Wenfang Tang, *Public Opinion and Political Change in China* (Redwood City: Stanford University Press, 2005); Wenfang Tang, *Populist Authoritarianism: Chinese Political Culture and Regime Sustainability* (Oxford: Oxford University Press, 2016); Yida Zhai, "Traditional Values and Political Trust in China," *Journal of Asian and African Studies* 53, no. 3 (2018): 350–65.

29. Shi, "Cultural Values and Political Trust"; Tianjian Shi and Jie Lu, "The Meanings of Democracy: The Shadow of Confucianism," *Journal of Democracy* 21, no. 4 (2010): 123–30.

30. Tang, *Populist Authoritarianism*; Yang and Tang, "Exploring the Sources of Institutional Trust in China"; Yang Zhong, *Political Culture and Participation in Urban China* (Singapore: Palgrave Macmillan, 2018); Yang Zhong, "Do Chinese People Trust Their Local Government, and Why? An Empirical Study of Political Trust in Urban China," *Problems of Post-Communism* 61, no. 3 (2014): 31–44; Yang Zhong and Yongguo Chen, "Regime Support in Urban China," *Asian Survey* 53, no. 2 (2013): 369–92.

31. Inglehart, *Modernization and Postmodernization*; Ronald Inglehart and Christian Welzel, *Modernization, Cultural Change, and Democracy: The Human Development Sequence* (New York: Cambridge University Press, 2005).

32. Chunlong Lu, "Democratic Values among Chinese People: Analysis of a Public Opinion Survey," *China Perspectives* 55 (2004): 1–13; Wu, Chang, and Pan, "Does China's Middle Class Prefer (Liberal) Democracy?"; Yida Zhai, "Popular Conceptions of Democracy and Democratic Satisfaction in China," *International Political Science Review* 40, no. 2 (2019): 246–62.

33. Youngho Cho, "How Well Are Global Citizenries Informed about Democracy? Ascertaining the Breadth and Distribution of Their Democratic Enlightenment and Its Sources," *Political Studies* 63, no. 1 (2015): 240–58; Min-Hua Huang, Yun-han Chu, and Yu-tzung Chang, "Popular Understandings of Democracy and Regime Legitimacy in East Asia," *Taiwan Journal of Democracy* 9, no. 1 (2013): 147–71; Jie Lu and Tianjian Shi, "The Battle of Ideas and

Discourses before Democratic Transition: Different Democratic Conceptions in Authoritarian China." *International Political Science Review* 36, no. 1 (2015): 20–41; Doh Chull Shin and Youngho Cho, "How East Asians Understand Democracy: From a Comparative Perspective," *Asien* 116 (2010): 21–40; Doh Chull Shin and Hannah June Kim, "How Global Citizenries Think about Democracy: An Evaluation and Synthesis of Recent Public Opinion Research," *Japanese Journal of Political Science* 19, no. 2 (2018): 222–49.

34. The WVS data can be obtained from its official website, accessed on October 22, 2010, http://www.worldvaluessurvey.org/wvs.jsp.

35. These six questions are grouped into three pairs, and each pair asks respondents to identify the most and second-most important options from the same four survey options. For example, the first pair of questions asks respondents to choose the first and second aims of their countries from items 1, 2, 3, and 4. Item 5 to 8 are used in the second pair of questions, and items 9 to 12 are used in the third pair.

36. Inglehart, *Culture Shift.*

37. After checking the data, the author ensures that this exception is not a calculation mistake, although it is not yet clear why this happened to the eldest generation.

38. Alastair Iain Johnston, "Is Chinese Nationalism Rising? Evidence from Beijing," *International Security* 41, no. 3 (2006): 7–43; Robert Weatherley, *Making China Strong: The Role of Nationalism in Chinese Thinking on Democracy and Human Rights* (New York: Springer, 2014); Jessica Chen Weiss, "How Hawkish Is the Chinese Public? Another Look at 'Rising Nationalism' and Chinese Foreign Policy," *Journal of Contemporary China* 28, no. 119 (2019): 679–95.

39. Zhaoxi Josie Liu, "Media Use and Postmaterialist Values in China and the US: A Comparative Study," *Chinese Journal of Communication* 5, no. 4 (2012): 383–98.

40. Nan Dirk De Graaf and Geoffrey Evans, "Why Are the Young More Postmaterialist? A Cross-National Analysis of Individual and Contextual Influences on Postmaterial Values," *Comparative Political Studies* 28, no. 4 (1996): 608–35; Sachiko Takeda, Marta Disegna, and Yumei Yang, "Changes in Chinese Work Values: A Comparison between the One-Child, Social Reform and Cultural Revolution Generations," *Evidence-based HRM* 7, no. 1 (2019): 24–41.

41. Russell J. Dalton, "Was There a Revolution? A Note on Generational Versus Life Cycle Explanations of Value Differences," *Comparative Political Studies* 9, no. 4 (1977): 459–74.

42. W. Holmes Finch, Jocelyn E. Bolin, and Ken Kelley, *Multilevel Modeling Using R* (Boca Raton: CRC Press, 2019).

43. Graaf and Evans, "Why Are the Young More Postmaterialist?"; Zhang, Brym, and Andersen, "Liberalism and Postmaterialism in China."

44. Yun-han Chu, Larry Diamond, Andrew J. Nathan, and Doh Chull Shin, eds., *How East Asians View Democracy* (New York: Columbia University Press, 2008); Yew Kuan Lee "Culture Is Destiny, an Interview with Fareed Zakaria," *Foreign Affairs* 73, no. 2 (1994): 109–26; Doh Chull Shin and To-ch'ŏl Sin, *Confucianism and Democratization in East Asia* (Cambridge: Cambridge University Press, 2012).

45. Clem Brooks and Jeff Manza, *Why Welfare States Persist: The Importance of Public Opinion in Democracies* (Chicago: University of Chicago Press, 2008); Gøsta Esping-Andersen, *The Three Worlds of Welfare Capitalism* (Princeton: Princeton University Press, 1990).

46. Christian Aspalter, "Welfare Regime Analysis: 30 Years in the Making," *International Social Work* 62, no. 1 (2017): 76–88; Esping-Andersen, *Three Worlds of Welfare Capitalism*; Torben Iversen and John D. Stephens, "Partisan Politics, the Welfare State, and Three Worlds of Human Capital Formation," *Comparative Political Studies* 41, no. 4–5 (2008): 600–37.

47. Xinping Guan, "China's Social Policy: Reform and Development in the Context of Marketization and Globalization," in *Transforming the Developmental Welfare State in East Asia*, ed. Huck-ju Kwon (New York: Palgrave Macmillan, 2005), 231–56; Ian Holliday, "Productivist Welfare Capitalism: Social Policy in East Asia," *Political Studies* 48, no. 4 (2000): 706–23.

48. Stephan Haggard and Robert R. Kaufman, *Development, Democracy, and Welfare States: Latin America, East Asia, and Eastern Europe* (Princeton: Princeton University Press, 2008).

49. It is common to treat people born after 1983 as millennials, but for the sake of simplicity, the year 1986 is used as the cutoff in this paper. If using the year 1983 as the cutoff, results are highly similar.

50. Inglehart, *Silent Revolution*; Inglehart, *Modernization and Postmodernization*; Inglehart, "Changing Values among Western Publics."

51. Inglehart, "After Postmaterialism."

52. Shirao Wang, "Chinese Statistics Bureau: An Increase in Gini Coefficient for 2016 Is 0.465 from 2015," accessed on November 10, 2020, http://www.chinanews.com/cj/2017/01-20/8130559.shtml.

53. Shi Li, "Dangdai Zhongguo de Shouru Fengpei Zhuangkuan (Current Income Distribution in China)," *Xueshujie* (*Academics*) 3 (2018): 5–19.

54. For example, Daron Acemoglu, Suresh Naidu, Pascual Restrepo, and James A. Robinson, "Democracy, Redistribution, and Inequality," in *Handbook of Income Distribution*, ed. Daron Acemoglu and James A. Robinson (New York: Elsevier, 2015), 1886–1966; Daron Acemoglu and James A. Robinson, *Economic Origins of Dictatorship and Democracy* (Cambridge: Cambridge University Press, 2006); Alberto Alesina and George-Marios Angeletos, "Fairness and Redistribution," *American Economic Review* 95, no. 4 (2005): 960–80; Carles Boix, *Democracy and Redistribution* (Cambridge: Cambridge University Press, 2003); Richard Wilkinson and Kate Pickett, *The Spirit Level: Why Equality Is Better for Everyone* (London: Penguin UK, 2010).

55. Shi, "Cultural Values and Political Trust"; John James Kennedy, "Maintaining Popular Support for the Chinese Communist Party: The Influence of Education and the State-Controlled Media," *Political Studies* 57, no. 3 (2009): 517–36; Daniela Stockmann and Mary E Gallagher, "Remote Control: How the Media Sustain Authoritarian Rule in China," *Comparative Political Studies* 44, no. 4 (2011): 436–67; Min Tang and Narisong Huhe, "Alternative Framing: The Effect of the Internet on Political Support in Authoritarian China," *International Political Science Review* 35, no. 5 (2014): 559–76.

Bibliography

Abramson, Paul R. "Critiques and Counter-Critiques of the Postmaterialism Thesis: Thirty-four Years of Debates." *UC Irvine: Center for the Study of Democracy*, 2011, https://escholarship.org/uc/item/3f72v9q4.

Abramson, Paul R., and Ronald Inglehart. "Education, Security, and Postmaterialism: A Comment on Duch and Taylor's 'Postmaterialism and the Economic Condition.'" *American Journal of Political Science* 38, no. 3 (1994): 797–814.

Abramson, Paul R., and Ronald Inglehart. "Generational Replacement and Value Change in Eight West European Societies." *British Journal of Political Science* 22, no. 2 (1992): 183–228.

Acemoglu, Daron, and James A. Robinson. *Economic Origins of Dictatorship and Democracy*. Cambridge: Cambridge University Press, 2006.

Acemoglu, Daron, Suresh Naidu, Pascual Restrepo, and James A. Robinson. "Democracy, Redistribution, and Inequality." In *Handbook of Income Distribution*, edited by Daron Acemoglu and James A. Robinson, 1886–966. New York: Elsevier, 2015.

Alesina, Alberto, and George-Marios Angeletos. "Fairness and Redistribution." *American Economic Review* 95, no. 4 (2005): 960–80.

Aspalter, Christian. "Welfare Regime Analysis: 30 Years in the Making." *International Social Work* 62, no. 1 (2019): 76–88.

Boix, Carles. *Democracy and Redistribution*. Cambridge: Cambridge University Press, 2003.

Brooks, Clem, and Jeff Manza. *Why Welfare States Persist: The Importance of Public Opinion in Democracies*. Chicago: University of Chicago Press, 2008.

Brown, Clair, Barry J. Eichengreen, and Michael Reich. *Labor in the Era of Globalization*. Cambridge: Cambridge University Press, 2009.

Cameron, David R. "The Expansion of the Public Economy: A Comparative Analysis." *American Political Science Review* 72, no. 4 (1978): 1243–61.

Cho, Youngho. "How Well Are Global Citizenries Informed About Democracy? Ascertaining the Breadth and Distribution of Their Democratic Enlightenment and Its Sources." *Political Studies* 63, no. 1 (2015): 240–58.

Chu, Yun-han, Larry Diamond, Andrew J. Nathan, and Doh Chull Shin, eds. *How East Asians View Democracy*. New York: Columbia University Press, 2008.

Clarke, Harold D., and Nitish Dutt. "Measuring Value Change in Western Industrialized Societies: The Impact of Unemployment." *American Political Science Review* 85, no. 3 (1991): 905–20.

Dalton, Russell J. "Was There a Revolution? A Note on Generational Versus Life Cycle Explanations of Value Differences." *Comparative Political Studies* 9, no. 4 (1977): 459–74.

Dominitz, Jeff, and Charles F. Manski. "Using Expectations Data to Study Subjective Income Expectations." *Journal of the American Statistical Association* 92, no. 439 (1997): 855–67.

Duch, Raymond M., and Michaell A. Taylor. "Postmaterialism and the Economic Condition." *American Journal of Political Science* 37, no 3, (1993): 747–79.

Esping-Andersen, Gøsta. *The Three Worlds of Welfare Capitalism*. Princeton: Princeton University Press, 1990.
Esping-Andersen, Gøsta, Duncan Gallie, Anton Hemerijck, and John Myles. *Why We Need a New Welfare State*. Oxford: Oxford University Press, 2002.
Finch, W. Holmes, Jocelyn E. Bolin, and Ken Kelley. *Multilevel Modeling Using R*. Boca Raton: CRC Press, 2019.
Gautié, Jérôme, and John Schmitt, eds. *Low-Wage Work in the Wealthy World*. New York: Russell Sage Foundation, 2010.
Gilbert, Neil. *Transformation of the Welfare State: The Silent Surrender of Public Responsibility*. Oxford: Oxford University Press, 2002.
Graaf, Nan Dirk De, and Geoffrey Evans. "Why Are the Young More Postmaterialist? A Cross-National Analysis of Individual and Contextual Influences on Postmaterial Values." *Comparative Political Studies* 28, no. 4 (1996): 608–35.
Guan, Xinping. "China's Social Policy: Reform and Development in the Context of Marketization and Globalization." In *Transforming the Developmental Welfare State in East Asia*, edited by Huck-ju Kwon, 231–56. New York: Palgrave Macmillan, 2005.
Haggard, Stephan, and Robert R. Kaufman. *Development, Democracy, and Welfare States: Latin America, East Asia, and Eastern Europe*. Princeton: Princeton University Press, 2008.
Hays, Jude, Sean Ehrlich, and Clint Peinhardt. *Globalization in the Study of Comparative and International Political Economy*. Mimeo, 2002.
Holliday, Ian. "Productivist Welfare Capitalism: Social Policy in East Asia." *Political Studies* 48, no. 4 (2000): 706–23.
Huang, Min-Hua, Yun-han Chu, and Yu-tzung Chang. "Popular Understandings of Democracy and Regime Legitimacy in East Asia." *Taiwan Journal of Democracy* 9, no. 1 (2013): 147–71.
Inglehart, Ronald. "Aggregate Stability and Individual-Level Flux in Mass Belief Systems: The Level of Analysis Paradox." *American Political Science Review* 79, no. 1 (1985): 97–116.
Inglehart, Ronald. "After Postmaterialism: An Essay on China, Russia and the United States: A Comment." *Canadian Journal of Sociology* 41, no. 2 (2016): 213–22.
Inglehart, Ronald. "Changing Values among Western Publics from 1970 to 2006." *West European Politics* 31, no. 1–2 (2008): 130–46.
Inglehart, Ronald. *Culture Shift in Advanced Industrial Society*. Princeton: Princeton University Press, 1990.
Inglehart, Ronald. *Modernization and Postmodernization in 43 Societies*. Princeton: Princeton University Press, 1997.
Inglehart, Ronald. *The Silent Revolution: Changing Values and Political Styles among Western Publics*. Princeton: Princeton University Press, 1977.
Inglehart, Ronald, and Pippa Norris. "Trump and the Xenophobic Populist Parties: The Silent Revolution in Reverse." *Perspectives on Politics* 15, no. 2 (2017): 443–54.
Iversen, Torben, and John D. Stephens. "Partisan Politics, the Welfare State, and Three Worlds of Human Capital Formation." *Comparative Political Studies* 41, no. 4–5 (2008): 600–37.

Johnston, Alastair Iain. "Is Chinese Nationalism Rising? Evidence from Beijing." *International Security* 41, no. 3 (2006): 7–43.

Kennedy, John James. "Maintaining Popular Support for the Chinese Communist Party: The Influence of Education and the State-Controlled Media." *Political Studies* 57, no. 3 (2009): 517–36.

Lee, Kuan Yew. "Culture is Destiny, an Interview with Fareed Zakaria." *Foreign Affairs* 73, no. 2 (1994): 109–26.

Li, Shi. "Dangdai Zhongguo de Shouru Fengpei Zhuangkuan. (Current Income Distribution in China)." *Xueshujie (Academics)* 3 (2018): 5–19.

Liu, Zhaoxi Josie. "Media Use and Postmaterialist Values in China and the US: A Comparative Study." *Chinese Journal of Communication* 5, no. 4 (2012): 383–98.

Lu, Chunlong. "Democratic Values among Chinese People: Analysis of a Public Opinion Survey." *China Perspectives*, no. 55 (2004): 40–48.

Mau, Steffen, Jan Mewes, and Nadine M. Schöneck. "What Determines Subjective Socio-Economic Insecurity? Context and Class in Comparative Perspective." *Socio-Economic Review* 10, no. 4 (2012): 655–82.

Rodrik, Dani. "Why Do More Open Economies Have Bigger Governments?" *Journal of Political Economy* 106, no. 5 (1998): 997–1032.

Scheve, Kenneth, and Matthew J. Slaughter. "Economic Insecurity and the Globalization of Production." *American Journal of Political Science* 48, no. 4 (2004): 662–74.

Shi, Tianjian. "Cultural Values and Political Trust: A Comparison of the People's Republic of China and Taiwan." *Comparative Politics* 33, no. 4 (2001): 401–19.

Shi, Tianjian, and Jie Lu. "The Meanings of Democracy: The Shadow of Confucianism." *Journal of Democracy* 21, no. 4 (2010): 123–30.

Shin, Doh Chull, and Hannah June Kim. "How Global Citizenries Think About Democracy: An Evaluation and Synthesis of Recent Public Opinion Research." *Japanese Journal of Political Science* 19, no. 2 (2018): 222–49.

Shin, Doh Chull, and To-ch'ŏl Sin. *Confucianism and Democratization in East Asia.* Cambridge: Cambridge University Press, 2012.

Shin, Doh Chull, and Youngho Cho. "How East Asians Understand Democracy: From a Comparative Perspective." *Asien* 116 (2010): 21–40.

Stockmann, Daniela, and Mary E Gallagher. "Remote Control: How the Media Sustain Authoritarian Rule in China." *Comparative Political Studies* 44, no. 4 (2011): 436–67.

Takeda, Sachiko, Marta Disegna, and Yumei Yang. "Changes in Chinese Work Values: A Comparison between the One-child, Social Reform and Cultural Revolution Generations." In *Evidence-Based HRM: A Global Forum for Empirical Scholarship*, edited by Thomas Lange, 24–41. Beijing: Emerald Publishing Limited, 2019.

Tang, Min, and Narisong Huhe. "Alternative Framing: The Effect of the Internet on Political Support in Authoritarian China." *International Political Science Review* 35, no. 5 (2014): 559–76.

Tang, Wenfang. *Populist Authoritarianism: Chinese Political Culture and Regime Sustainability.* Oxford: Oxford University Press, 2016.

Tang, Wenfang. *Public Opinion and Political Change in China.* Redwood City: Stanford University Press, 2005.

Ting, Kwok-Fai, and Catherine C.H. Chiu. "Materialistic Values in Hong Kong and Guangzhou: A Comparative Analysis of Two Chinese Societies." *Sociological Spectrum* 20, no. 1 (2000): 15–40.

Weatherley, Robert. *Making China Strong: The Role of Nationalism in Chinese Thinking on Democracy and Human Rights.* New York: Springer, 2014.

Weiss, Jessica Chen. "How Hawkish Is the Chinese Public? Another Look at 'Rising Nationalism' and Chinese Foreign Policy." *Journal of Contemporary China* 28, no. 119 (2019): 679–95.

Wilkinson, Richard, and Kate Pickett. *The Spirit Level: Why Equality Is Better for Everyone.* London: Penguin UK, 2010.

Wong, Ka-Ying, and Po-San Wan. "New Evidence of the Postmaterialist Shift: The Experience of Hong Kong." *Social Indicators Research* 92, no. 3 (2009): 497–515.

Wu, Wen-Chin, Yu-Tzung Chang, and Hsin-Hsin Pan. "Does China's Middle Class Prefer (Liberal) Democracy?" *Democratization* 24, no. 2 (2017): 347–66.

Zhai, Yida. "Popular Conceptions of Democracy and Democratic Satisfaction in China." *International Political Science Review* 40, no. 2 (2019): 246–62.

Zhai, Yida. "Traditional Values and Political Trust in China." *Journal of Asian and African Studies* 53, no. 3 (2018): 350–65.

Zhang, Tony Huiquan, Robert Brym, and Robert Andersen. "Liberalism and Postmaterialism in China: The Role of Social Class and Inequality." *Chinese Sociological Review* 49, no. 1 (2017): 65–87.

Zhong, Yang. "Do Chinese People Trust Their Local Government, and Why? An Empirical Study of Political Trust in Urban China." *Problems of Post-Communism* 61, no. 3 (2014): 31–44.

Zhong, Yang. *Political Culture and Participation in Urban China.* Singapore: Palgrave Macmillan, 2018.

Zhong, Yang, and Yongguo Chen. "Regime Support in Urban China." *Asian Survey* 53, no. 2 (2013): 369–92.

FIVE

Contained Emancipative Social Values:
Waves of Conservative and Liberal
Trends in China

JOHN JAMES KENNEDY

Introduction

In Chapter 1, Inglehart and Zhong show that people in more traditional
societies tend to favor greater respect for authority and less acceptance
of divorce and homosexuality. In this chapter, the focus is on emancipative social values as opposed to postmaterialist. While postmaterialist values are related to political freedom and participation as well as
creativity and care for the environment, emancipative values emphasize freedom of choice and equality of opportunities, including gender
equality and social acceptance.[1] Moreover, emancipative values, including gender equality over patriarchy and social tolerance over conformity,
are critical for the development of liberal reforms especially within the
Confucian-influenced cultural zone (see Chapter 1, Figure 1.1). China
as well as Hong Kong, South Korea, Japan, and Taiwan are part of this
cultural zone and have relatively similar values. While all five countries
and regions have experienced rapid economic growth and urbanization
over the last few decades, the seventh wave of the World Values Survey
(WVS) shows that respondents in China still hold more traditional values
compared to the other countries/regions. However, emancipative values
are emerging in China, but they have gone through dynamic changes
since the first WVS was distributed in China in 1990.

The seventh wave of the WVS on China shows two distinct trends. First, while the previous waves display an overall increase in liberal values and tolerance in China, the seventh wave (2018) shows a more conservative trend. For example, in 1990, 90 percent of respondents reported that homosexuality was "never acceptable," but in 2013 that number decreased to 48 percent. This suggests a significant increase in social tolerance. However, in 2018, the percentage of respondents who believe "homosexuality is never acceptable" increased to 67 percent. The responses to survey questions that reflect emancipative values, such as divorce, religious tolerance, gender equality, and respect for authority, follow the same pattern. This points to the rise of more conservative and traditionalist policies and propaganda since 2012 (i.e., the Xi Jinping era) rather than a resurgence of Confucian values. This is even more apparent when compared to Hong Kong, South Korea, Japan, and Taiwan, where we do not see this same trend. Second is the demographic change in respondents, such as level of education, income, and age, when it comes to more conservative and liberal views on social tolerance and equality. For example, in the China 1990 survey, a respondent's level of education and income had no influence on their acceptance of homosexuality. There was a near universal lack of tolerance for same-sex relationships. However, in 2018, higher levels of education and income showed a strong positive influence on attitudes toward accepting homosexuality. Indeed, despite the general conservative trend, there is a clear distinction between respondents who hold conservative and liberal values in the seventh WVS wave. Younger respondents with higher levels of education and income tend to hold stronger emancipative and postmaterialist values than the rest of the sample population. This is the same trend observed in Hong Kong, South Korea, Japan, and Taiwan.

The results from the China seventh wave WVS show a return to traditional attitudes toward gender equality and social tolerance along some dimensions. However, this trend does not reflect Asian Exceptionalism or even a return of Confucian values in China.[2] Instead, this reflects a more conservative political environment especially through television, print, and social media over the last five years between the 2013 and 2018 WVS. The Chinese Communist Party (CCP), under Xi Jinping since 2012, has made a concerted effort to restrict and even repeal liberal reforms in the name of national security and the "China Dream." Yet, despite the ongoing nationalist campaign, younger respondents with higher levels of education and income still display more liberal sentiments. This suggests more *contained* emancipative values in China.

The level of education and income has been rising in China since the 1980s. According to the 1995 WVS, less than 5 percent of respondents graduated from college and only 16 percent completed high school for university preparation (as opposed to vocational high school). In 2018, 22 percent of respondents received a college degree and 23 percent completed high school for university preparation. At the same time, the China WVS from 1990 to 2013 shows a clear rise in emancipative values such as gender equality over patriarchy, tolerance over conformity, and autonomy over authority (see below). However, the majority of the population has not reached higher levels of education and income. Thus, despite the positive correlation between higher education, income, and emancipative values, these values maybe constrained to a smaller proportion of citizens. Moreover, as the central Party-government continues to limit liberal reforms, some of these citizens seem to be resisting the current conservative trend. The fact that the CCP has recently been targeting higher education, such as placing greater limits on academic freedom and international interactions, suggests that the central leadership is aware of this correlation. Thus, the social and political campaigns designed to foster nationalism and traditional principles may further constrain emancipative values in China.

This chapter proceeds as follows. The first section discusses emancipative values as defined by Welzel.[3] Two key factors that influence the emergence of these values are higher education and generational shifts (that is, younger people with different values than their parents). The second section examines respect for authority and compares China with Hong Kong, South Korea, Japan, and Taiwan, as well as change over the last six China WVS waves. The seventh wave shows a sharp increase in this measure since Xi Jinping came to power. The third section investigates the trends regarding sexuality and gender equality. We observe some increase in conservative values regarding acceptance of divorce and homosexuality, especially when compared with Hong Kong, South Korea, Japan, and Taiwan. Moreover, higher levels of education and income have a positive influence on acceptance. There is a similar pattern regarding gender inequality, but gender and age have a greater influence on these values than level of education and income. The fourth section considers the social tolerance in China. Again, there is a relative decrease in intolerance toward people with different religions and sexualities, followed by an increase in 2018. Also, younger and more educated respondents tend to have greater levels of tolerance. Finally, we examine what respondents believe are important qualities children should have instilled in them growing up. The most mentioned qualities are tolerance and respect for others, independence, and a good work ethic.

Emancipative Values

As Christian Welzel writes, "People are cognitively empowered when rising education and knowledge enable them to make better informed choices in life. As this happens, people recognize the utility of equal freedoms and begin to value them accordingly. As a manifestation of this, emancipative values emerge."[4]

At the national level, the emergence of emancipative values represents a cultural shift from patriarchy to gender equality and from conformity to tolerance. This occurs through the slow and continuous spread of higher education and relatively equal educational opportunities that eventually results in a generational shift.[5] However, social inequality and unequal access to education within a nation means that rising education and knowledge is limited to a certain segment of the population. Thus, diffusion of emancipative values within a country may be constrained by the access to higher education and professional employment opportunities. Although China has increased both the number of universities and the number of individuals with access to them, higher educational opportunities remain elusive for many rural and urban residents. Indeed, aggregate growth in higher education does not necessarily translate to fair or reasonable distribution of educational opportunities. Limited access to universities in China can vary by geographical region, rural and urban environment, social class, type of school, gender, and ethnicity.[6] This is also related to the generational shift. Children whose parents completed higher education are more likely to attend college. Likewise, children whose parents do not have a university education are less likely to attend college. In the 2018 WVS, there is a significant correlation (0.54) between the respondent's highest level of education and their parents' education level. Finally, China still maintains the National College Entrance Exam, which also limits access to universities due to unequal access to resources and exam preparation. In fact, students from wealthier families, who can afford extra tutoring and invest in shadow education, tend to do better on the exam and get into more prestigious universities.[7] Thus, limited and unequal access to higher education may slow the emergence of societal emancipative values in China.

At the same time, government control over compulsory education and the media can also influence and reinforce state/Party values, especially among individuals without higher education. Indeed, compulsory education strengthens national and traditional values.[8] In China, compulsory education is nine years, and core Party and national values are taught and expressed in the classroom. It is post-compulsory, such as high school and college in the China case, that has the greatest influence on the development of emancipative values. Yet, high school and university education can also instill nationalist and traditional values.[9] For example, the nationalist Patriotic Education Campaign conducted in high schools and universities nationwide began under Jiang Zemin in the 1990s and continues under Xi Jinping.[10] Nevertheless, the population that completed compulsory education or high school but did not go on to complete university education is more susceptible to government messaging. Indeed, given the combination of compulsory education and the increased intensity of nationalist messaging from the central government media outlets since 2012, we might expect the majority of the population to hold more nationalist and traditional values. That is, there may be an expected increase in more traditional conservative values from the 2013 to the 2018 WVS due to nationalist campaigns.

One alternative explanation for the increase in conservatism and the lack of widespread emancipative values in China is Asian Exceptionalism. This suggests that East Asian cultures are more resistant to "Western" emancipative values due to collectivist and Confucian ideals.[11] If Asian Exceptionalism is hindering the development of emancipative values in China, then we should observe little change in these traditional Asian values over time. In addition, there should be little difference between a respondent's level of education and income regarding their attitudes toward gender equality, social tolerance, and respect for authority. However, if we observe changes in these values over time as well as generational differences, then this reflects more dynamic cultural changes. Moreover, the driving force behind these cultural shifts may be due to economic and social modernization as well as government influence through education and political campaigns. An analysis of the China WVS waves from 1990 to 2018 suggests more dynamic cultural changes and diverse values within the samples, especially in 2018. This pattern is observed in four general values: respect for authority, gender and sexuality, social tolerance, and qualities of children.

Respect for Authority

Respect of authority is a measure of deference to the central and even local government leaders, especially in authoritarian regimes.

Moreover, decline in deference reflects emancipative values such as greater autonomy over authority.[12] Since 1990, the WVS has asked an authority question in every wave including 2018. The survey question is: "Listed below are some changes that one may experience in their lifestyle and in the near future. Do you think this change is good, bad, or does not matter?" On the list is "greater respect for authority." Table 5.1 displays the trend from 1990 to 2018. The lowest level of respect for authority was in 1990, with only 24 percent who believed greater respect was "good." The 1990 survey was conducted only one year after the June 4, 1989, Tiananmen Square incident, and the lower level of respect for authority seems to be in response to that.[13] At the time, confidence in the central government may have also been lower, but (for obvious reasons) the 1990 WVS did not ask any questions regarding trust or confidence in the central government. However, respect for authority increased in 1995 and 2001, and then decreased in 2007 and 2013. The most striking change is from 2013 to 2018, with a 20 percent increase in respondents who believe greater respect for authority is "good." This suggests the success of Xi Jinping's nationalist messaging, including the ongoing anti-corruption campaign.

Still, one issue with the data is the percentage of those who answered "do know" (DNK) in 2007. Almost 30 percent of respondents answered DNK regarding "respect for authority." It is unclear whether or not these respondents truly did not know or if they simply refused to answer. Several other questions regarding gender, politics, and religion also have relatively high percentages of DNK in 2007. Many of the respondents who answered DNK for the 2007 WVS questions on importance of politics and

Table 5.1. Greater Respect for Authority

	1990	1995	2001	2007	2013	2018
	Percentage (Frequency)					
Good	24 (236)	41 (609)	53 (532)	43 (864)	41 (947)	61 (1,842)
Do Not Mind	39 (391)	43 (647)	15 (153)	20 (393)	28 (637)	20 (616)
Bad	34 (340)	16 (244)	15 (150)	8 (160)	19 (435)	18 (546)
Do Not Know	3 (33)	0 (0)	17 (165)	29 (569)	12 (281)	1 (32)
Total	100 (1,000)	100 (1,500)	100 (1,000)	100 (1,991)	100 (2,300)	100 (3,036)

Source: World Values Surveys.

religion also reported DNK for respect for authority. This was the year before the 2008 Beijing Olympics, and it is possible respondents were unwilling to answer seemingly critical or sensitive questions. Moreover, after a closer look at the demographics, the respondents who reported DNK tend to be older and less educated. Nevertheless, the general trend in respect for authority started relatively low in 1990 with a large increase early 2000s, followed by a decrease and then a dramatic increase in 2018.

In addition to the variation in responses over time, there was also a significant change in respondent demographics from 1990 to 2018 with regard to respect for authority. In 1990, education and income had no influence on this measure. Only age had an influence, that is, younger respondents were more likely to believe respect for authority was "bad." Yet, in 2018, education had a much stronger influence on respect for authority. In Table 5.2, the ordered logit regression shows education is positive and statistically significant. This means respondents with higher education are much more likely to believe respect for authority is "bad." However, Table 5.2 also shows that respondents with higher incomes are more likely to have higher respect for authority. One explanation is that wealthier middle-class respondents desire social stability and view respect for authority as a way to maintain stable economic development.[14] However, along other dimensions of emancipative values, such as support for divorce and homosexuality, respondents with more education and higher income tend to hold more liberal views.

Table 5.2. Influence of Gender, Education, Age, and Income on Respect for Authority[1]

	1990	2018
	Coefficient (Z-score)	
Gender	0.18	-0.16*
(0, 1=female)	(1.48)	(2.26)
Education	-0.01	0.29***
	(0.74)	(6.82)
Age	-0.01**	-0.01*
	(2.61)	(2.01)
Rural	0.01	0.10
(0, 1=rural)	(0.13)	(1.23)
Income	-0.04	-0.07***
	(1.16)	(3.40)

$p < 0.05$ = *, $p < 0.01$ = **, $p < 0.001$ = ***
N (1990) is 947; N (2018) is 2,958
[1]Respect for authority is "good" = 1, "does not matter" = 2, and "bad" = 3 (Ordered Logit Regression)

Comparatively, China has the highest level of respect for authority of all the countries and regions in the Confucian-influenced zone. Table 5.3 shows the difference in respect for authority across China, Hong Kong, Taiwan, South Korea, and Japan. For example, only 2 percent of the respondents in Japan believe "greater respect for authority" is "good" as opposed to over 60 percent in China. Taiwan and South Korea also display much lower percentages of "good." As Inglehart and Zhong suggest in Chapter 1, this reflects the difference in Freedom House scores. The freedom measure combines political rights and civil liberties scores. Japan, Taiwan, and South Korea are ranked as more free, while China is ranked as comparatively not free. Hong Kong's WVS 2018 responses to the respect for authority survey question are similar to the China's WVS 1990 responses. Given the growing tensions with Hong Kong residents and the increasing influence of Beijing on Hong Kong society, it is not surprising that fewer Hong Kong respondents believe greater respect for authority is "good."

While there is a clear distinction between China and the other Confucian-influenced countries regarding levels of respect for authority, there is greater similarity across these countries and regions regarding the influence of education on this measure. Table 5.4 displays the ordered logit regression and the influence of gender, education, age, and income on attitudes toward authority. More educated respondents in China, Hong Kong, Taiwan, and Japan tend to think greater respect for authority is "bad." This suggests that higher education has a positive influence on emancipative values in the Confucian-influenced zone. Moreover, when it comes to greater respect for authority, the Chinese

Table 5.3. Greater Respect for Authority in Comparative Perspective

	China	Hong Kong	Taiwan	S. Korea	Japan
	Percent (Frequency)				
Good	61	23	19	18	2
	(1,842)	(477)	(229)	(225)	(25)
Do Not Mind	20	42	15	41	17
	(616)	(877)	(182)	(510)	(226)
Bad	18	34	63	41	81
	(546)	(698)	(772)	(510)	(1,091)
Do Not Know	1	1	3	0	0
	(32)	(24)	(40)	(0)	(11)
Total	100	100	100	100	100
	(3,036)	(2,075)	(1,223)	(1,245)	(1,353)

Source: World Values Surveys.

Table 5.4. Influence of Gender, Education, Age, and Income on Respect for Authority in Comparative Perspective[1]

	China	Hong Kong	Taiwan	S. Korea	Japan
			Coefficient (Z-Score)		
Gender	-0.16*	-0.04	-0.10	0.11	-0.06
(0, 1=female)	(2.26)	(0.52)	(0.83)	(1.03)	(0.36)
Education	0.29***	0.28***	0.47***	-0.05	0.41***
	(6.82)	(5.03)	(6.26)	(0.65)	(3.45)
Age	-0.01*	0.01*	0.01**	-0.01**	-0.01**
	(2.01)	(1.94)	(2.64)	(2.63)	(2.94)
Rural	0.10		-0.32		0.08
(0, 1=rural)	(1.23)		(1.82)		(0.29)
Income	-0.07***	-0.06**	0.03	-0.11**	0.02
	(3.40)	(2.30)	(0.77)	(2.88)	(0.40)

$p < 0.05$ = *, $p < 0.01$ = **, $p < 0.001$ = ***
[1]Respect for authority is "good" = 1, "does not matter" = 2, and "bad" = 3 (Ordered Logit Regression)

respondents who are more highly educated hold the same attitudes as those in Hong Kong, Taiwan, and Japan. The exception is South Korea, where education has no effect.

Gender and Sexuality

Acceptance of gender equality and homosexuality is another key dimension of emancipative values. In China, divorce reflects women's empowerment, giving them the legal ability to escape bad marriages, which might include domestic violence or infidelity.[15] Indeed, in November 2019, the president of China's Supreme People's Court revealed that women initiated over 70 percent of divorces in China.[16] Social acceptance of divorce signifies gender equality and autonomy in relation to strict family or communal traditions. Modernization and higher education especially also have a positive influence on the acceptance of same-sex relationships.[17] In the 2018 WVS, higher education and income have a positive and significant influence on acceptance of divorce and homosexuality. However, the trend since 1990 is uneven.

The survey question on accepting divorce or homosexuality was asked in all six waves of the China WVS from 1990 to 2018. The question states, "Please tell me, to what extent can you accept the following behaviors? The numbers on this scale range from 1 to 10, indicating the varying degrees from completely unacceptable to completely acceptable." Table 5.5 shows the responses. The acceptance of divorce is

Table 5.5. Proportion of People Who Believe Divorce and Homosexuality Are
Never Acceptable

	1990	1995	2001	2007	2013	2018
	Percentage (Frequency)					
Divorce Is Never	15	13	56	52	31	39
Acceptable	(147)	(203)	(564)	(1,030)	(704)	(1,184)
Total	100	100	100	100	100	100
	(1,000)	(1,500)	(1,000)	(2,000)	(2,300)	(3,020)
Homosexuality Is	90	81	82	62	48	67
Never Acceptable	(900)	(1,219)	(815)	(1,231)	(1,100)	(2,036)
Total	100	100	100	100	100	100
	(1,000)	(1,500)	(1,000)	(2,000)	(2,300)	(3,036)

Source: World Values Surveys.

relatively high in 1990 and 1995, followed by a significant increase in
the unacceptance of divorce in 2001 and 2007. While the acceptance
of divorce increases again after 2007, it remains significantly lower than
in the 1990s. Yet, the survey responses do not reflect the divorce rate
in China. The crude divorce rate, which is the number of divorces per
1,000 population, was .09 in 1990 and steadily increased, especially
after 2003, to 3.2 in 2017.[18] Before 2003, couples had to go through
third-party mediation to get a divorce, but after the new divorce law in
2003, this is no longer necessary; rather, only both parties need to agree
to get a divorce. Soon after, divorced rates climbed. Ironically, acceptance of divorce decreased (i.e., became more conservative) during this
time. Indeed, over 50 percent of respondents reported that divorce is
"never acceptable" in 2007. This suggests that despite (or because of)
the increase in the divorce rate, the social stigma of divorce remained.
Nevertheless, the acceptance of divorce increased in 2013, with a 20 percent decline in respondents who believe divorce is "never acceptable"
compared to 2007. Although the level of acceptance is higher compared to the 2000s, about 40 percent still report that divorce is "never
acceptable" in 2018.

When compared with Hong Kong, Taiwan, South Korea, and Japan,
Chinese respondents are much more conservative regarding divorce
(see Table 5.6). In Taiwan, attitudes toward divorce have consistently
become more liberal, while China has moved in the opposite direction.
Indeed, the 2018 Taiwan WVS is similar to China's more liberal views
in the 1990 and 1995 WVS responses. Although gender equality and
the social status of women are still critical issues in South Korea and
Japan, attitudes toward divorce are fairly liberal. In Japan, the majority

Table 5.6. Divorce in Comparative Perspective

	China	Hong Kong	Taiwan	S. Korea	Japan
	Percent (Frequency)				
Never Acceptable	39	9	14	4	3
	(1,184)	(181)	(180)	(50)	(46)
Mostly Unacceptable	20	16	16	25	10
	(612)	(335)	(199)	(304)	(128)
Neutral	15	32	35	28	26
	(469)	(673)	(427)	(345)	(345)
Mostly Acceptable	18	37	28	42	30
	(566)	(753)	(343)	(534)	(412)
Always Acceptable	6	6	6	1	24
	(189)	(121)	(74)	(12)	(322)
Do Not Know	0	0	0	0	7
	(16)	(12)	(0)	(0)	(103)
Total	100	100	100	100	100
	(3,036)	(2,075)	(1,223)	(1,245)	(1,353)

Source: World Values Surveys.

of respondents believe divorce is generally acceptable. Thus, except for China, most respondents in the Confucian-influenced zone countries are neutral toward or generally accepting of divorce.

Examining the social attitudes toward homosexuality in China reveals a pattern of growing acceptance from 1990 to 2013 followed by a sharp increase in conservative values in 2018. Table 5.5 displays the responses for the survey question on whether or not homosexuality is "never acceptable" or "completely acceptable." In 1990, there was an almost universal lack of acceptance of homosexuality in China. This reflected the legal status of gay and lesbian relationships in China at the time. Homosexuality was considered a mental illness until 2001, and people caught engaging in homosexual acts could be persecuted under the crime of "hooliganism" until 1997.[19] However, by 2013 less than 50 percent believed same-sex relationships were never acceptable. Although not universal, there has been a growing acceptance of homosexuality among more educated Chinese citizens, especially university students.[20] Nevertheless, lack of acceptance increased dramatically from 2013 to 2018, dropping by almost 20 percent. This reversal seems to reflect the increased conservative messaging from the central government in television and print media, focusing on traditional family values and relationships.[21] In early 2019, China's popular blog site Weibo attempted to ban all LGBTQ content and messaging.[22] Although Weibo reversed its

decision after online protests from the site's users, the move demonstrates the growing conservative trend.

In comparison with Hong Kong, Taiwan, South Korea, and Japan,
respondents in China are much more conservative regarding the acceptance of homosexuality, as Table 5.7 shows. Respondent attitudes in Hong
Kong, Taiwan, and Japan are neutral or generally acceptant of homosexuality. This reflects emancipative values. However, in South Korea
72 percent of respondents find homosexuality either entirely or mostly
unacceptable. There are two overlapping reasons for this response. One
is that South Korea is also considered a Confucian society, even more so
than China. The other is that South Koreans who are more religious and
who identify with the conservative political party tend to be less acceptant of homosexuality.[23] Whatever the reason, South Korean attitudes
toward homosexuality are closer to China's than those in the more democratic Hong Kong, Japan, and Taiwan.

In China, despite the general surge in conservative values, younger
respondents with more education and income display significantly higher
levels of acceptance in the 2018 survey. Only 19 percent of respondents
who believe homosexuality is unacceptable have a college education, but
of those who believe homosexuality is acceptable, 47 percent have a college education. There is a similar pattern with divorce. In Table 5.8 the
ordered logit regression models display the key demographic variables,

Table 5.7. Homosexuality in Comparative Perspective

	China	Hong Kong	Taiwan	S. Korea	Japan
	Percent (Frequency)				
Never Acceptable	67	16	29	24	9
	(2,036)	(339)	(353)	(298)	(116)
Mostly Unacceptable	16	16	17	48	9
	(465)	(339)	(210)	(602)	(126)
Neutral	6	24	25	13	18
	(196)	(493)	(312)	(167)	(240)
Mostly Acceptable	7	36	21	15	27
	(201)	(734)	(254)	(168)	(378)
Always Acceptable	4	7	8	0	27
	(122)	(147)	(94)	(4)	(358)
Do Not Know	0	1	0	0	10
	(11)	(23)	(0)	(0)	(135)
Total	100	100	100	100	100
	(3,036)	(2,075)	(1,223)	(1,245)	(1,353)

Source: World Values Surveys.

Table 5.8. Influence of Gender, Education, Age, and Income on Acceptance of Divorce and Homosexuality

	Divorce		Homosexuality	
	1990	2018	1990	2018
	Coefficient (t-score)			
Gender	-0.05	-0.01	-0.11	-0.01
(0, 1=female)	(0.37)	(0.09)	(1,91)	(0.90)
Education	-0.02	0.38***	-0.02*	0.38***
	(0.90)	(6.33)	(2.30)	(6.33)
Age	-0.02***	-0.01**	-0.01**	-0.01**
	(4.43)	(2.56)	(2.60)	(-2.56)
Rural	-0.69***	-0.32**	-0.10	-0.31**
(0, 1=rural)	(4.28)	(2.79)	(1.62)	(2.79)
Income	0.04	0.11***	-0.01	0.11***
	(1.00)	(3.76)	(0.26)	(3.76)

p < 0.05 = *, p < 0.01 = **, p < 0.001 = ***

N (1990) is 947; N (2018) is 2,958

Divorce and Homosexuality: "never acceptable" = 1 to "always acceptable" = 10 (Ordinary Least Squares Regression)

such as gender, education, age, rural residence, and income, and the influence these have on acceptance of divorce and homosexuality in 1990 and 2018. In 1990, education and income have no influence. Younger respondents are more acceptant than older ones with regards to divorce, and urban respondents are much more acceptant than rural residents. In fact, Table 5.8 shows that rural residents tend to maintain conservative values from 1990 to 2018. Indeed, the emergence of emancipative values includes the shift from agrarian to more modern urban environments. Yet, there is considerable change in 2018 regarding the effects of education, income, and age. These variables have a strong positive influence on acceptance of divorce and homosexuality, suggesting the emergence of emancipative values for this smaller segment of the population. Moreover, government control over the media with a greater focus on traditional family values may further constrain emancipative values to this minority population.

One example of emerging unconstrained emancipative values within a traditional Confucian/Chinese society is Taiwan. In 1995, the WVS for Taiwan shows that 64 percent of respondents considered homosexuality as "never acceptable." For divorce, 33 percent reported that this was unacceptable. Yet, in 2012, only 23 percent deem gay and lesbian relationships as "never acceptable," while 13 percent consider divorce as "completely unacceptable." Most of the respondents who accept homosexuality and divorce in Taiwan are younger, more educated respondents. Indeed, higher education is also more widespread in Taiwan, with 44 percent of 2012 WVS respondents either completing university or having some college education. Contemporary Taiwan has a democratic political system and a free press. This development has allowed for the emergence of unconstrained emancipative values within a Chinese society.

China displays more similarities than differences regarding the factors that influence attitudes toward divorce and homosexuality when compared with Hong Kong, Taiwan, South Korea, and Japan. Tables 5.9 and 5.10 show that education and age have a similar effect across all countries and regions in the Confucian-influenced zone. Education has the most positive significant influence. That is, the more educated respondents in China share similar emancipative values with Hong Kong, Taiwan, South Korea, and Japan. In these countries and regions, higher educated respondents are typically urban and middle class. This reflects postmaterialist values and development. The China sample reveals that this change is taking place in educated individuals rather than society as a whole. Segments within society are developing emancipative values, while the general population (survey sample) display more traditional values. Older respondents hold more conservative attitudes than the younger ones. This is not a surprise, and we might expect this pattern. It is also the same across the Confucian-influenced zone for attitudes toward both divorce and homosexuality.

Table 5.9. Influence of Gender, Education, Age, and Income on Acceptance of Divorce in Comparative Perspective

	Divorce				
	China	Hong Kong	Taiwan	S. Korea	Japan
	Coefficient (t-score)				
Gender	-0.01	0.07	0.43***	0.11	0.26
(0, 1 =female)	(0.09)	(0.66)	(3.41)	(1.10)	(1.71)
Education	0.38***	0.39***	0.59***	0.20**	0.23
	(6.33)	(5.93)	(7.30)	(2.51)	(1.87)
Age	-0.01**	-0.01*	-0.02***	-0.01***	-0.34***
	(2.56)	(2.23)	(4.49)	(3.51)	(7.33)
Rural	-0.32**		-0.07		-0.15
(0, 1=rural)	(2.79)		(0.36)		(0.57)
Income	0.11***	-0.13	-0.02	-0.10**	-0.04
	(3.76)	(0.45)	(0.51)	(2.59)	(1.32)

p < 0.05 = *, p < 0.01 = **, p < 0.001 = ***
Divorce: "never acceptable" = 1 to "always acceptable" = 10 (Ordinary Least Squares Regression)

Table 5.10. Influence of Gender, Education, Age, and Income on Acceptance of Homosexuality in Comparative Perspective

	China	Hong Kong	Taiwan	S. Korea	Japan
			Homosexuality		
			Coefficient (t-score)		
Gender	-0.01	0.23*	0.62***	0.10	0.54***
(0, 1=female)	(0.90)	(2.13)	(4.49)	(0.90)	(3.44)
Education	0.38***	0.35***	0.49***	-0.02	0.51***
	(6.33)	(4.83)	(5.91)	(0.21)	(3.90)
Age	-0.01**	-0.04***	-0.67***	-0.02***	-0.07***
	(2.56)	(11.77)	(13.87)	(5.76)	(16.37)
Rural	-0.31**		-0.33		-0.11
(0, 1=rural)	(2.79)		(1.56)		(0.38)
Income	0.11***	0.06*	0.12**	0.11**	-0.04
	(3.76)	(1.94)	(2.74)	(2.58)	(1.50)

$p < 0.05$ = *, $p < 0.01$ = **, $p < 0.001$ = ***

Homosexuality: "never acceptable" = 1 to "always acceptable" = 10 (Ordinary Least Squares Regression)

The WVS provides a series of statements related to gender equality, which is another important dimension of emancipative values. The question asks: "Do you agree or disagree with the following statements?" The response range is "completely agree, agree, disagree, completely disagree, or do not know." The statements reflect a patriarchal view such that an agreeing with a statement reveals conservative values while disagreeing indicates more liberal or emancipative attitudes toward gender equality. The five key statements are as follows: (1) "When a mother works for pay, the children suffer;" (2) "On the whole, men make better political leaders than women do;" (3) "A university education is more important for a boy than for a girl;" (4) "When jobs are scarce, men should have more right to a job than women;" and (5) "If a woman earns more money than her husband, it causes problems." Each of these statements was asked from 1990 or 1995 to 2018, and in general the responses have been fairly consistent across all waves for four of the five statements. For example, regarding the statement "men make better leaders than women," respondents were split 50/50 across all five surveys. For "university education more important for boys," over 70 percent of respondents disagreed with this statement across all five surveys (1995 to 2018). For "women earning more," over 60 percent of respondents in both 1995 and 2018 disagreed with this statement. Regarding the statement "when jobs are scarce," about 40 percent of respondents agreed across six waves from 1990 to 2018. However, the statement "children suffer with a working mother" revealed a more uneven response. In 2001, 89 percent agreed with this statement, while only 42 percent agreed in 2013; then in 2018, agreement jumped up to 60 percent. This increase in conservative values reflects the same pattern seen in acceptance of divorce and homosexuality.

Table 5.11 displays the variation in responses along the five dimensions of gender equality in 2018. The vast majority of respondents believe in equal higher educational opportunity for sons and daughters (see "University" column in Table 5.11). This may reflect the family planning campaigns throughout the 1990s and 2000s promoting the idea that sons and daughters are equal, especially in the countryside. Studies in the 2000s suggest that rural parents tend to make equal education investments for sons and daughters.[24] Given the traditional preference for sons, this suggests a significant value change. However, when it comes to women in leadership positions and working mothers, there is a much higher percentage of respondents who agree with the patriarchal view. While Mao Zedong said that "women hold up half the sky," the WVS shows that only half of the respondents agree. The gender composition of central leadership in China also reflects this view. After the 19th Party Congress, only one of the 25-member Politburo is a woman (Sun Chunlan), and out of 204 Central Committee members there are only 10 women (5 percent). The WVS also reveals a more conservative view of women in the workplace, with an increase in more traditional views from 2013 to 2018. Female participation in the labor force is one dimension of gender equality.[25] The recent conservative trend is reflected by the

Table 5.11. Values toward Gender Equality in the 2018 WVS

	Suffer	Leaders	Scarce	Earns	University
	Percentage (Frequency)				
Strongly Agree	14	10	10	3	5
	(412)	(311)	(308)	(106)	(155)
Agree	46	40	35	23	16
	(1,387)	(1,225)	(1,059)	(704)	(484)
Disagree	35	44	42	54	61
	(1,075)	(1,324)	(1,273)	(1,640)	(1,841)
Strongly Disagree	5	5	6	8	18
	(158)	(165)	(191)	(244)	(553)
Do Not Know	0	0	7	11	0
	(4)	(11)	(205)	(342)	(3)
Total	100	100	100	100	100
	(3,036)	(3,036)	(3,036)	(3,036)	(3,036)

national percentage of female employment in the labor force. According to the World Bank, 73 percent of women fifteen years and older participated in the work force in 1990, but the percentage declined to 61 percent in 2018. While this suggests an increase in patriarchal values, this percentage is still higher than South Korea with 53 percent and Japan with 51 percent female participation rates. Still, the WVS does not suggest a general trend toward widespread values supporting gender equality.

However, between 1990 and 2018 the WVS does display a clear generational and gender shift regarding who supports gender equality and emancipative values. The order logit regression model in Table 5.12 displays how gender, education, age, rural residency, and income influence this measure. In 1990 and 1995, there was no difference between men and women or between younger and older respondents regarding gender equality. Yet in 2018, the data displays a strong statistically significant gender and generational shift, whereby younger respondents and women are more likely to support gender equality. While gender inequality remains an important issue in China, over the last three decades women's empowerment and identity have made positive strides.[26] Thus we might expect women to develop stronger values regarding gender equality. Interestingly, rural residency has no significant influence. Given the traditional values associated with villagers in the Chinese countryside, we might expect rural respondents to be more conservative than

Table 5.12. Gender Equality in the Areas of Education, Employment, and Leadership

	Girls College Education		Jobs Scarce		Better Leaders	
	1995	2018	1990	2018	1995	2018
	Coefficient (Z-score)					
Gender	0.19	0.37***	0.98***	0.35***	0.08	0.31***
(0, 1=female)	(1.88)	(4.97)	(7.39)	(5.02)	(0.76)	(4.48)
Education	0.01	0.05	-0.04	0.26***	-0.01	-0.01
	(0.44)	(1.40)	(1.89)	(6.68)	(0.48)	(0.34)
Age	-0.01	-0.01**	-0.01	-0.12***	-0.01*	-0.02***
	(1.77)	(2.66)	(2.03)	(6.57)	(2.12)	(6.61)
Rural	0.18	0.08	0.21	-0.13	0.05	-0.03
(0, 1=rural)	(1.66)	(1.11)	(1.41)	(1.70)	(0.43)	(0.34)
Income	-0.01	-0.06*	-0.06	0.01	-0.03	-0.01
	(0.15)	(2.07)	(1.68)	(0.19)	(0.96)	(0.60)

p < 0.05 = *, p < 0.01 = **, p < 0.001 = ***
N (1990) is 947; N (1995) is 1,372; N (2018) is 2,958
Girls College, Jobs, and Leaders: "strongly agree" = 1 to "strongly disagree" = 5 (Ordered Logit Regression)

their urban counterparts. This suggests that rural to urban migration and urbanization since the 1990s may have tempered more traditional conservative values in the countryside. Unexpectedly, income and education have no influence on patriarchal values.

Social Tolerance

Religious, racial, ethnic, and sexual tolerance are essential elements of emancipative values. This reflects openness and acceptance of people beyond their immediate and extended family. However, the level of social tolerance can vary widely within a nation. Even in democracies, the level of acceptance and tolerance of others may vary and fluctuate over time as well. Within authoritarian regimes, tolerance of others reflects the emergence of emancipative values. The six waves of the China WVS show that along some dimensions, such as accepting people with a different race, religion, or language, most respondents display liberal values. However, when it comes to sexuality and AIDs, most respondents remain conservative. In addition, the six WVS waves exhibit the same pattern of a slowly decreasing proportion of respondents who display intolerance from 1990 to 2013 followed by a sharp conservative increase from 2013 to 2018. Similar to attitudes toward divorce and homosexuality, younger respondents with higher education tend to be more accepting of others.

One measure of tolerance is the willingness to live near people who are different from yourself. This exemplifies accepting a diverse community, especially in close proximity like neighbors. The WVS asked the same general question on social tolerance in all surveys from 1990 to 2018: "Who would you NOT like to be neighbors with?" If the respondent mentions a specific group, then they are unwilling to have them as neighbors; if the respondent does not mention the specific group, then they would not mind having them as a neighbor. The list includes people who have a different religion, sexual orientation, race, or marital status, as well as foreign workers.

Regarding race and religion, the 2018 WVS reveals relatively acceptant views, with over 70 percent of respondents reporting they do not mind living near people with a different race or religion. This is the same across all six China WVS waves. Table 5.13 presents the distribution of responses for the seventh wave. Although the WVS shows relatively high acceptance of different races and foreign workers, this does not reflect some of the studies on the challenges endured by African students and

Table 5.13. WVS 2018 and Tolerance: The People Respondents Would Not Want for a Neighbor

	Race	Foreigners	Religion	Unmarried	Homo	AIDs
	Percentage (Frequency)					
Mentioned: Do Not Want as Neighbor	18 (554)	26 (778)	31 (921)	40 (1,206)	71 (2,150)	77 (2,329)
Not Mentioned	80 (2,416)	72 (2,192)	67 (2,049)	58 (1,767)	28 (843)	22 (675)
Do Not Know	2 (66)	2 (64)	2 (66)	2 (63)	1 (34)	1 (28)
Total	100 (3,036)	100 (3,036)	100 (3,036)	100 (3,036)	100 (3,036)	100 (3,036)

businesspeople in China. Since the 1980s and into the 2000s, African students and migrants have faced institutional and public racism at universities and within Chinese communities.[27] Thus, there seems to be a contradiction between the previous research and the WVS results on racial tolerance. Yet, recent studies demonstrate the complexity of foreign worker experiences in China, especially for African migrants.[28] Indeed, Min Zhou et al. (2016) directly address this contradiction: "The Chinese tend to perceive Africans negatively in general, but they also look upon Africans' overall presence in a positive way and express openness to interacting with them."[29] This suggests that while the Chinese may have negative stereotypes of foreigners, most may not mind having foreigners and people of a different race as neighbors.

Like previous WVS waves, most respondents in 2018 are willing to accept neighbors with a different religion or faith. However, the proportion of those who would not want to have neighbors with a different religion increased sharply from 2013 to 2018 (see Table 5.14). This may reflect the current campaign to gain greater control over religious institutions including mosques, temples, and churches, especially in Xinjiang. Although the CCP allows religious institutions and practices, the central leadership has been placing greater limits and controls over religious practices. This includes new legal restrictions as well as more public campaigns.[30] After the violent anti-religious campaigns during the Cultural Revolution (1966–1976), the central leadership began rebuilding mosques, temples, and even churches in the 1980s and 1990s. This was a limited state-sanctioned religious resurgence where the CCP allowed the development of religious institutions as long as these were registered

Table 5.14. Would Not Like to Have Neighbors with a Different Religion[1]

	1990	2007	2013	2018
Mentioned: Do Not Want as Neighbor	12 (121)	16 (327)	9 (208)	31 (921)
Not Mentioned	88 (879)	84 (1,664)	91 (2,092)	67 (2,049)
Do Not Know	0 (0)	0 (0)	0 (0)	2 (66)
Total	100 (1,000)	100 (1,991)	100 (2,300)	100 (3,036)

[1]In 1990, the question asked if respondents would not like to have Muslims as neighbors. In 1995 and 2001, this question was not asked. In 2007, 2013, and 2018, the question only referred to neighbors with a "different religion."

with the local Party-government.[31] However, after 2012, the central leaders added greater restrictions to religious institutions and practices. This may explain the resurgence in less tolerant views of religion.

The level of intolerance is highest with regard to sexuality, including homosexuals, people with AIDs, and unmarried couples living together. The level of intolerance for homosexuals is over 60 percent for all waves except in 2013, when the it was close to 50 percent. However, intolerance then jumped about 20 percent in 2018 (see Table 5.15). We observe a similar increase in intolerance regarding willingness to live next to unmarried couples. In 2013, only 18 percent do not want to live next to an unmarried couple, but this percentage increased to 40 percent in 2018. In both cases, we observe the same slightly liberal trend in the 2000s with a sharp conservative increase in 2018. For AIDS, there is

Table 5.15. Would Not Like to Have Homosexual Neighbors

	1990	1995	2001	2007	2013	2018
	Percentage (Frequency)					
Mentioned: Do Not Want as Neighbor	72 (719)	61 (911)	73 (732)	66 (1,324)	52 (1,188)	71 (2,150)
Not Mentioned	28 (281)	39 (589)	27 (268)	34 (667)	48 (1,112)	28 (843)
Do Not Know	0 (0)	0 (0)	0 (0)	0 (0)	0 (0)	1 (34)
Total	100 (1,000)	100 (1,500)	100 (1,000)	100 (1,991)	100 (2,300)	100 (3,036)

no liberal trend. Except for 1995, over 70 percent of respondents for every wave would not want to have someone with AIDs as their neighbor. Although there has been a growing number of government campaigns to increase AIDs awareness, including using celebrities to reduce the social stigma, discrimination and fear of people with AIDs remain prevalent in China.[32]

While the proportions of intolerance remain relatively constant, the factors that influence these values differ in 1990 and 2018. Education and age (generational) effects have the strongest positive influence on tolerance. Table 5.16 displays the logit regression analysis. In 1990, education, income, and rural residency had no influence on tolerance of people or neighbors with a different religion. Tolerance was relatively high, and there was no difference between young and old, rural and urban, or level of education. However, in 2018, age, rural residency, and education do have a significant influence on religious tolerance. Rural respondents are *less* willing to have neighbors with a different religion. The diversity of religious practices in rural China has increased since the 1980s and 1990s, including state-sanctioned Christian churches, Buddhist temples, mosques, as well as folk religions.[33] Thus, there may be a greater variation in religious practices in the countryside than in urban areas, and this may explain why some rural respondents are less willing to live next people with different religions.

Younger as well as higher educated respondents are much more willing to have neighbors with a different religion. This presents an

Table 5.16. Would NOT Like to Have as Neighbors

	Different Religion		People with AIDS		Homosexuals	
	1990	2018	1990	2018	1990	2018
	Coefficient (Z-score)					
Gender	0.23	0.11	0.64	0.09	0.06	-0.01
(0, 1=female)	(1.16)	(1.41)	(0.09)	(1.07)	(0.44)	(0.04)
Education	-0.04	-0.21***	0.04	-0.18***	0.06**	-0.23***
	(1.23)	(4.38)	(1.75)	(3.48)	(2.62)	(4.77)
Age	0.01	0.01***	-0.01*	0.01***	-0.01	0.02***
	(0.77)	(3.82)	(2.12)	(3.61)	(1.58)	(6.28)
Rural	-0.38	0.38***	-0.14	-0.11	-0.35*	0.11
(0, 1=rural)	(1.54)	(4.34)	(0.83)	(1.09)	(2.17)	(1.22)
Income	-0.02	-0.02	-0.12**	0.04	-0.08*	0.01
	(0.45)	(0.89)	(2.88)	(1.83)	(1.95)	(0.54)

$p < 0.05$ = *, $p < 0.01$ = **, $p < 0.001$ = ***
N (1990) is 947; N (1995) is 1,372; N (2018) is 2,958
Religion, AIDs, and Homosexuals: "mentioned" = 1 to "not mentioned" = 0 (Logit Regression)

interesting contradiction. Most respondents, especially those with college and high school educations, are more tolerant of different religions, but over 80 percent do not consider religion important in their lives. For example, all six waves of the China WVS asked "How important is religion in your life?" In every wave, less than 5 percent answered "very important" and less than 11 percent said "rather important." Thus, the vast majority of the respondents believe religion is not important. While educated Chinese have greater individual religious tolerance, they may have less acceptance of religious institutions. This is more aligned with the central government control over religious activities. Xiuhua Wang and Paul Froese's examination of Chinese attitudes toward religion found that "highly educated people are more empathetic of the individual's religious beliefs, but also more certain that religious leaders and institutions should be restricted in their political activities."[34] Thus there is religious tolerance, but also support for government control over religious institutions.

While intolerance for people with AIDs is consistent across all six waves, there is a significant difference in the demographic influence on this measure in 1990 and 2018. The level of education and rural residency have no influence in 1990, but older generation and higher-income respondents tend to be more tolerant. In the 1990s, there was little information about AIDs, and there seems to be greater empathy from older respondents. Yet in 2018, younger respondents tend to be more tolerant than the older generation, as do those with higher education. This suggests growing tolerance among this group. Still the majority of college-educated respondents (over 60 percent) would not want to have people with AIDs as neighbors. This suggests that greater AIDs awareness does not necessarily translate into more widespread tolerance.

The ordered logit regression model in Table 5.16 deipicts a dramatic shift regarding the influence of rural residency, age, and education on tolerance of homosexuals between 1990 and 2018. In 1990, those with more education were *less* tolerant of homosexuals. In the 1990s, there was a much lower proportion of college-educated respondents; at this time, higher education was basically high school. In addition, rural residents were *more* tolerant than urban respondents. One explanation is that in rural areas, especially in poorer villages, there is a history of involuntary bachelorhood or "bare branches." This is due to poverty and excess males in the less affluent regions. Some scholars have shown a correlation between homosexuality and surplus males.[35]

However, Thérèse Hesketh points out that this "suggestion is not that the shortage of women will produce homosexuals, but rather that increasing tolerance toward homosexuality, together with the surplus of males, may lead to large numbers of covert homosexuals openly expressing their sexuality."[36] This may explain the relative tolerance (or lack of significant intolerance) for living next to homosexuals exhibited by rural Chinese residents. Still, there is a different between tolerance and acceptance. Table 5.8 shows that, in 2018, rural respondents were less likely than urban residents to accept homosexuality.

A university education is associated with greater tolerance for homosexuality in 2018, similar to what we see in Table 5.8. Youth and a university education have a particularly strong positive influence. Figure 5.1 displays the predicted margins regarding the influence of education and age on tolerance of homosexuality. College education has a clear positive influence on members of the younger generation, who display greater levels of tolerance, while respondents who only completed compulsory education exhibit the lowest level. However, respondents over the age of sixty show higher levels of intolerance regardless of how educated they are. This finding is similar to previous studies on higher education, youth, and tolerance toward homosexuality in China.[37]

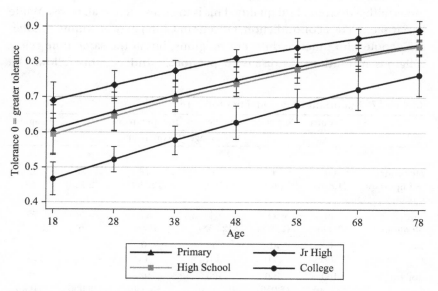

Figure 5.1. Influence of Education and Age on Tolerance of Homosexuality

CHINA AS NUMBER ONE?

Qualities of Children

The WVS data suggests a strong generational influence on acceptance and tolerance as well as respect for authority, with the younger
respondents displaying greater emancipative values. The values that are
instilled in children when they are young is another important generational measure. The WVS asks a related question: "What do you think
are important child qualities that should be cultivated at home?" The
respondent is given a list of qualities such as tolerance and respect for
others, religious faith, obedience, independence, hard work ethic, and
imagination. If the respondent mentions a specific quality, then this is a
value they believe should be passed along to children; if the respondent
does not mention the specific quality, then this is not an important quality they want pass down to the next generation.

Table 5.17 shows the distribution of perceived important child qualities in 2018. The table is set up to compare tolerance versus religion,
obedience versus independence, and hard work versus imagination.
Tolerance and respect for others is relatively high across all six of the
China WVS waves. While tolerance is a desired child virtue for most
respondents, there is an almost universal rejection of religion as an
important quality for children. This is consistent with the WVS question
asking whether or not religion is important in your life. Over 80 percent
deem religion as unimportant, and over 90 percent do not consider religious faith a desired child quality. This is the same across all waves. While
it may seem like a contradiction, citizens in China may be willing to toler-
ate people who practice different religions, but at the same time reject
religious institutions, as discussed previously. Indeed, this follows the

Table 5.17. Important Child Qualities for 2018

	Tolerance	Religion	Obedience	Independence	Work	Imagine
	Percentage (Frequency)					
Mentioned as Important Quality	60 (1,816)	1 (40)	6 (169)	78 (2,359)	71 (2,159)	22 (663)
Not Mentioned	40 (1,206)	99 (2,982)	94 (2,853)	22 (663)	29 (863)	78 (2,359)
Do Not Know	0 (14)	0 (14)	0 (14)	0 (14)	0 (14)	0 (14)
Total	100 (3,036)	100 (3,036)	100 (3,036)	100 (3,036)	100 (3,036)	100 (3,036)

central government approach of allowing individuals to practice their religion as long as it is within strictly controlled state-sanctioned institutions. Of course, the Chinese education system and state-controlled media also view religious institutions with suspicion. Therefore, we might expect the majority to reject religious faith as an important child quality at home and in schools.

Over the last six China WVS waves, respondents overwhelmingly support independence over obedience as an important child quality. In 1990, 84 percent selected independence as an important quality, and 78 percent made this selection in 2018. There is a related pattern for obedience, with 8 percent in 1990 believing this is an important quality and only 6 percent in 2018. This suggests a difference between obedience and respect for authority (see Table 5.1). While respect for authority varied from 1990 to 2018, with a recent increase in respondents who believe this is good, respondents have consistently *not* mentioned obedience as an important child quality. This suggests that respect for authority varies with changes in central leadership and nationalist campaigns, but obedience remains relatively unimportant. This response seems to reject the traditional Confucian value of obedient children. Instead, respondents tend to encourage children's independence over obedience, and this is closer to instilling emancipative rather than Confucian values.

Nevertheless, traditional values are still apparent. The vast majority of respondents believe hard work is a more important quality for children than imagination (see Table 5.17). A number of scholars have discussed the importance of the Confucian work ethic in China and how this is an important business and family value.[38] At the same time, encouraging this work ethic may also stifle imagination and the arts. At the heat of this dichotomy is the notion that hard work is connected with a practical vocation, and that this is more important than the creative arts (i.e., imagination). However, this is not restricted to a Chinese work ethic or an East Asian cultural norm. In the sixth WVS wave, 40 percent of Taiwanese respondents considered hard work an important child quality, as did 66 percent of Americans. When it comes to imagination, only 30 percent of American respondents considered this important for children. Still, hard work has remained one of the most important child qualities across all six China WVS waves, while imagination remains close to the bottom of the list.

Table 5.18 displays the factors that influence important child qualities in 1990 and 2018. Generational differences is the most significant factor over and above education and income. Older respondents in both years

Table 5.18. Factors That Influence the Selection of Important Child Qualities

	Tolerance		Hard Work		Imagination	
	1990	2018	1990	2018	1990	2018
	Coefficient (Z-score)					
Gender	0.22	0.25***	-0.16	-0.01	0.01	-0.15
(0, 1=female)	(1.65)	(3.23)	(1.13)	(0.10)	(0.10)	(1.72)
Education	0.01	0.04	-0.02	-0.18	0.01	0.06
	(0.17)	(0.94)	(1.02)	(1.01)	(0.48)	(1.07)
Age	0.01	-0.01***	0.04***	0.01**	-0.03***	-0.02**
	(1.12)	(3.68)	(7.55)	(3.05)	(5.48)	(3.17)
Rural	-0.03	-0.38	0.60***	0.14	-0.32	0.05
(0, 1=rural)	(0.19)	(1.44)	(3.60)	(1.53)	(1.86)	(0.48)
Income	-0.04	0.01	-0.01	-0.02	-0.05	-0.01
	(0.99)	(0.54)	(0.20)	(0.77)	(1.03)	(0.74)

p < 0.05 = *, p < 0.01 = **, p < 0.001 = ***
N (1990) is 947; N (1995) is 1,372; N (2018) is 2,958
Tolerance, Hard Work, and Imagination: "mentioned" = 1 to "not mentioned" = 0 (Logit Regression)

are more likely than younger ones to select hard work as an important child quality. This is a value we might expect the older generation to pass along to their children. While only 27 percent of respondents in 1990 and 22 percent in 2018 consider imagination an important child quality, those who do tend to be younger. This is more of a generational difference than a shift. On the other hand, tolerance does appear to reflect a generational shift. In 1990, age has no influence on tolerance as an important child quality, but in 2018 it has a much greater influence, with younger respondents increasingly more likely deem this important. In addition, women are more likely than men to value tolerance as an important child quality.

Overall, there is a general generational shift in tolerance from 1990 to 2018. This is similar to the shift observed regarding tolerance of different neighbors (see Table 5.16). The younger generation tends to be more tolerant and acceptant of others. Moreover, they are also more likely to pass these values on to their children.

Conclusion

The seventh WVS wave reveals how higher education and income are associated with emancipative values, but also how current political developments, such as nationalist campaigns, can contribute to the reemergence of more conservative values. One clear trend is the difference between sixth wave in 2013 and the seventh wave in 2018. There is a significant increase in the unacceptance and intolerance, especially around homosexuality, religion, and divorce. In the same vein, respect for authority is an increasingly important virtue among respondents in 2018. This reflects the current conservative political climate, especially after 2012. The vast majority of respondents get their daily news from state television broadcasts that can shape (and reinforce) perceptions and values. This in conjunction with public education may strengthen conservative values regarding sexuality, gender equality, and respect for authority.

When compared with the other Confucian-influenced countries, respondents in China hold stronger conservative and traditional values. The descriptive tables show much greater support for "respect for authority" in China as opposed to the more democratic societies in the Confucian-influenced zone. The same is true with attitudes toward divorce and homosexuality. The descriptive tables display less acceptant views in China compared with Hong Kong, Taiwan, South Korea, and Japan. However, the statistical analysis reveals more liberal views and greater acceptance among the more educated Chinese middle class.

As Ronald Inglehart and Christian Welzel have suggested, respondents in the China sample with a university education and higher income tend to hold more liberal values, as seen in the seventh wave.[39] There is also a clear generational shift between 1990 and 2018. While age had little correlation with emancipative values in the 1990s, younger respondents are more likely to hold these values in 2018. Younger respondents also tend to be more educated and use the internet as a news source. In the seventh wave, over 75 percent get their daily and weekly news from television broadcasts, while over 20 percent get their daily news from the internet. Most of the internet users tend to be younger and more educated. Of course, internet use in China is also monitored and content is constrained, but many of these users still tend to hold more liberal values. Indeed, younger respondents with a university education seem to resist the current conservative trend.

Although there are signs that emancipative values are emerging in China, these values are restricted to a relatively small segment of the population. Indeed, higher education is constrained by limited access and quality. Though the number of college students has increased since the 1990s, most students who complete compulsory education in China will not attend college. For those who do attend, many will graduate from smaller specialized universities. The quality of higher education also varies across China, from top universities to smaller vocational colleges. Thus, the general knowledge that comes from a university education is not consistent. The combination of the current nationalist campaigns and the limited access to college could explain why emancipative values are constrained.

Notes

1. Ronald Inglehart and Christian Welzel, *Modernization, Cultural Change, and Democracy: The Human Development Sequence* (New York: Cambridge University Press, 2005); Amy C. Alexander and Christian Welzel, "Eroding Patriarchy: The Co-Evolution of Women's Rights and Emancipative Values," *International Review of Sociology* 25, no. 1 (2015): 144–65.

2. Eduard J. Bomhoff and Mary Man-Li Gu, "East Asia Remains Different: A Comment on the Index of 'Self-Expression Values,' by Inglehart and Welzel," *Journal of Cross-Cultural Psychology* 43, no. 3 (2012): 373–83; Christian Welzel, "The Asian Values Thesis Revisited: Evidence from the World Values Surveys," *Japanese Journal of Political Science* 12, no. 1 (2011): 1–31.

3. Christian Welzel, "The Myth of Asian Exceptionalism: Response to Bomhoff and Gu," *Journal of Cross-Cultural Psychology* 43, no. 7 (2012): 1039–54.

4. Welzel, "The Myth of Asian Exceptionalism: Response," 1039.

5. Inglehart and Welzel, *Modernization, Cultural Change, and Democracy*; Ronald Inglehart, "Changing Values among Western Publics, 1970–2006: Postmaterialist Values and the Shift from Survival Values to Self-Expression Values," *West European Politics* 31, no. 1–2 (2008): 130–46; Ronald Inglehart, *Modernization and Postmodernization: Cultural, Economic, and Political Change in 43 Societies* (Princeton: Princeton University Press, 1997).

6. Yan Luo, Fei Guo, and Jinghuan Shi, "Expansion and Inequality of Higher Education in China: How Likely Would Chinese Poor Students Get To Success?" *Higher Education Research & Development* 37, no. 5 (2018): 1015–34; Houxiong Wang, "Access to Higher Education in China: Differences in Opportunity," *Frontiers of Education in China* 6, no. 2 (2011): 227–47; Xiaogang Wu, "Higher Education, Elite Formation and Social Stratification in Contemporary China: Preliminary Findings from the Beijing College Students Panel Survey," *Chinese Journal of Sociology* 3, no. 1 (2017): 3–31.

7. Wei Zhang and Mark Bray, "Equalising Schooling, Unequalising Private Supplementary Tutoring: Access and Tracking through Shadow Education in China," *Oxford Review of Education* 44, no. 2 (2018): 221–38.

8. V. O. Key, *Public Opinion and American Democracy* (New York: Knopf, 1961); Jessica Li and Jean Madsen, "Chinese Workers' Work Ethic in Reformed State-Owned Enterprises: Implications for HRD," *Human Resource Development International* 12, no. 2 (2009): 171–88.

9. Elizabeth J. Perry, "Higher Education and Authoritarian Resilience: The Case of China, Past and Present" (Harvard-Yenching Institute Working Paper Series, 2015), https://dash.harvard.edu/handle/1/30822717.

10. Suisheng Zhao, "A State-Led Nationalism: The Patriotic Education Campaign in Post-Tiananmen China," *Communist and Post-Communist Studies* 31, no. 3 (1998): 287–302; Linda Walton, "The 'Spirit' of Confucian Education in Contemporary China: Songyang Academy and Zhengzhou University," *Modern China* 44, no. 3 (2018): 313–42; Chuyu Liu and Xiao Ma, "Popular Threats and Nationalistic Propaganda: Political Logic of China's Patriotic Campaign," *Security Studies* 27, no. 4 (2018): 633–64.

11. Bomhoff and Gu, "East Asia Remains Different"; Doh Chull Shin, "The Third Wave in East Asia Comparative and Dynamic Perspectives," *Taiwan Journal of Democracy* 4, no. 2 (2008): 91–131; Yida Zhai, "Values of Deference to Authority in Japan and China," *International Journal of Comparative Sociology* 58, no. 2 (2017): 120–39.

12. Ronald Inglehart, "Postmodernization Erodes Respect for Authority, but Increases Support for Democracy," in *Critical Citizens: Global Support for Democratic Government*, ed. Pippa Norris (Oxford: Oxford University Press, 1999), 236–56.

13. Of course, not everyone knew about the June 4th incident, especially in the countryside, but the 1990 WVS oversampled the larger urban areas (the WVS sample is 70 percent urban, while according to the census over 70 percent of the population lived in the rural areas). Thus it is likely these respondents in larger urban areas knew about the protests and crackdowns.

14. Wenfang Tang, *Populist Authoritarianism: Chinese Political Culture and Regime Sustainability* (Oxford: Oxford University Press, 2016); Andrew J. Nathan, "The Puzzle of the Chinese Middle Class," *Journal of Democracy* 27, no. 2 (2016): 5–19.

15. Neil J. Diamant, *Revolutionizing the Family: Politics, Love, and Divorce in Urban and Rural China, 1949–1968* (Berkeley: University of California Press, 2000); Deborah Davis, "On the Limits of Personal Autonomy: PRC Law and the Institution of Marriage," in *Wives, Husbands, and Lovers: Marriage and Sexuality in Hong Kong, Taiwan, and Urban China*, ed. Deborah Davis and Sara Friedman (Redwood City: Stanford University Press, 2014), 41–61.

16. Lijia Zhang, "China's Divorce Rate Is Spiking Because Women No Longer Have to Accept Unsatisfying Marriages. This Should Be Celebrated, Not Stifled," *South China Morning Post*, November 27, 2019, https://www.scmp.com/comment/opinion/article/3039370/chinas-divorce-rate-spiking-because-women-no-longer-have-accept).

17. Phillip M. Ayoub and Jeremiah Garretson, "Getting the Message Out: Media Context and Global Changes in Attitudes toward Homosexuality," *Comparative Political Studies* 50, no. 8 (2017): 1055–85; Ronald Inglehart and Wayne E. Baker, "Modernization, Cultural Change, and the Persistence of Traditional Values," *American Sociological Review* 65, no. 1 (2000): 19–51.

18. Li Ma, Jani Turunen, and Ester Rizzi, "Divorce Chinese Style," *Journal of Marriage and Family* 80, no. 5 (2018): 1287–97.

19. Yinhe Li, "Regulating Male Same-Sex Relationships in the People's Republic of China," in *Sex and Sexuality in China*, ed. Elaine Jeffreys (New York: Routledge, 2007), 90–109.

20. Kai Lin, Deeanna M. Button, Mingyue Su, and Sishi Chen, "Chinese College Students' Attitudes toward Homosexuality: Exploring the Effects of Traditional Culture and Modernizing Factors," *Sexuality Research and Social Policy* 13, no. 2 (2016): 158–72.

21. Kang Hu and Xinling Li, "The Effects of Media Use and Traditional Gender Role Beliefs on Tolerance of Homosexuality in China," *Chinese Sociological Review* 51, no. 2 (2019): 147–72.

22. Christian Shepherd, "China LGBT Community Fears Crackdown after Weibo Content Vanishes," *Financial Times*, April 15, 2019, https://www.ft.com/content/19ff4b36-5f7a-11e9-b285-3acd5d43599e.

23. Timothy S. Rich, "Religion and Public Perceptions of Gays and Lesbians in South Korea," *Journal of Homosexuality* 64, no. 5 (2017): 606–21.

24. Emily Hannum, Peggy Kong, and Yuping Zhang, "Family Sources of Educational Gender Inequality in Rural China: A Critical Assessment," *International Journal of Educational Development* 29, no. 5 (2009): 474–86; Junxia Zeng, Xiaopeng Pang, Linxiu Zhang, Alexis Medina, and Scott Rozelle, "Gender Inequality in Education in China: A Meta-Regression Analysis," *Contemporary Economic Policy* 32, no. 2 (2014): 474–91.

25. Emily Honig and Gail Hershater, *Personal Voices: Chinese Women in the 1980s* (Redwood City: Stanford University Press, 1988).

26. Tamara Jacka, *Rural Women in Urban China: Gender, Migration, and Social Change* (New York: Routledge, 2014); Vilma Seeberg and Shujuan Luo, "Migrating to the City in North West China: Young Rural Women's Empowerment," *Journal of Human Development and Capabilities* 19, no. 3 (2018): 289–307.

27. Yinghong Cheng, "From Campus Racism to Cyber Racism: Discourse of Race and Chinese Nationalism," *The China Quarterly* 207 (2011): 561–79; Barry Sautman, "Anti-Black Racism in Post-Mao China," *The China Quarterly* 138 (1994): 413–37.

28. Min Zhou, Shabnam Shenasi, and Tao Xu, "Chinese Attitudes toward African Migrants in Guangzhou, China," *International Journal of Sociology* 46, no. 2 (2016): 141–61; Kelly Liang and Philippe Le Billon, "African Migrants in China: Space, Race and Embodied Encounters in Guangzhou, China," *Social & Cultural Geography* 21, no. 10 (2018): 1–27.

29. Zhou et al., "Chinese Attitudes toward African Migrants," 141.

30. Eleanor Albert and Lindsay Maizland, "Religion in China," *Council on Foreign Relations*, September 25, 2020, https://www.cfr.org/backgrounder/religion-china.

31. Daniel L. Overmyer, "Religion in China Today: Introduction," *The China Quarterly* 174 (2003): 307–16.

32. Li Li, Li-Jung Liang, Chunqing Lin, Zunyou Wu, and Yi Wen, "Individual Attitudes and Perceived Social Norms: Reports on HIV/AIDS-Related Stigma among Service Providers in China," *International Journal of Psychology* 44, no. 6 (2009): 443–50; Anuradha Chaddah and Zunyou Wu, "HIV-Related Stigma and Discrimination in China: A Persistent Puzzle," in *HIV/AIDS in China: Beyond the Numbers*, ed. Zunyou Wu (Singapore: Springer, 2017), 95–107.

33. Yongjia Liang, "Religious Revival in Rural China and the Fate of 'Religion' in China," *Chinese Journal of Sociology* 3, no. 2 (2017): 268–90; Chongqing Wu, "The Transmission of Information in Chinese Folk Religion: Reflections on Fieldwork in Putian, Fujian," *Modern China* 45, no. 3 (2019): 295–315.

34. Xiuhua Wang and Paul Froese, "Attitudes toward Religion and Believers in China: How Education Increases Tolerance of Individual Religious Differences and Intolerance of Religious Influence in Politics," *Religion and Education* 47, no. 1 (2019): 1–20; 2.

35. Bret Hinsch, *Passions of the Cut Sleeve: The Male Homosexual Tradition in China* (Berkeley: University of California Press, 1992); Quanbao Jiang and Jesús J. Sánchez-Barricarte, "Bare Branches and Social Stability: A Historical Perspective from China," *Frontiers of History in China* 6, no. 4 (2011): 538–61.

36. Thérèse Hesketh, "Too Many Males in China: The Causes and the Consequences," *Significance* 6, no. 1 (2009): 9–13.

37. Kai Lin, Deeanna M. Button, Mingyue Su, and Sishi Chen, "Chinese College Students' Attitudes toward Homosexuality: Exploring the Effects of Traditional Culture and Modernizing Factors," *Sexuality Research and Social Policy* 13, no. 2 (2016): 158–72; Min Zhou and Tianyang Hu, "Social Tolerance of Homosexuality: A Quantitative Comparison of Mainland China, Singapore, and Taiwan," *Chinese Sociological Review* 52, no. 3 (2019): 1–29.

38. Stevan Harrell, "Why Do the Chinese Work So Hard? Reflections on an Entrepreneurial Ethic," *Modern China* 11, no. 2 (1985): 203–26; Li and Madsen, "Chinese Workers' Work Ethic."

39. Inglehart and Welzel, *Modernization, Cultural Change, and Democracy*.

Bibliography

Albert, Eleanor, and Lindsay Maizland. "Religion in China." *Council on Foreign Relations*, September 25, 2020, https://www.cfr.org/backgrounder/religion-china.

Alexander, Amy C., and Christian Welzel. "Eroding Patriarchy: The Co-Evolution of Women's Rights and Emancipative Values." *International Review of Sociology* 25, no. 1 (2015): 144–65.

Ayoub, Phillip M., and Jeremiah Garretson. "Getting the Message Out: Media Context and Global Changes in Attitudes toward Homosexuality." *Comparative Political Studies* 50, no. 8 (2017): 1055–85.

Bomhoff, Eduard J., and Mary Man-Li Gu. "East Asia Remains Different: A Comment on the Index of 'Self-Expression Values,' by Inglehart and Welzel." *Journal of Cross-Cultural Psychology* 43, no. 3 (2012): 373–83.

Chaddah, Anuradha, and Zunyou Wu. "HIV-Related Stigma and Discrimination in China: A Persistent Puzzle." In *HIV/AIDS in China*, edited by Zunyou Wu, 95–107. Singapore: Springer, 2017.

Cheng, Yinghong. "From Campus Racism to Cyber Racism: Discourse of Race and Chinese Nationalism." *The China Quarterly* 207 (2011): 561–79.

Davis, Deborah. "On the Limits of Personal Autonomy: PRC Law and the Institution of Marriage." In *Wives, Husbands, and Lovers: Marriage and Sexuality in Hong Kong, Taiwan, and Urban China*, edited by Deborah S. Davis and Sara L. Friedman, 41–61. Redwood City: Stanford University Press, 2014.

Diamant, Neil J. *Revolutionizing the Family: Politics, Love, and Divorce in Urban and Rural China, 1949–1968*. Berkeley: University of California Press, 2000.

Hannum, Emily, Peggy Kong, and Yuping Zhang. "Family Sources of Educational Gender Inequality in Rural China: A Critical Assessment." *International Journal of Educational Development* 29, no. 5 (2009): 474–86.

Harrell, Stevan. "Why Do the Chinese Work So Hard? Reflections on an Entrepreneurial Ethic." *Modern China* 11, no. 2 (1985): 203–26.

Hesketh, Thérèse. "Too Many Males in China: The Causes and the Consequences." *Significance* 6, no. 1 (2009): 9–13.

Hinsch, Bret. *Passions of the Cut Sleeve: The Male Homosexual Tradition in China.* Berkeley: University of California Press, 1992.

Honig, Emily, and Gail Hershater. *Personal Voices: Chinese Women in the 1980s.* Redwood City: Stanford University Press, 1988.

Hu, Kang, and Xinling Li. "The Effects of Media Use and Traditional Gender Role Beliefs on Tolerance of Homosexuality in China." *Chinese Sociological Review* 51, no. 2 (2019): 147–72.

Inglehart, Ronald. "Changing Values among Western Publics, 1970–2006: Postmaterialist Values and the Shift from Survival Values to Self-Expression Values." *West European Politics* 31, no. 1 (2008): 130–46.

Inglehart, Ronald. *Modernization and Postmodernization: Cultural, Economic, and Political Change in 43 Societies.* Princeton: Princeton University Press, 1997.

Inglehart, Ronald. "Postmodernization Erodes Respect for Authority, but Increases Support for Democracy." In *Critical Citizens: Global Support for Democratic Government,* edited by Pippa Norris, 236–56. Oxford: Oxford University Press, 1999.

Inglehart, Ronald, and Christian Welzel. "Changing Mass Priorities: The Link between Modernization and Democracy." *Perspectives on Politics* 8, no. 2 (2010): 551–67.

Inglehart, Ronald, and Christian Welzel. *Modernization, Cultural Change, and Democracy: The Human Development Sequence.* New York: Cambridge University Press 2005.

Inglehart, Ronald, and Wayne E. Baker. "Modernization, Cultural Change, and the Persistence of Traditional Values." *American Sociological Review* 65, no. 1 (2000): 19–51.

Jacka, Tamara. *Rural Women in Urban China: Gender, Migration, and Social Change.* New York: Routledge, 2014.

Jiang, Quanbao, and Jesús J. Sánchez-Barricarte. "Bare Branches and Social Stability: A Historical Perspective from China." *Frontiers of History in China* 6, no. 4 (2011): 538–61.

Key, V. O. *Public Opinion and American Democracy.* New York: Knopf, 1960.

Li, Jessica, and Jean Madsen. "Chinese Workers' Work Ethic in Reformed State-Owned Enterprises: Implications for HRD." *Human Resource Development International* 12, no. 2 (2009): 171–88.

Li, Li, Li-Jung Liang, Chunqing Lin, Zunyou Wu, and Yi Wen. "Individual Attitudes and Perceived Social Norms: Reports on HIV/AIDS-Related Stigma among Service Providers in China." *International Journal of Psychology* 44, no. 6 (2009): 443–50.

Li, Yinhe. "Regulating Male Same-Sex Relationships in the People's Republic of China." In *Sex and Sexuality in China,* edited by Elaine Jeffreys, 90–109. New York: Routledge, 2007.

Lin, Kai, Deeanna M. Button, Mingyue Su, and Sishi Chen. "Chinese College Students' Attitudes toward Homosexuality: Exploring the Effects of Traditional Culture and Modernizing Factors." *Sexuality Research and Social Policy* 13, no. 2 (2016): 158–72.

Liang, Kelly, and Philippe Le Billon. "African Migrants in China: Space, Race and Embodied Encounters in Guangzhou, China." *Social & Cultural Geography* 21, no. 5 (2020): 602–28.

Liang, Yongjia. "Religious Revival in Rural China and the Fate of 'Religion' in China." *Chinese Journal of Sociology* 3, no. 2 (2017): 268–90.

Liu, Chuyu, and Xiao Ma. "Popular Threats and Nationalistic Propaganda: Political Logic of China's Patriotic Campaign." *Security Studies* 27, no. 4 (2018): 633–64.

Luo, Yan, Fei Guo, and Jinghuan Shi. "Expansion and Inequality of Higher Education in China: How Likely Would Chinese Poor Students Get To Success?" *Higher Education Research & Development* 37, no. 5 (2018): 1015–34.

Ma, Li, Jani Turunen, and Ester Rizzi. "Divorce Chinese Style." *Journal of Marriage and Family* 80, no. 5 (2018): 1287–97.

Nathan, Andrew J. "The Puzzle of the Chinese Middle Class." *Journal of Democracy* 27, no. 2 (2016): 5–19.

Overmyer, Daniel L. "Religion in China Today: Introduction." *The China Quarterly* 174 (2003): 307–16.

Perry, Elizabeth J. "Higher Education and Authoritarian Resilience: The Case of China, Past and Present." *Harvard-Yenching Institute Working Paper Series*, 2015, https://dash.harvard.edu/handle/1/30822717.

Rich, Timothy S. "Religion and Public Perceptions of Gays and Lesbians in South Korea." *Journal of Homosexuality* 64, no. 5 (2017): 606–21.

Sautman, Barry. "Anti-Black Racism in Post-Mao China." *The China Quarterly* 138 (1994): 413–37.

Seeberg, Vilma, and Shujuan Luo. "Migrating to the City in North West China: Young Rural Women's Empowerment." *Journal of Human Development and Capabilities* 19, no. 3 (2018): 289–307.

Shepherd, Christian. "China LGBT Community Fears Crackdown after Weibo Content Vanishes." *Financial Times*, April 15, 2019, https://www.ft.com/content/19ff4b36-5f7a-11e9-b285-3acd5d43599e.

Shin, Doh Chull. "The Third Wave in East Asia Comparative and Dynamic Perspectives." *Taiwan Journal of Democracy* 4, no. 2 (2008): 91–131.

Tang, Wenfang. *Populist Authoritarianism: Chinese Political Culture and Regime Sustainability*. Oxford: Oxford University Press, 2016.

Walton, Linda. "The 'Spirit' of Confucian Education in Contemporary China: Songyang Academy and Zhengzhou University." *Modern China* 44, no. 3 (2018): 313–42.

Wang, Houxiong. "Access to Higher Education in China: Differences in Opportunity." *Frontiers of Education in China*, 6, no. 2 (2011): 227–47.

Wang, Xiuhua, and Paul Froese. "Attitudes toward Religion and Believers in China: How Education Increases Tolerance of Individual Religious Differences and Intolerance of Religious Influence in Politics." *Religion and Education* 47, no. 1 (2019): 1–20.

Welzel, Christian. "The Asian Values Thesis Revisited: Evidence from the World Values Surveys." *Japanese Journal of Political Science* 12, no. 1 (2011): 1–31.

Welzel, Christian. "The Myth of Asian Exceptionalism: Response to Bomhoff and Gu." *Journal of Cross-Cultural Psychology* 43, no. 7 (2012): 1039–54.

Wu, Chongqing. "The Transmission of Information in Chinese Folk Religion: Reflections on Fieldwork in Putian, Fujian." *Modern China* 45, no. 3 (2019): 295–315.

Wu, Xiaogang. "Higher Education, Elite Formation and Social Stratification in Contemporary China: Preliminary Findings from the Beijing College Students Panel Survey." *Chinese Journal of Sociology* 3, no. 1 (2017): 3–31.

Zeng, Junxia, Xiaopeng Pang, Linxiu Zhang, Alexis Medina, and Scott Rozelle. "Gender Inequality in Education in China: A Meta-Regression Analysis." *Contemporary Economic Policy* 32, no. 2 (2014): 474–91.

Zhai, Yida. "Values of Deference to Authority in Japan and China." *International Journal of Comparative Sociology* 58, no. 2 (2017): 120–39.

Zhang, Wei, and Mark Bray. "Equalising Schooling, Unequalising Private Supplementary Tutoring: Access and Tracking through Shadow Education in China." *Oxford Review of Education* 44, no. 2 (2018): 221–38.

Zhao, Suisheng. "A State-Led Nationalism: The Patriotic Education Campaign in Post -Tiananmen China." *Communist and Post-Communist Studies* 31, no. 3 (1998): 287–302.

Zhang, Lijia. "China's Divorce Rate Is Spiking Because Women No Longer Have to Accept Unsatisfying Marriages. This Should Be Celebrated, Not Stifled." *South China Morning Post*, November 27, 2019, https://www.scmp.com/comment/opinion/article/3039370/chinas-divorce-rate-spiking-because-women-no-longer-have-accept.

Zhou, Min, Shabnam Shenasi, and Tao Xu. "Chinese Attitudes toward African Migrants in Guangzhou, China." *International Journal of Sociology* 46, no. 2 (2016): 141–61.

Zhou, Min, and Tianyang Hu. "Social Tolerance of Homosexuality: A Quantitative Comparison of Mainland China, Singapore, and Taiwan." *Chinese Sociological Review* 52, no. 1 (2020): 27–55.

SIX | Mapping the Changes of Trust in Transitional China

ALFRED M. WU, EDUARDO ARARAL, AND BIAO HUANG

Introduction

Over the past two decades, trust in people and the government in China has been a puzzle. The literature suggests that the Chinese population has high levels of trust in the government compared to other countries, particularly in the Western world.[1] Although trust in the government has been under the spotlight, studying this alone does not show a complete picture. In reality, public governance in China has been questioned on numerous occasions, the example being the mishandling of Covid-19 in the early days of the pandemic, which led to some backlash domestically. Most notably, people felt deprived of government information, while some whistleblowers had already warned the government in Wuhan during the early stages of the Covid-19 outbreak. Nevertheless, if looking at many international surveys, trust in the Chinese government has demonstrated an unfailingly good record. Based on an in-depth analysis of the World Values Surveys (WVS) from 1995 to 2021, we aim to untangle the changes regarding trust in public and political institutions; furthermore, we also attempt to study the changes in interpersonal trust in China with a comparative perspective.

A number of studies on China document high levels of citizen satisfaction with the government. For example, the study by the Harvard's Ash Center in 2020 suggests that the level of trust in government has increased substantially between 2003 and 2016, particularly during the leadership of Xi Jinping. The widespread anti-corruption campaign was positively received by the population, strengthening the integrity of public officials. As indicated in this study, the percentage of interviewees who perceived public officials in China as "clean" was 35.4 percent in 2011. However, after Xi's Tiger Hunt (the anti-corruption campaign) started in late 2012, this percentage increased to 44.2 percent in 2015 and 65.3 percent in 2016. When the general public interacted with local government officials, they reported increasingly positive experiences during the Xi regime. In the survey item entitled "impressions of interactions with local officials," the satisfaction level of eventual outcome was 47.9 percent in 2011, increasing to 69.8 percent in 2015 and 75.1 percent in 2016. People in poor inland provinces, together with those from affluent coastal areas, trust their governments and rate government performance highly.[2]

In another study, Jesse Turiel et al. suggest that people in coastal regions were particularly satisfied with government performance.[3] More so, in recent years, even people in inland provinces with lower income have reported high levels of government satisfaction. This refutes the speculations that low-income people, or people in inland areas, may be dissatisfied with Chinese government performance due to the fact that poor people are deprived of the economic benefits of China's rapid growth, therefore laying the foundation for unrest and social instability. In reality, according to various survey data, the Chinese people, in different segments of society, generally trust the government.

Interpersonal trust is equally puzzling in the Chinese context due to the nature of the Chinese regime. In particular, we raise two interesting questions. First, does the Communist system increase or decrease trust in family members? Second, is the level of trust in strangers higher or lower compared to other contexts? The literature suggests that, in most post-Communist regimes, people tend to protect themselves carefully because of life experiences under government suppression; therefore, they have less trust in strangers, but more trust in family members or close friends. However, anecdotal evidence suggests a more complicated picture. For example, people in China increasingly engage in social activities that involve mingling with strangers, particularly in urban areas. Young people get used to co-working spaces where interacting with strangers is a new normal.

Our study paints a nuanced picture of trust in China. In terms of trust in public and political institutions, there was a substantial decline before Xi Jinping took power in 2012. However, it has significantly increased during his leadership, not least because of the anti-corruption campaign, which was largely positively received by the general public, leading to more confidence in the government. We also find some variations in terms of confidence in public and political institutions based on social status and educational attainment. At the same time, interpersonal trust has steadily increased over the examined period. While trust in family members has experienced a slight decline, in recent years the public has displayed higher trust in strangers, people of other religions, and people of other nationalities. This could be due to the influence of globalization and urbanization. The buoyant economy in China during the examined period might explain increased interpersonal trust and confidence in public and political institutions, given that Chinese propaganda has consistently highlighted spectacular economic achievements and improved livelihoods due to good Chinese governance.

Literature Review

In the existing literature, the concept of trust is questioned in both content and methodology. In addition, under the Communist regime, it is even more challenging to evaluate and understand trust, as propaganda and other factors could complicate the measurement and conceptualization of subject indicators. In the Chinese context, trust is more contested, as its measures and implications are complicated. Some studies link trust in China with the Chinese culture, while some compare trust in China with other Communist regimes, assuming similarities in trust levels across Communist or post-Communist countries.[4]

There is a large body of conceptual and empirical literature on trust.[5] Trust is conceptualized and understood in many ways depending on the methodology and the disciplinary orientation used to study it. Social psychologists study trust in experimental settings through interpersonal relations. They suggest that trust is a function of individual dispositions, social intelligence, character, and morals.[6] Others examine trust as a function of personal and social biases. Charles Ballew and Alexander Todorov, for example, link rapid judgments of competence based on facial appearances with a willingness to trust political candidates.[7] Therefore, we can conclude that trust is both fluid and dynamic.

In the business literature, trust is analyzed in the context of market transactions. Oliver Williamson defined trust in terms of credible commitments, where trust is a property of a market transaction.[8] He suggests that the degree of trust depends on the degree of the completeness of contracts. Incomplete contracts create mistrust due to the potential for opportunism. To gain from an exchange, parties to the transaction seek to find ways of addressing the problems of opportunism and make their commitments more credible.[9] Similarly, in the literature on industrial organization, trust is understood as a function of the institutional structure. In countries where the rule of law prevails, trust among firms is more likely.[10] Under a benign institutional structure, trust is likely to enhance institutional characteristics such as the rule of law.

Game theorists and international relations scholars have modeled trust in terms of completeness of information, pay-off structure, whether the game is a single shot or repeated, and whether it is played simultaneously or sequentially.[11] Elinor Ostrom, Robert Putnam, and Mark Granovetter have each pointed to factors such as norms, networks, group size, the history of cooperation, and face-to-face communication as structural variables to help explain variations of trust in settings characterized by collective action.[12] Social capital and trust are often conflated, making it challenging to use empirical research to deal with the problem of endogeneity. Karen Cook et al. address the central question of "what comes first, social capital or trust?" They argue that empirical analysis on trust should focus on groups, networks, and institutions instead of individuals.[13] In their earlier work, they consider trust as a relational interpretation of preexisting incentives.[14] In many contexts, it is observed that interpersonal trust is fundamentally shaped by institutions, particularly the political system and governance structures.

Political trust has been at the forefront of many academic debates. The state of research on political trust is summarized by Warren Miller. He writes that trust exists as "an independent variable in search of a dependent variable."[15] It means that trust can be used to explain many outcomes, such as government performance and crisis management. The majority of existing empirical studies cover attitudes toward particular institutions or politicians, or use behavioral experiments that analyze trust by observing subjects' behavior in a laboratory context. In both cases, the study of trust is often framed as a binary variable (trust or no trust) or in terms of the Likert scale (high, medium, or low trust). These kinds of studies add important insights to the ongoing debate. Nevertheless, to complement the studies, treating trust as an independent variable, future researchers should measure and compare trust in different contexts. For example, some studies in the Chinese context using the different measurements of trust suggest that trust in government may be overestimated due to social desirability under the authoritarian regime.[16]

In summary, the literature on trust is still very much contested conceptually, empirically, and methodologically. It is clear that trust has various dimensions, including perceptions about the trustworthiness of the other party, how the game is set up (e.g., prisoner's dilemma leads to non-cooperation), and the set of institutions involved, as well as the formal and informal rules of the game, and their enforcement mechanisms. The methodology to study trust has evolved from large-N surveys, comparative studies, and longitudinal studies to laboratory experiments. However, more research is needed to develop a more coherent theory on trust.

In this study, we have not accounted for measures like the issue of social desirability. Interpersonal trust and confidence in public and political institutions may therefore be complicated by a number of factors, including, but not limited to, propaganda and peer pressure (social desirability). The previous literature on trust in different fields informs our study; nevertheless, the measurement and impact of trust in people and government tend to be situated in a specific yet fluid context. We should therefore compare trust in different contexts. However, as we acknowledge the difficulty associated with comparing different contexts, we argue that China, as the largest developing Communist country, should be interpreted and understood carefully in its own respect.

Interpersonal and Political Trust in China

This study utilizes data from the World Values Surveys (WVS hereafter) Waves 3 to 7, conducted in mainland China in 1995, 2001, 2007, 2013, and 2018. The number of respondents was 1,500 in Wave 3; 1,000 in Wave 4; 1,991 in Wave 5; 2,300 in Wave 6; and 3,036 in Wave 7 (9,827 observations in total). To map the evolution of trust in China, this study includes questions that reflect trust and confidence in people and the government in China. The first question reads, "Generally speaking, would you say that most people can be trusted or that you need to be very careful in dealing with people?" Like most other studies, we view this question as an indication of general interpersonal trust. The options are "1 = most people can be trusted" and "2 = need to be very careful." The second group of questions refers to trust in close people and relative strangers. They read, "How much do you trust your family/your neighborhood/people you know personally/people you meet for the first time/people of another religion/people of another nationality?" The responses are measured on a four-point scale: "1 = trust completely," "2 = trust somewhat," "3 = do not trust very much," "4 = do not trust at all." The third group of questions reflects people's confidence in public and political organizations: "How much confidence do you have in the armed forces/ the police/the courts/the government/political parties?" The responses are also measured on a four-point scale: "1 = a great deal," "2 = quite a lot," "3 = not very much," "4 = none at all."

As a caveat, it should be mentioned that this study uses reverse scoring for the sake of clarity. Because the options of the questions above are descending, which means the lower the number, the higher the trust/ confidence, we reverse the numbers for the convenience of understanding when analyzing the data. It means that for interpersonal trust, in the following analysis, 4 means "trust completely" while 1 means "do not trust at all." The higher the number, the higher trust/confidence. In the raw data, 4 means "do not trust at all" while 1 means "trust completely."

We first present the change of the means of each question in a descriptive way (a pooled dataset). Then, we compare the means of each year/group by adopting ordered logistic regression (robust standard errors are used), because the values of each question are ordinal, and other covariates could be controlled when employing regression models. For example, assuming that we would like to compare whether the mean of answers to the question "Generally speaking, would you say that most people can be trusted or that you need to be very careful in dealing with people?" differs significantly between 2013 and 2018, we regress the answer to this question on the variable of year (2013 as reference) and controls. If the variable year 2018 contributes significantly to the dependent variable (the score of this question), then the answer to this question in 2018 is significantly different from that in 2013. This method is also used in comparing the means of these answers in different groups of people. For example, when comparing the differences in confidence toward the government among people with different educational backgrounds, we regress the answer to the question "How much confidence do you have in the government?" on educational levels (no education as reference) and controls. If the variables of educational level (primary school, lower secondary school, upper secondary school, university) are negatively associated with the confidence toward government, it then shows that educated people have significantly less confidence in the government than people with no education. Demographic variables such as sex, age, and membership in political parties are controlled for.[17] Table 6.1 lists the descriptive statistics of the variables.

Table 6.1. Descriptive Statistics of Trust in China

Variables	Mean (SD)/Percentage		
Interpersonal trust			
Generally speaking, would you say that most people can be trusted or that you need to be very careful in dealing with people?	1.60 (.49)		
1 = need to be very careful	38.95%		
2 = most people can be trusted	57.33%		
Trust in close people			
How much you trust your family	3.87 (.37)		
How much you trust your neighborhood		3.04 (.62)	
How much you trust people you know personally			2.99 (.59)
1 = do not trust at all	0.05%	0.57%	0.61%
2 = do not trust very much	0.57%	10.64%	10.91%
3 = trust somewhat	8.46%	46.49%	48.44%
4 = trust completely	63.84%	14.54%	11.51%
Trust in relative strangers			
How much you trust people you meet for the first time	1.93 (.60)		
How much you trust people of another religion		1.95 (.69)	
How much you trust people of another nationality			1.90 (.68)
1 = do not trust at all	14.55%	13.62%	15.11%
2 = do not trust very much	46.83%	29.85%	30.64%
3 = trust somewhat	8.07%	9.87%	8.30%
4 = trust completely	0.78%	0.64%	0.61%
Confidence in public and political organizations			
How much confidence you have in the armed forces	3.36 (.62)		
How much confidence you have in the police		3.00 (.72)	
How much confidence you have in the courts			3.07 (.70)
1 = none at all	0.78%	2.22%	1.50%
2 = not very much	3.89%	14.42%	10.13%
3 = quite a lot	40.96%	45.22%	40.12%
4 = a great deal	34.15%	19.03%	18.27%
How much confidence you have in the government	3.37 (.62)		
How much confidence you have in political parties		3.22 (.67)	
1 = none at all	0.66%	1.00%	
2 = not very much	4.18%	7.68%	

(*Continued*)

Table 6.1. (*Continued*)

Variables	Mean (SD)/Percentage	
3 = quite a lot	40.79%	42.60%
4 = a great deal	35.47%	26.49%
Demographic Variables		
Male	52.21%	
Age	43.12 (14.18)	
Educational level	3.04 (1.20)	
1 = No education	10.54%	
2 = Primary school	24.91%	
3 = Lower secondary school	27.77%	
4 = Upper secondary school	22.68%	
5 = University	13.75%	
Social class	2.38 (.88)	
1 = Lower class	18.34%	
2 = Working class	29.18%	
3 = Lower middle class	41.10%	
4 = Upper middle class	6.30%	
5 = Upper class	0.33%	
Membership of political parties	10.45%	

Note: Reverse scoring is used in this study. The higher the number, the higher the trust/confidence.

Interpersonal Trust

Interpersonal trust is fundamental for studying overall trust. In China, interpersonal trust has generally increased since 2007 (Wave 5, 2005–2008), from 52.41 percent in 2007 to 65.44 percent in 2018 (Wave 7, 2017–2021). The mean comparison demonstrates that general interpersonal trust in 2007 (52.41 percent) is significantly different from that in 2013 (Wave 6, 2010–2014), which is 64.44 percent; however, the difference of general interpersonal trust between 1995 (Wave 3, 1995–1998) and 2007 is statistically insignificant, as is that between 2013 and 2018. The jump in interpersonal trust between 2007 and 2018 is substantial.

For comparison across countries and regions, we chose Japan, Taiwan, and Hong Kong in Asia, which share some similar socioeconomic conditions with mainland China; Germany, which is an important EU economy; and the United States, the world's largest economy. It can be seen that, in China, the percentage of respondents who stated that most people can be trusted is the highest among a number of economies with similar socioeconomic characteristics, as well as selected important countries and regions in the world (see Figure 6.1). Though the existing literature suggests that generalized trust is overestimated in China,[18] the survey data we utilize does show the largest increase in the last three surveys, with an increase of 13.03 percent (Germany also records a substantial increase of interpersonal trust, 11.86 percent in the examined period). In the United States, interpersonal trust has been slowly rising over the past two decades, with 35.94 percent believing that most people can be trusted in the 1995–1998 survey and 39.74 percent in the 2017–2021 survey. The only exception with regard to the rising trend is observed between Wave 5 (2005–2008) and Wave 6 (2010–2014), as the 2007–2008 financial crisis may have negatively affected interpersonal trust. Germany has the lowest percentage of interpersonal trust among the selected countries and regions in the Wave 3 survey (1995–1998). However, this percentage has jumped in the last three waves since 2005, from 34.09 percent in Wave 5 to 45.95 percent in Wave 7, which is very similar to the situation in China. This may be because during this period, Germany's economic standing grew steadily, as did China's, and they were among the few economies in the world that remained relatively unscathed during the 2007–2008 financial crisis. The change in Japan's interpersonal trust differs from that of China and the other selected countries and regions. The percentage of people saying that most people can be trusted is 42.32 percent in the Wave 3 survey (1995–1998)

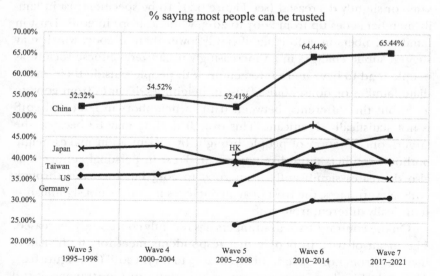

Figure 6.1. General Interpersonal Trust in China and Selected Countries/Regions

and 43.06 percent in the Wave 4 survey (2000–2004), second only to China in those waves; however, according to data from the latest three waves, trust has gradually fallen in Japan to just 35.60 percent at the time of Wave 7 (2017–2021), higher than only Taiwan, which has the lowest percentage in the latest three waves. This is probably related to the fact that social problems such as a rapidly aging population and increasing social anxiety have become prominent. Regarding Taiwan and Hong Kong, which share cultural similarities with mainland China, general interpersonal trust shows two different situations. In Taiwan, although the percentage of respondents saying most people can be trusted is 38.20 percent in Wave 3 (1995–1998), it declines significantly in the next decade and reaches its lowest point of 24.42 percent in the Wave 5 (2005–2008) survey. After that, the number improves in the following two surveys, up to 30.99 percent in the 2017–2021 survey, but it is still the lowest among the regions being compared here. As for Hong Kong, interpersonal trust is 41.06 percent in the Wave 5 survey (2005–2008), higher than that of the United States, Germany, Japan, and Taiwan. In the Wave 6 survey (2010–2014), it rises to 48.34 percent, but plummets to 39.50 percent in the Wave 7 survey (2017–2021), lower than Germany and the United States. The decline may be related to Hong Kong's economic downturn and social unrest in recent years.

Although there has been a significant increase in overall interpersonal trust in China, trust in close relationships has either remained the same or slightly decreased (see Figure 6.2). To be specific, trust in family members goes up from 2007 to 2013, while it drops in 2018. Trust in family members in 2018 is significantly lower than in 2007, which may suggest subtle changes in an increasingly urbanized Chinese society, as people tend to have more interactions with people outside their immediate families or households. Trust in neighbors declines from 2007 to 2018, but the difference between trust in neighbors in 2013 and 2018 is not statistically significant. This overall decline may be because the larger concentration of people brought by urbanization makes neighborhood conflicts more likely to occur. Trust in personal connections also decreases significantly from 2007 to 2013 but increases through 2018. Nevertheless, the trust in acquaintances in 2007 is not significantly statistically different from 2018.

On the contrary, trust in strangers has recently consistently increased. The mean of trust in people that respondents meet for the first time increases from 1.91 in 2007 and 1.92 in 2013 to 1.95 in 2018 (see Figure 6.2). Although this phenomenon deserves attention, trust in strangers is still substantially lower than trust in close relations.

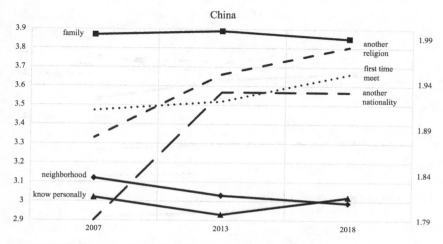

Figure 6.2. Trust in Close People and Strangers (China)
Note: The left-hand vertical axis corresponds to the data represented by the solid line, while the right-hand vertical axis corresponds to the data represented by the dashed line.

The mean of trust in people of other religions has also gone up significantly, from 1.88 in 2007 to 1.95 in 2013 and 1.98 in 2018 (see Figure 6.2). Similarly, the mean of trust in people of other nationalities is significantly higher in 2013 and 2018 than that in 2007. The existing literature suggests that China's xenophobia and relatively low trust among people who meet for the first time are due to cultural homogeneity.[19] This is true to some extent, particularly in comparison with other nations. Nevertheless, our data suggests that xenophobia has become less of an issue in China over time. Almost scoring 2 in 2018 in terms of trust in people of another religion means that people are more tolerant of coexisting with people of different religions. As China and the United States are big countries (in terms of population and GDP), we include a comparison about interpersonal trust. The data indicates that almost all kinds of interpersonal trust in the United States have slightly declined during the past two decades (see Figure 6.3). As stated above, this may be due to the impact of the 2007–2008 financial crisis, which leads to social discontent and increased distrust among citizens, especially toward those with whom we have close relationships, such as family members.

Altogether, over the past decade, trust in strangers, people of other religions, and people of other nationalities has increased in China. However, compared to the United States, the gap between trust in close

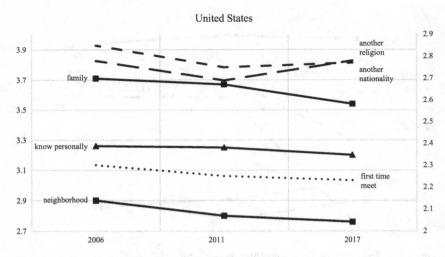

Figure 6.3. Trust in Close People and Strangers (United States)
Note: The left-hand vertical axis corresponds to the data represented by the solid line, while the right-hand vertical axis corresponds to the data represented by the dashed line.

relationships and strangers in China is still substantial. China's story about interpersonal trust echoes previous findings from other Communist regimes. Due to the authoritarian nature of government, repression makes people wary of being reported to the authorities by strangers or people outside of the household. Therefore, trust in strangers is significantly lower than trust in close relations, as found in cross-country studies of Communist and post-Communist regimes.[20] Nevertheless, in some contexts, repression has become much more targeted in recent years. People who are scrutinized mostly come from the media and nongovernmental organizations (NGOs), and as a result the average person is more relaxed and will view the regime as benign. The majority of people who are not targeted are more likely to interact with strangers without the fear of being reported. Furthermore, China has strengthened its regulations and improved penalties for behaviors that undermine social trust, such as telecommunications fraud and shoddy products. These factors may help improve the level of trust in strangers.

Rapid urbanization also explains the increase of trust in strangers. Urbanization has been a key feature of China's development policy in the past few decades, and as a result, we have seen rapid urbanization in recent years.[21] The year 2011 marked a turning point, where China's urban population surpassed the rural population. The share of its urban population in the total population increased from less than 20 percent in 1978 to 60 percent in 2018.[22] Urban lives are fundamentally different from rural lives, in the sense that urban people are dealing with strangers all the time, while rural people are mostly interacting with close relations or fellow villagers. Therefore, urbanized people in China must adapt to living and interacting with strangers.

Confidence in Public and Political Organizations

Confidence in public and political organizations is important for understanding state-society relations, which are crucial for regime stability. Comparatively speaking, confidence in public and political organizations is high in China.[23] Nevertheless, our study suggests some intriguing patterns appearing between 1995 and 2018. Confidence in public and political organizations went down slightly before bouncing back and even reaching new heights under the Xi regime.

Confidence in public and political organizations fluctuates during the examined period. It mostly decreases from 2001 to 2013, but goes up significantly after 2013, reaching a peak in 2018. Taking the government as an example, the mean of confidence in the government is 3.36 in 2001 and 3.32 in both 2007 and 2013, but rises to 3.44 in 2018 (see Figure 6.4). The changes of confidence in armed forces, political parties, courts, and police are all presented in Figure 6.4 as well. The evolution of confidence in public and political organizations, to some extent, illustrates that the Chinese people gradually cast doubt on their

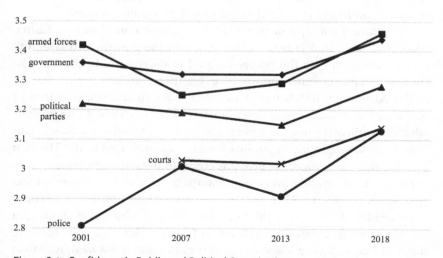

Figure 6.4. Confidence in Public and Political Organizations

confidence in government.[24] However, this confidence regained ground in the Xi Jinping era.

The Harvard surveys indicate a similar pattern. They evaluated citizen satisfaction with government performance based on the four-point Likert scale, and found that the level of satisfaction has increased substantially over the past decade.[25] This is particularly true for local governments, such as those of counties or townships, which are usually much less popular than the central government.[26] Nevertheless, the level of satisfaction in recent years is much higher than before. The Harvard surveys also evaluated people's perceptions of local officials. In 2003, the results were negative, with half of the interviewees stating that public officials were "talk only." Nevertheless, in the last round of the survey (in 2016), more than half of the interviewees viewed local officials as "practical problem solvers." By any standard, this is a good record with regard to public perceptions of officials.

The overall increased confidence in public and political organizations may be caused by improved public services at different levels of government in China. Particularly after agricultural taxes were removed in 2006, public officials have been viewed more positively when residents approach them for public services. In the past, a constant tussle occurred between public officials in rural areas and farmers. In the meantime, because fiscal capacity has improved across the board, public officials in the urban area have been viewed much more positively, as they would provide better services than they did before. A study by Dan Chen also suggests that when residents view public services provided by local governments positively, they tend to trust local governments more.[27]

Combatting corruption may work to improve confidence in China. Xiao et al. note that citizen satisfaction with the government is significantly correlated with the perceived level of corruption in the Chinese context.[28] The anti-corruption drive has been an important feature of the Xi regime, which has prosecuted more than a few hundred of senior public officials, including ministers, since late 2012.[29] The unprecedented anti-corruption campaign has received positive feedback both from ordinary people and public officials.[30] As indicated in the Harvard surveys, anti-corruption has brought credit to the current regime.[31] The approval rating of the government campaign to reduce corruption was 71.5 percent in 2016.[32] At the same time, around two-thirds of interviewees considered Chinese public officials "clean," which is a significant improvement from previous records in China.[33] However, the literature suggests that exposing scandals of corrupt officials has a negative effect on public trust in government.[34] This difference is likely to depend on whether trust is placed on institutions or on individual officials.[35]

For this section, a caveat with regard to education levels is in order. Although overall confidence in the government has increased over the examined period (data from 2001 to 2018), the pooled data analysis shows that the level of confidence decreases with education; the proportion of people with the most confidence in the government are also the ones with no formal education. Educated people, on the other hand, are much more cautious about government performance (see Figure 6.5). Based on survey data in China, Yang Zhong also notes that better-educated people and high-income people tend to trust their governments less than their counterparts.[36] Some studies in non-Chinese contexts identify a similar trend: Education, together with high income, is associated with lower confidence in public organizations.[37] Since 1999, when the Chinese government rolled out the policy of the massification of higher education, the percentage of higher-education degree holders in the total population has increased substantially.[38] As better education can bring about better lives, more people with higher education and high income do not guarantee that they support the regime, according to many opinion surveys in China over the past decades. Rather, people with higher education degrees may act as "loyal critics"[39] in the country. They are skeptical of political and public organizations, but at the same time, they are generally appreciative of government performance.

Lastly, when evaluating confidence by social class, we find that those who perceive themselves as a lower class have the least confidence in

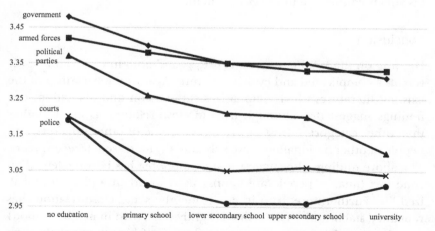

Figure 6.5. Trust in Public and Political Organizations by Levels of Education

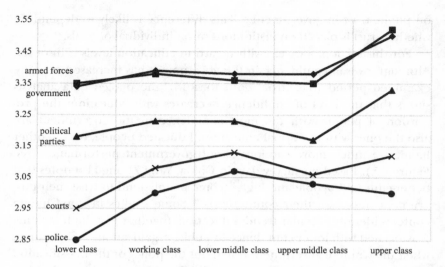

Figure 6.6. Trust in Public and Political Organizations by Social Class

public and political organizations (see Figure 6.6). This is contrary to the often-mentioned claim by the CCP, the ruling party in China. Like other Communist parties, the CCP portrays itself as the vanguard of the proletariat.[40] Lower-class people may suffer from economic hardship, which negatively impacts their confidence in public and political organizations. They may also have poor experiences when interacting with governments, while upper-class individuals may use their connections (*guanxi*) to access better public services; therefore, in general, social status affects confidence in the government.

Conclusion

Drawing on the WVS waves between 1995 and 2018 in China, this study reveals a complicated and evolving picture. Against the backdrop of the existing literature, which emphasizes suppression and alienation, our findings suggest that although trust in close relations is much higher than other categories, trust in strangers, people of other religions, and people of other nationalities have substantially increased in recent years. The above findings also suggest that xenophobia has become less of an issue in China, as people are getting used to urban and even globalized life. Furthermore, trust in family members and close relations has remained stable and even declined slightly (e.g., trust in neighborhood) over the years. In general, interpersonal trust in China has gone through some significant changes, probably due to globalization and urbanization, but the percentage of respondents stating that most people can be trusted is significantly higher in China than in some other countries and regions in both Asia and the West.

In terms of confidence in public and political institutions, compared with countries and regions, data suggests that Chinese confidence in public and political organizations is much higher all the time. However, it varies to some extent according to social status and educational attainment. Particularly people with higher educational attainments and people who view themselves as part of a lower class have less confidence in public and political organizations. Nevertheless, despite some differences, the overall confidence in public and political institutions remains very high in China. Furthermore, the Xi regime has effectively promoted popular confidence in political and public institutions, as confidence has remained quite high in recent years. This finding echoes other similar research conducted in China. The improvement of fiscal capacity, better public services at the local level, as well as the massive anti-corruption campaign, may all have helped boost public confidence in the CCP and the government. Slightly before Xi Jinping entered office in 2012, confidence in political and public institutions had declined; however, the Xi regime has showcased that confidence in government can be restored and strengthened through improvements in government performance. Nonetheless, one note of caution: As mentioned previously, research in the Chinese context suggests that the measurement of trust could be very tricky, and people tend to comply with social desirability.[41] Moreover, this study could not evaluate the impact of the propaganda by the CCP to boost public opinion in favor of its policies. Therefore, trust and confidence levels tend to be overestimated in studies like this one.

Furthermore, as the literature suggests, trust should be understood from a perspective of groups, networks, and institutions. Institutions, particularly the political system and government structure, can significantly shape trust in society. For example, authoritarian governments tend to have more propaganda on government performance and achievements in fighting corruption (instead of the failure in controlling corruption). The propaganda also significantly impacts the media consumption of Chinese citizens, and as a result, people collectively view the government very positively. Moreover, critical citizens may be subject to peer pressure to change their unfavorable positions.

However, we need to consider our study's finding that education attainments are negatively associated with confidence in political and public institutions. This shows that higher education levels may reduce the impact of propaganda on people's trust in governmental organizations. As more people in China receive better and higher education, we can expect that more Chinese people will trust official institutions less in the years to come.

Against the backdrop of assessing trust in a Communist regime, trust can also be understood more accurately from a cultural perspective. For example, the existing literature finds more "trustful" cultures in Western Europe and less "trustful" cultures in countries like Turkey and Nigeria. In places with high levels of interpersonal trust, people tend to pay attention to social cohesion and tolerance for others. At the same time, in low-trust societies, people are concerned with maintaining social order. China has been viewed as embodying a level of trust similar to that of the United States.[42] Interestingly, comparing interpersonal trust in the United States, which has been declining over the examined period, in China the levels of trust in strangers, people of other religions, and people of other nationalities have increased notably. This indicates that under urbanization and globalization, interpersonal trust in China has been moving in a positive direction. Nevertheless, we also need to bear in mind the role of authoritarianism and the political structure in affecting individual trust and collective culture. Ultimately, the issue of social desirability and the measurement of trust could be a topic for additional exploration. Finally, the gap between trust in strangers and trust in close relations in China, as compared with the data in the United States, is substantial. It indicates that although Chinese society has been influenced by globalization and urbanization, it is still a very traditional Asian society that relies a lot on close relations (family members and relatives) for various supports, whether financial or emotional.

In terms of policy implications, as noted in the business literature discussed before, trust is positively correlated with the degree of the completeness of contracts. More specifically, complete social contracts stimulate more trust. In the meantime, incomplete or opaque contracts reduce trust in the long run. That is the reason behind the decline of trust in political and public institutions before the Xi regime, as rampant corruption and substantial government failures occurred during that period. Nevertheless, complete social contracts need to go hand in hand with the rule of law and transparent governance.

Notes

1. Edward Cunningham, Tony Saich, and Jesse Turiel, *Understanding CCP Resilience: Surveying Chinese Public Opinion through Time* (Harvard Kennedy School Ash Center for Democratic Governance and Innovation, 2020), https://ash.harvard.edu/files/ash/files/final_policy_brief_7.6.2020.pdf; Yang Zhong, *Political Culture and Participation in Urban China* (Singapore: Springer, 2018).

2. Cunningham et al., *Understanding CCP Resilience*; Zhong, *Political Culture.*

3. Jesse Turiel, Edward Cunningham, and Anthony Saich, "To Serve the People: Income, Region and Citizen Attitudes towards Governance in China (2003–2016)," *The China Quarterly* 240 (2019): 906–35.

4. Carsten Herrmann-Pillath, "Social Capital, Chinese Style: Individualism, Relational Collectivism and the Cultural Embeddedness of the Institutions–Performance Link," *China Economic Journal* 2, no. 3 (2010): 325–50; Qing Yang and Wenfang Tang, "Exploring the Sources of Institutional Trust in China: Culture, Mobilization, or Performance," *Asian Politics & Policy* 2, no. 3 (2010): 415–36.

5. Denise M. Rousseau, Sim B. Sitkin, Ronald S. Burt, and Colin Camerer, "Not So Different after All: A Cross-Discipline View of Trust," *Academy of Management Review* 23, no. 3 (1998): 393–404.

6. Eric M. Uslaner, *The Moral Foundations of Trust* (Cambridge: Cambridge University Press, 2002); Toshio Yamagishi, *Trust: The Evolutionary Game of Mind and Society* (New York: Springer, 2011).

7. Charles C. Ballew and Alexander Todorov, "Predicting Political Elections from Rapid and Unreflective Face Judgments," *Proceedings of the National Academy of Sciences* 104, no. 46 (2007): 17948–53.

8. Oliver E. Williamson, "Calculativeness, Trust, and Economic Organization," *The Journal of Law and Economics* 36, no. 1 (1993): 453–86.

9. Williamson, "Calculativeness."

10. Henry Farrell and Jack Knight, "Trust, Institutions, and Institutional Change: Industrial Districts and the Social Capital Hypothesis," *Politics & Society* 31, no. 4 (2003): 537–66.

11. Andrew H. Kydd, *Trust and Mistrust in International Relations* (Princeton: Princeton University Press, 2007).

12. Elinor Ostrom, *Governing the Commons: The Evolution of Institutions for Collective Action* (Cambridge: Cambridge University Press, 1990); Robert Putnam, "The Prosperous Community: Social Capital and Public Life," *The American Prospect* 13, no. 4 (1993): 35–42; Mark Granovetter, *Society and Economy Framework and Principles* (Cambridge, MA: Harvard University Press, 2017).

13. Karen S. Cook, Margaret Levi, and Russell Hardin, *Whom Can We Trust?: How Groups, Networks, and Institutions Make Trust Possible* (New York: Russell Sage Foundation, 2009).

14. Karen S. Cook, Russell Hardin, and Margaret Levi, *Cooperation without Trust?* (New York: Russell Sage Foundation, 2005).

15. Margaret Levi and Laura Stoker, "Political Trust and Trustworthiness," *Annual Review of Political Science* 3, no. 1 (2000): 501.

16. Lianjiang Li, "Distrust in Government and Preference for Regime Change in China," *Political Studies* 69, no. 2 (2021a): 326–43; Neil Munro, "Does Refusal Bias Influence the Measurement of Chinese Political Trust?" *Journal of

Contemporary China 27, no. 111 (2018): 457–71; Kerry Ratigan and Leah Rabin, "Re-Evaluating Political Trust: The Impact of Survey Nonresponse in Rural China," *The China Quarterly* 243 (2020): 823–38.

17. When comparing means of answers by year, educational level and social class are included as control variables. When comparing means of answers by group, years are included as control variables.

18. H. Christoph Steinhardt, "How Is High Trust in China Possible? Comparing the Origins of Generalized Trust in Three Chinese Societies," *Political Studies* 60, no. 2 (2012): 434–54; Eric M. Uslaner, "Measuring Generalized Trust: In Defense of the 'Standard' Question," in *Handbook of Research Methods on Trust*, ed. Fergus Lyon, Guido Möllering, and Mark N.K. Saunders (Northampton, MA: Edward Elgar Publishing, 2012), 72–82.

19. See Herrmann-Pillath, "Social Capital, Chinese Style."

20. Christian Bjørnskov, "The Multiple Facets of Social Capital," *European Journal of Political Economy* 22, no. 1 (2006): 22–40.

21. Lin Ye and Alfred M. Wu, "Urbanization, Land Development, and Land Financing: Evidence from Chinese Cities," *Journal of Urban Affairs* 36, no. 1 (2014): 354–68.

22. See World Bank and the Development Research Center of the State Council, the People's Republic of China, *Urban China: Toward Efficient, Inclusive, and Sustainable Urbanization* (Washington, DC: The World Bank, 2014), https://www.worldbank.org/content/dam/Worldbank/document/EAP/China/WEB-Urban-China.pdf; Ye and Wu, "Urbanization, Land Development."

23. Zhong, *Political Culture*; Hedda Flatø, "Trust Is in the Air: Pollution and Chinese Citizens' Attitudes Towards Local, Regional and Central Levels of Government," *Journal of Chinese Governance* 7, no. 2 (2021): 180–211.

24. Here, we use government as an umbrella concept that incorporates the public and political organizations.

25. Cunningham et al., *Understanding CCP Resilience*.

26. Lianjiang Li, "Reassessing Trust in the Central Government: Evidence from Five National Surveys," *The China Quarterly* 225 (2016): 100–21.

27. Dan Chen, " 'Supervision by Public Opinion' or by Government Officials? Media Criticism and Central-Local Government Relations in China," *Modern China* 43, no. 6 (2017): 620–45.

28. Hanyu Xiao, Ting Gong, Chilik Yu, Wen-Jong Juang, and Baishun Yuan, "Citizens' Confidence in Government Control of Corruption: An Empirical Analysis," *Social Indicators Research* 152, no. 3 (2020): 877–97.

29. Lina Vyas and Alfred M. Wu, "Anti-Corruption Policy: China's Tiger Hunt and India's Demonetization," *International Journal of Public Administration* 43, no. 11 (2020): 1000–11.

30. See Cunningham et al., *Understanding CCP Resilience*; Vyas and Wu, "Anti-Corruption Policy."

31. Cunningham et al., *Understanding CCP Resilience*.

32. Cunningham et al., *Understanding CCP Resilience*.

33. Cunningham et al., *Understanding CCP Resilience*.

34. Yuhua Wang and Bruce J. Dickson, "How Corruption Investigations Undermine Regime Support: Evidence from China," *Political Science Research and Methods* 10, no. 1 (2022): 33–48.

35. Jie Chen, *Popular Political Support in Urban China* (Redwood City: Stanford University Press, 2004); Lianjiang Li, "Decoding Political Trust in China: A Machine Learning Analysis," *The China Quarterly* 249 (2021b): 1–20; Jie Lu and Bruce Dickson, "Revisiting the Eastonian Framework on Political Support: Assessing Different Measures of Regime Support in Mainland China," *Comparative Politics* 52, no. 4 (2020): 671–701; Jiangnan Zhu, Huang Huang, and Dong Zhang, " 'Big Tigers, Big Data': Learning Social Reactions to China's Anticorruption Campaign through Online Feedback," *Public Administration Review* 79, no. 4 (2019): 500–13.

36. Zhong, *Political Culture*.

37. Bianca Clausen, Aart Kraay, and Zsolt Nyiri, "Corruption and Confidence in Public Institutions: Evidence from a Global Survey," *The World Bank Economic Review* 25, no. 2 (2011): 212–49.

38. Lin Ye, Alfred M. Wu, and Xinhui Yang, "University Enrolment Expansion and Returns to Higher Education: Evidence from China," in *Massification of Higher Education in Asia*, ed. Alfred M. Wu and John N. Hawkins (Singapore: Springer, 2018), 113–28.

39. Zhong and Zhan use the concept of "authoritarian critical citizens" to explain the declining trust in the Chinese central government. See Pei Zhong and Jing Vivian Zhan, "Authoritarian Critical Citizens and Declining Political Trust in China," *China Review* 21, no. 2 (2021): 117–52.

40. See The Tenth National Congress of the Communist Party of China, "Constitution of the Communist Party of China," Marxists, August 28, 1973, https://www.marxists.org/subject/china/documents/cpc/CONSTITUTION_ CPC.htm.

41. Li, "Distrust in Government"; Munro, "Does Refusal Bias Influence the Measurement of Chinese Political Trust?"; Ratigan and Rabin, "Re-Evaluating Political Trust."

42. Ronald Inglehart, *Modernization and Postmodernization: Cultural, Economic, and Political Change in 43 Societies* (Princeton: Princeton University Press, 1997); Steven T. Mortenson, "Interpersonal Trust and Social Skill in Seeking Social Support among Chinese and Americans," *Communication Research* 36, no. 1 (2009): 32–53.

Bibliography

Ballew, Charles C., and Alexander Todorov. "Predicting Political Elections from Rapid and Unreflective Face Judgments." *Proceedings of the National Academy of Sciences* 104, no. 46 (2007): 17948–53.

Bjørnskov, Christian. "The Multiple Facets of Social Capital." *European Journal of Political Economy* 22, no. 1 (2006): 22–40.

Chen, Dan. " 'Supervision by Public Opinion' or by Government Officials? Media Criticism and Central-Local Government Relations in China." *Modern China* 43, no. 6 (2017): 620–45.

Chen, Jie. *Popular Political Support in Urban China.* Redwood City: Stanford University Press, 2004.

Clausen, Bianca, Aart Kraay, and Zsolt Nyiri. "Corruption and Confidence in Public Institutions: Evidence from a Global Survey." *The World Bank Economic Review* 25, no. 2 (2011): 212–49.

Cook, Karen S., Margaret Levi, and Russell Hardin. *Whom Can We Trust?: How Groups, Networks, and Institutions Make Trust Possible*. New York: Russell Sage Foundation, 2009.

Cook, Karen S., Russell Hardin, and Margaret Levi. *Cooperation without Trust?* New York: Russell Sage Foundation, 2005.

Cunningham, Edward, Tony Saich, and Jesse Turiel. *Understanding CCP Resilience: Surveying. Chinese Public Opinion through Time*. Cambridge: Ash Center for Democratic Governance and Innovation at Harvard University's John F. Kennedy School of Government, 2020.

Farrell, Henry, and Jack Knight. "Trust, Institutions, and Institutional Change: Industrial Districts and the Social Capital Hypothesis." *Politics & Society* 31, no. 4 (2003): 537–66.

Flatø, Hedda. "Trust Is in the Air: Pollution and Chinese Citizens' Attitudes towards Local, Regional and Central Levels of Government." *Journal of Chinese Governance* 7, no. 2 (2022): 180–211.

Granovetter, Mark. *Society and Economy Framework and Principles*. Cambridge: Harvard University Press, 2017.

Herrmann-Pillath, Carsten. "Social Capital, Chinese Style: Individualism, Relational Collectivism and the Cultural Embeddedness of the Institutions–Performance Link." *China Economic Journal* 2, no. 3 (2010): 325–50.

Inglehart, Ronald. *Modernization and Postmodernization: Cultural, Economic, and Political Change in 43 Societies*. Princeton: Princeton University Press, 1997.

Kydd, Andrew H. *Trust and Mistrust in International Relations*. Princeton: Princeton University Press, 2007.

Levi, Margaret, and Laura Stoker. "Political Trust and Trustworthiness." *Annual Review of Political Science* 3, no. 1 (2000): 475–507.

Li, Lianjiang. "Decoding Political Trust in China: A Machine Learning Analysis." *The China Quarterly* 249 (2022): 1–20.

Li, Lianjiang. "Distrust in Government and Preference for Regime Change in China." *Political Studies* 69, no. 2 (2021): 326–43.

Li, Lianjiang. "Reassessing Trust in the Central Government: Evidence from Five National Surveys." *The China Quarterly* 225 (2016): 100–21.

Lu, Jie, and Bruce Dickson. "Revisiting the Eastonian Framework on Political Support: Assessing Different Measures of Regime Support in Mainland China." *Comparative Politics* 52, no. 4 (2020): 671–701.

Mortenson, Steven T. "Interpersonal Trust and Social Skill in Seeking Social Support among Chinese and Americans." *Communication Research* 36, no. 1 (2009): 32–53.

Munro, Neil. "Does Refusal Bias Influence the Measurement of Chinese Political Trust?" *Journal of Contemporary China* 27, no. 111 (2018): 457–71.

Ostrom, Elinor. *Governing the Commons: The Evolution of Institutions for Collective Action*. Cambridge: Cambridge University Press, 1990.

Putnam, Robert D. "The Prosperous Community: Social Capital and Public Life." *American Prospects* 4, no. 13 (1993): 35–42.

Ratigan, Kerry, and Leah Rabin. "Re-Evaluating Political Trust: The Impact of Survey Nonresponse in Rural China." *The China Quarterly* 243 (2020): 823–38.

Rousseau, Denise M., Sim B. Sitkin, Ronald S. Burt, and Colin Camerer. "Not So Different after All: A Cross-Discipline View of Trust." *Academy of Management Review* 23, no. 3 (1998): 393–404.

Steinhardt, H. Christoph. "How Is High Trust in China Possible? Comparing the Origins of Generalized Trust in Three Chinese Societies." *Political Studies* 60, no. 2 (2012): 434–54.

The Tenth National Congress of the Communist Party of China. "Constitution of the Communist Party of China." *Marxists*, August 28, 1973, https://www.marxists.org/subject/china/documents/cpc/CONSTITUTION_CPC.htm.

Turiel, Jesse, Edward Cunningham, and Anthony Saich. "To Serve the People: Income, Region and Citizen Attitudes toward Governance in China (2003–2016)." *The China Quarterly* 240 (2019): 906–35.

Uslaner, Eric M. "Measuring Generalized Trust: In Defense of the 'Standard' Question." In *Handbook of Research Methods on Trust*, edited by Fergus Lyon, Guido Mšllering, and Mark N. K. Saunders, 72–82. Cheltenham: Edward Elgar Publishing, 2012.

Uslaner, Eric M. *The Moral Foundations of Trust.* Cambridge: Cambridge University Press, 2002.

Vyas, Lina, and Alfred M. Wu. "Anti-Corruption Policy: China's Tiger Hunt and India's Demonetization." *International Journal of Public Administration* 43, no. 11 (2020): 1000–11.

Wang, Yuhua, and Bruce J. Dickson. "How Corruption Investigations Undermine Regime Support: Evidence from China." *Political Science Research and Methods* 10, no. 1 (2022): 33–48.

Williamson, Oliver E. "Calculativeness, Trust, and Economic Organization." *Journal of Law and Economics* 36, no. 1 (1993): 453–86.

World Bank and Development Research Center of the State Council, the People's Republic of China. *Urban China: Toward Efficient, Inclusive, and Sustainable Urbanization.* Washington: World Bank, 2014.

Xiao, Hanyu, Ting Gong, Chilik Yu, Wen-Jong Juang, and Baishun Yuan. "Citizens' Confidence in Government Control of Corruption: An Empirical Analysis." *Social Indicators Research* 152, no. 3 (2020): 877–97.

Yamagishi, Toshio. *Trust: The Evolutionary Game of Mind and Society.* Singapore: Springer, 2011.

Yang, Qing, and Wenfang Tang. "Exploring the Sources of Institutional Trust in China: Culture, Mobilization, Or Performance?" *Asian Politics & Policy* 2, no. 3 (2010): 415–36.

Ye, Lin, Alfred M. Wu, and Xinhui Yang. "University Enrolment Expansion and Returns to Higher Education: Evidence from China." In *Massification of Higher Education in Asia*, edited by Alfred M. Wu and John N. Hawkins, 113–28. Singapore: Springer, 2018.

Ye, Lin, and Alfred M. Wu. "Urbanization, Land Development, and Land Financing: Evidence from Chinese Cities." *Journal of Urban Affairs* 36, no. S1 (2014): 354–68.

Zhong, Pei, and Jing Vivian Zhan. "Authoritarian Critical Citizens and Declining Political Trust in China." *China Review* 21, no. 2 (2021): 117–52.

Zhong, Yang. *Political Culture and Participation in Urban China.* Singapore: Springer, 2018.

Zhu, Jiangnan, Huang Huang, and Dong Zhang. " 'Big Tigers, Big Data': Learning Social Reactions to China's Anticorruption Campaign through Online Feedback." *Public Administration Review* 79, no. 4 (2019): 500–13.

SEVEN | Attitudes toward Religion, Science, and Technology in China

YANG ZHONG

Introduction

Various forms of religious beliefs and practices have existed since the hunting and gathering era. Like many modern Chinese terms and concepts, *zongjiao*, the Chinese term for religion, was imported from Japan.[1] The modern concept of science as a systematic way of pursuing knowledge based on testable empirical explanations emerged during the Renaissance in the fifteenth and sixteenth centuries, although activities of a scientific nature were going on for a long time before then. Like *zongjiao*, *kexue*, the Chinese term for science, also came from Japan.

In general, there are two main competing perspectives about the relationship between religion and science.[2] The conflict thesis argues that science and religion have completely different logics and worldviews, and they are fundamentally at odds with each other. Science seeks to understand and explain the world based on verifiable facts, while religion, based on faith, believes that supernatural, transcendent, and immaterial forces shape the world.[3] One of the most prominent examples of the conflict between science and religion is the seventeenth-century Roman Catholic Church's persecution of Galileo for promoting Copernicus's theory that the Earth revolves around the Sun. Another obvious and long-standing debate between many scientists and ardent Christian religious believers is about the origin of human life, namely the clash between the theory of evolution and Christian creationist theory. The former argues that life

evolves through natural selection, while the latter believes that God created all forms of life on Earth.

An opposing view about the relationship between science and religion, advocated by some scientists and religious leaders, holds that science and religion are not necessarily in conflict and can coexist.[4] Science
seeks to find the truth through empirical examinations of testable
propositions. Religion, on the other hand, is faith-based and involves
supernatural forces and personal spiritual experience. Since science and
religion operate in completely different realms, they can coexist peace-
fully. One indication that science and religion are compatible with each
other is the fact that some (although still a minority of) scientists say they
believe in God.[5] And, according to Pew Research Center survey findings,
38 percent of the American adult population says religion and science
are compatible, and 68 percent of them do not see conflict between science and their own religious beliefs.[6]

From the very beginning, the World Values Survey (WVS) has contained questions about people's attitudes toward religion and science.
The questions seem designed to test classical modernization theories
that pit religion and science against each other. According to modernization theorists, the modernization process contributes to secularization.[7] Belief in science is one of the values held by modern people.[8]
Max Weber believes secularization or disenchantment to be a necessary
part of the modernization process. According to Weber, Protestantism
was, in his time, the only religion whose ethic saw material gains as a
sign of salvation, which promoted early capitalist development.[9] Weber
points out that the version of Confucianism then prevailing in China—
before the transformations brought by the Nationalist and Communist
revolutions—was not conducive to modern capitalist development. This
thesis obviously does not apply to the contemporary world, and has
been disputed for some time. Robert Bellah, for example, argues that
the Tokugawa religion, combining Japanese Confucianism and Japanese
Buddhism, played a major role in Japanese industrialization and modernization after the Meiji Restoration.[10] Michio Morishima contends, in
particular, that Confucian traits of loyalty, nationalism, and social collectivism contributed to Japanese economic success.[11]

Unlike some other studies on religions in contemporary China, this
chapter, using WVS data on China, primarily traces and explains changes
and continuities of the Chinese people's religious values and attitudes
toward science and technology in the past three decades. The other
difference between this and some other studies on religious beliefs in

China is that this study presents comparative findings between China and some other countries. This chapter starts with a brief discussion of the relationship between religion and science, followed by a review of the treatment of religion and science in the context of modernization theories. A brief history of the developments in religion and science in contemporary China follows. The next section presents the main findings concerning Chinese people's views on religion and science, based on Waves 2 through 7 of the WVS conducted in China. The views of Chinese people toward religion and science will also be compared with WVS findings in other regions and countries so that we can understand Chinese attitudes on these subjects from a comparative perspective. The final section of the chapter summarizes key findings and conclusions.

Religion and Science in Contemporary China

The Chinese government officially accords five religions in China: Buddhism, Daoism (or Taoism), Islam, Catholicism, and Protestant Christianity. Other than the five officially recognized religions, Chinese people practice numerous folk religions, such as ancestral worshipping; worshipping real historical or fictional figures, such as Guanyu, Jigong, and Mazu; and worshipping indigenous gods such as Huangdi, Wendi, Wudi, Longwang, Tudishen, Caishen, and Yanwang. For the majority of Chinese history, the Chinese people were able to practice their religious beliefs freely. Christianity was probably the one religion that experienced the most systematic and continuous discrimination prior to 1949. Due to its foreign origin and potential clash with Chinese traditions, the introduction of Christianity into China faced many obstacles from both Chinese authorities and the general population. Historically, Chinese emperors worried that they would lose control over the Chinese Christian population to foreign authorities, especially the Vatican.[12] At the grassroots level, many Chinese felt that Christianity posed a threat to traditional Chinese cultural values and Chinese cultural identity, since the Christianization of China meant replacing Chinese religions with a Western one.[13] For example, the Taiping Rebellion with its Christian overcoat posed a serious threat to the Qing government. Bringing Christianity to China was further complicated by the fact that it was accompanied by an influx of Western colonial forces. Hatred toward Christianity and foreign influence culminated in the Boxer Rebellion during the late nineteenth and early twentieth centuries, which killed thousands of Chinese Christians as well as international missionaries.

Although the new Chinese Communist government did not explicitly ban any religion in China after 1949, it adopted an atheist position toward religious beliefs and began to heavily regulate religious activity. The new government set up semi-official religious associations for each officially recognized religion. For example, Chinese Protestant Christians were forced to join the pro-government and religiously liberal Three-Self Patriotic Movement (self-governing, self-supporting, and self-propagation, or TSPM), and Chinese Catholics had to sever their ties with the Vatican and join the Chinese Catholic Patriotic Association churches.[14] Chinese Christians who refused to join the officially sanctioned churches had to form their own "house churches," which operated illegally according to official regulations. During the Cultural Revolution from 1966 to 1976, all religious activities were disbanded, and the semi-official religious associations were suspended. Clergy of all religious persuasions experienced persecution; religious sites were destroyed, and scriptures were burned. However, even the Cultural Revolution failed to stop all private religious activities and beliefs. It was discovered, for example, that many Chinese Christians had secret religious meetings at private homes even at the height of the Cultural Revolution.[15]

The end of the Cultural Revolution led to the gradual revival of religions in China in the late 1970s and the rapid increase of the Chinese religious population from the 1980s onward. In fact, religions have come back to China with a vengeance over the past forty years. A survey by the Pew Global Attitudes Project found that close to 60 percent of the Chinese public considers religion to be very or somewhat important in their lives.[16] According to the Pew Research Center, half of the world's Buddhist believers (about 245 million, or 18 percent of the Chinese population) are found in China.[17] Another 285 million Chinese (or 21 percent of the Chinese population) are Daoist or followers of other Chinese folk religions.[18] Christianity is another fast-growing religion in China. An extensive survey study conducted by the official Institute of World Religions (IWR) of the Chinese Academy of Social Sciences put the Chinese Protestant Christian population at 23 million, or 1.8 percent of the total population in China (in addition to 5.7 million Catholics).[19] Another estimate claims that Chinese Christian population is as high as 130 million.[20] On top of these religious groups, Chinese Muslims are estimated to be around 23 million, projected to increase to 30 million by 2030.[21] Even though religions in China have enjoyed a certain degree of freedom and the religious population has experienced a rapid increase, the Chinese government has never completely relinquished its control over religions and religious activities during the reform era.

In contrast to religion, which the Chinese government has never encouraged since 1949, science has been actively promoted in China over the past few decades. China prides itself on being the inventor of gunpowder, papermaking, printing, and the magnetic compass. Indeed, according to Joseph Needham, who devoted his life to studying the development of science and technology in China, historical China was rich in technological inventions (though Needham has been criticized for exaggerating Chinese scientific and technological achievements).[22] Needham is also well-known for raising the "Needham puzzle": *Why did modern science not happen in China?* Explanations for this question vary from the Chinese script, the geographic features of China, and the Chinese economic system to China's sociopolitical institutions. Regardless of the explanations, it is a fact that China lagged behind the West in science and technological discoveries and inventions after the sixteenth and seventeenth centuries. It was the Christian missionaries from the West who introduced modern science and technology to China in the sixteenth century. Lack of modern technologies and industries are often blamed for China's loss in wars with foreign powers, such as the two Opium Wars, the invasion of the Eight-Nation Alliance, and the First Sino-Japanese War in contemporary China.

Facing humiliating defeats in wars with foreign powers, the Qing government began to promote modern science and technology toward the end of the nineteenth century by introducing a science curriculum in Chinese schools and importing Western technologies. Even though the Qing government was trying to learn from the Japanese experiences after the Meiji Restoration in hope of saving the dynasty, its efforts proved to be too little and too late. Science (nicknamed "Mr. Science") and democracy (nicknamed "Mr. Democracy") became twin goals during the May Fourth Movement in 1919. Belief in "saving China through science" (*kexue jiuguo*) grew even stronger during the Republican era, before the Chinese Communist Party (CCP) came to power in 1949.[23]

Efforts to promote science and technology continued in the "new China." In the 1950s, scientific progress and technological advancements were primarily made in cooperation with the Soviet Union, which sent ten thousand experts in diverse fields to China to help China's scientific and economic development.[24] In the following two decades, China emphasized self-reliance in its scientific endeavors due to its international isolation and Mao's revolutionary ideology. It is worth noting that China did achieve some scientific breakthroughs in Mao's era. China became a nuclear power in the 1960s and successfully launched its first satellite in the 1970s. Even so, there is no question that China was lagging far behind the West in science and technology by the end of the Cultural Revolution and the beginning of the reform era in the late 1970s. The most destructive blow to China's scientific and technological advances prior to the reform era came in large part from the closing of all China's universities and the Chinese Academy of Sciences, as well as the persecution of intellectuals during the Cultural Revolution.

In the late 1970s, when the reform era started, science and technology became paramount concerns. Among the Four Modernizations (i.e., modernization of agriculture, industry, science and technology, and national defense), modern science and technology was viewed as the key to China's economic development. In his speech at the opening ceremony of China's national conference on science in 1978, Deng Xiaoping stated:

> The key to the four modernizations is the modernization of science and technology. Without modern science and technology, it is impossible to build modern agriculture, modern industry or modern national defense. Without the rapid development of science and technology, there can be no rapid development of the economy.[25]

Universities and research institutions reopened, and scientists were treated with honor and esteem. Science courses became the most emphasized subjects in Chinese middle schools and high schools, and mathematics, physics, and chemistry became the most popular majors among Chinese college students. After devoting significant amounts of human and non-human resources to developing science and technology in the past forty years, China has become one of the world's technological powerhouses. China is second only to the United States in terms of research and development (R&D) and accounts for 20 percent of the total R&D expenditure in the world.[26] China has also surpassed the United States in the number of published academic research papers.[27] China is currently a world technological leader in areas such as artificial intelligence, 5G, biotechnology, and quantum computing.[28] China's success in scientific and technological advances during the reform era can be contributed to, among other things, concerted and organized government involvement in science and technology innovation, significant government spending on scientific activities, and international scientific cooperation.

In fact, the Chinese government's rhetoric promoting science has risen to a level of science supremacy in the past few decades. The word "science" or "scientific" has been used to rationalize and justify any action or government policy, such as scientific management, scientific running of schools, scientific decision-making, scientific training, and scientific planning. This trend of pan-scientification accelerated especially after Hu Jintao introduced the concept of "scientific development" in 2003. The idea that science is supreme and is the answer to every problem in society ignores the possibility that there are other realms of reasoning and thinking. Mathematics, philosophy, and theology are other forms of rational thought, and science alone cannot decide ultimate values and moral issues. Moreover, scientific advancement has also brought negative consequences to humankind and has caused significant damage to the environment, although it has also improved our lives in many positive ways.

Attitudes toward Religion and Religious Values among Chinese People

From the start, the WVS has included attitudes toward religion and religious values as an important part of its investigation of changing values around the world, though the number of questions on religion varies from one wave to the next, and not all religious questions were asked in all six waves of the WVS conducted in China. We will start with a spiritual (not exactly religious) question in the survey, asking how often people think about the meaning and purpose of life. This question was asked from the second wave through the sixth wave of surveys conducted in China. As Table 7.1 shows, 31 percent of the Chinese people said they thought about the meaning and purpose of life "often" in 1990. However, the number dropped to 10 percent in 2012, when the WVS asked this question for the last time. It seems that a diminishing share of the Chinese have been thinking about the meaning and purpose of life during the last two decades.

Religiosity is often said to consist of believing, belonging, and behaving. Believing refers to a person believing in a particular religion and holding religious values; belonging refers to being part of a particular

Table 7.1. How Often Do You Think about the Meaning and Purpose of Life? (Percentage of Chinese Public Saying "Often" from 1990 to 2012)

	% "Often"
1990	31
1995	25
2001	32
2007	27
2012	10

religious sect; and behaving involves how a religious person practices their religion, such as participating in religious activities. Figure 7.1 reports the trend of people in China claiming to be religious believers. In the second WVS, conducted in 1990 (the first time the WVS was conducted in China), only 5 percent of the respondents said they were religious, while 49 percent reported that they were not religious and 42 percent claimed to be atheists. This question was not asked in the third wave of the WVS in China, but it was included in the fourth wave, completed in 2001. That year, the percentage of people who said they held religious beliefs jumped to 13.7 percent, and the proportion claiming to be atheists dropped to 25 percent. In the next survey, completed in 2007, close to a quarter of Chinese people reported that they were religious, while the number of atheists dropped to 16 percent. The next two waves of WVS conducted in China, in 2012 and 2018, found that 12.5 percent and 16 percent respectively said they were religious, and about a third of them claimed to be atheist. The overall trend over the past three decades is that more Chinese people claim to hold religious beliefs, and fewer say they are atheists. This runs contrary to the worldwide trend of decreasing religiosity in the past decade.[29]

One of the explanations offered by Ronald Inglehart to explain the worldwide decline of religion is people's increased sense of security.[30] As the living standard rises in China, so too has Chinese people's sense of security. Then why has religion become more popular in China since

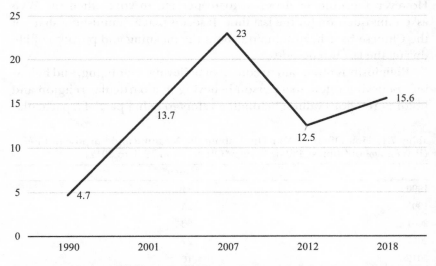

Figure 7.1. Percentage of Chinese Public Saying They Are a Religious Person, 1990–2018

the 1990s? The rising number of religious believers in China might be viewed as a natural rebound after China loosened up severe constraints put on religions during the Cultural Revolution. Another possible reason might be the need for spirituality during the rapid social and economic transformation of the country in the reform era.

Next, let us examine the belonging aspect of religiosity: To which religious denominations do the Chinese people belong? Table 7.2 shows the distribution of religious sects in China from 1990 to 2018. Chinese Buddhists have experienced the most significant increase during this period, going from 1 percent in 1990 to 9.2 percent in 2013. Protestant Christians also saw their numbers steadily increasing. In the meantime, the numbers of self-reported Muslims (except for the 2007 survey) and Catholic believers stayed more or less the same during this period. In other words, Buddhists and Protestant Christians made the largest gains in China, while Islamic and Catholic populations experienced limited growth. One possible reason for this is the fact that the Chinese authorities placed stronger restrictions and regulations on the Muslim and Catholic believers due to their sensitive status in China. Taoism was not given as an option in the surveys except for 2007. It seems clear that more Chinese people have become religious over the past three decades. As Table 7.2 shows, the proportion with no religious affiliation was 96.8 percent in 1990, and that number fell to 80.6 percent in 2013 and 86 in 2018. The combined number of religious believers has increased from 3 percent to 13 percent since 1990.

The WVS has consistently asked three questions to tap people's religiosity. One question asks how often respondents attend religious services

Table 7.2. Percentages Identifying with Given Religious Denominations, 1990–2018 (%)

	No religious denomination	Buddhist	Muslim	Protestant	Roman Catholic	Taoist	Other Religions
China (1990)	96.8	1	1.3	0.1	0.4		0.4
China (2001)	93	2.1	0.4	2.5	0.8		0.2
China (2007)	88.2	2.9	4.4	3.5		0.4	0.1
China (2013)	80.6	9.2	0.5	2.5	0.8		0.7
China (2018)	86	8.8	1.4	2.1	0.2		0.2

Table 7.3. How Often Do You Attend Religious Services?
(Percentage of Chinese Public Saying "Never" from 1990 to 2018)

	Never
1990	93
2001	89
2007	86
2012	83
2018	79

other than weddings and funerals. Given that the number of self-identified religious people in China is fairly low, we cannot expect many people to participate in religious activities. Indeed, as Table 7.3 shows, only a small percentage of Chinese people attend religious activities on a regular basis. But it is worth noting that the percentage of people who claimed that they never attend religious activities or refused to give an answer dropped from 93 percent in 1990 to 79 percent in 2018. Two other questions asked in the surveys concern how important a general god figure is, and how important religion is in the respondent's life. As Figure 7.2 indicates, religiosity among the Chinese people trends upward from 1990 to 2018.

Next, let us examine the Chinese people's religious tolerance. Religious conflicts are abundant in the world, but China has not experienced such conflicts. One major reason is that only a small percentage of the Chinese population is religious. Another reason is that religions are strictly under the control and watchful eyes of the Chinese government.

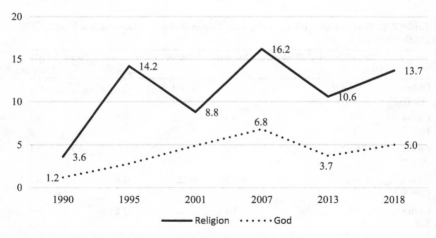

Figure 7.2. Trends in Religiosity in China, 1990–2018

Table 7.4. Logistic Regression on Belief in God

	B	S.E.	Wald	df	Sig	Exp (B)
Gender	-.486	.107	20.659	1	.000	.615
Age	-.003	.004	.316	1	.574	.997
Marital status	-.073	.140	.272	1	.602	.930
Education	-.205	.062	11.057	1	.001	1.228
Social class	.143	.095	2.261	1	.133	1.153
Employment	-.288	.152	3.561	1	.059	.750
Constant	2.220	.611	13.213	1	.000	9.204

Still another reason probably has something to do with higher levels of religious tolerance among the Chinese people. The WVS conducted in China in 2012 and 2018 both asked whether the only acceptable religion is the respondent's own religion. Only about 5 percent in the 2012 survey and 13 percent in the 2018 survey believed that their own religion is the only acceptable religion; most respondents rejected such a notion.

Who among the Chinese people tends to be most religious? The 2018 survey contains a question asking respondents whether they believe in a god figure (which may be a Buddhist god, a Christian God, Allah, or a superbeing in Chinese culture). Less than 18 percent of the Chinese public claims they believe in God, while the rest do not. Let us analyze this in terms of gender, age, educational level, marital status, social class, and employment in the public (government) sector as predictors of religious belief. A logit regression model (see Table 7.4) presents the predictors of belief in God. It turns out that women, people with less education, and people who work in the private sector tend to believe in God or a god figure. Marital status, age, and social class, on the other hand, do not seem to be strong predictors.

Religious Values in Comparative Perspective

How do the religious values of the people of mainland China compare with those of other Chinese societies, such as Hong Kong and Taiwan? People in all three places share a Chinese cultural tradition and history, but both Hong Kong and Taiwan allow religious freedom. Another difference is that both Hong Kong and Taiwan did not experience the Cultural Revolution, the anti-Confucian campaign, and other movements designed to eradicate traditional Chinese culture as mainland China did. In this sense, both Hong Kong and Taiwan have maintained Chinese traditions more than mainland China has. The main purpose of comparing public attitudes in these three places is to explore the possible impact of political systems on people's religious values. In addition to comparing mainland Chinese with the Hong Kongers and Taiwanese regarding their religious values, we will also compare them with popular religious values in the United States as an external reference. The United States has a very different culture and historical tradition from mainland China, Hong Kong, and Taiwan. If religious values held by Hong Kongers and Taiwanese are closer to those held by Americans, it would seem possible that the Chinese political system has shaped religious values in a different direction from that of the other three places. Most of these comparisons use WVS Wave 7 data.

We first compare responses to the question about how often people think about meaning and purpose of life. Table 7.5 contains some telling statistical numbers. About one-third of the people in both Hong Kong and Taiwan claim to think about the meaning and purpose of life, and less than 20 percent and 25 percent respectively say they never do so. Interestingly enough, the WVS conducted in the United States exhibits similar findings. By contrast, less than 10 percent of mainland Chinese say they think about meaning and purpose of life, while over 40 percent never do so. The findings suggest that people in Hong Kong and Taiwan have stronger spiritual interests than the people of mainland China.

This probably reflects the fact that more people in Hong Kong, Taiwan, and the United States profess to be broadly religious, that is, believe in God or a god figure, life after death, and heaven and hell (see Table 7.6). Large percentages of the people in Hong Kong (52 percent), Taiwan (82 percent), and the United States (76 percent) believe in God or a god figure, compared to only 17 percent of mainland Chinese. Moreover, the percentages of the people in Hong Kong, Taiwan, and the United States believing in life after death, heaven, and hell range between 40 and 70 percent, while only around 10 percent of people in mainland China have such beliefs. When asked about the importance

Table 7.5. How Often Do You Think about the Meaning and Purpose of Life? (Comparative Perspective) (Percent Saying "Often")

	Often
China (2018)	10
Hong Kong (2018)	30
Taiwan (2019)	31
U.S. (2017)	36

Table 7.6. Broad Religious Belief in Comparative Perspective (%)

	Believe in God	Believe in Life after Death	Believe in Heaven	Believe in Hell
China (2018)	17	12	12	14
Hong Kong (2018)	52	40	48	49
Taiwan (2019)	82	57	63	68
U.S. (2017)	76	65	66	70

Table 7.7. How Important Is God in Your Life? (Comparative Perspective) (Mean scores on 10-point scale)

China (2018)	2.77
Hong Kong (2018)	4.84
Taiwan (2019)	6.06
U.S. (2017)	4.60

of God or a god figure in their lives on a scale of 1 (least important) to 10 (most important), the mean score for Chinese respondents is only 2.77, while mean scores for Hong Kongers, Taiwanese, and Americans are 4.84, 6.06, and 4.60 respectively (see Table 7.7). In addition, much larger percentages of people in both Hong Kong and Taiwan claim that religion is important in their lives (see Figure 7.3). The people of mainland China seem to be much less religious than the people of either Hong Kong or Taiwan, which probably reflects the fact that the mainland

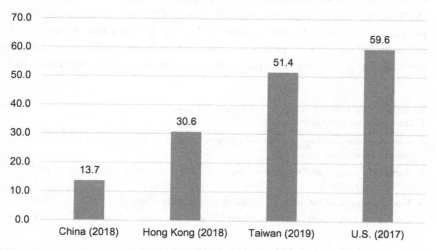

Figure 7.3. Importance of Religion in Life in Comparative Perspective

Chinese have lived in a largely atheist environment with religious practices under strict governmental regulation and control.

Attitudes toward Science and Technology

Science-related questions have appeared in all waves of the WVS except for the 1990 wave. One question that has been asked in both 2012 and 2018 is whether respondents agree with the statement that science and technology are making their lives healthier, easier, and more comfortable. On a scale of 1 (completely disagree) to 10 (completely agree), an overwhelming majority of respondents tend to agree with this statement (see Table 7.8). Similarly, Table 7.8 also indicates that the majority of the Chinese people tend to agree that science and technology provide more opportunities for the next generation. As a result, it is not surprising that majority of the Chinese people disagree with the statement that it is *not* important for them to know about science in their daily lives (see Table 7.8). The positive views on science and technology held by the majority of the Chinese people may reflect the intense propaganda efforts of the Chinese government to emphasize the supremacy of science and technology for modernizing China in the reform era. Since religion sometimes competes with a scientific belief system, it might also reflect the fact that most of the Chinese people are not religious.

As mentioned earlier, scientific advances (such as nuclear weapons) can sometimes have negative effects on humanity. Moreover, science cannot offer clear solutions to moral dilemmas. One question asked in WVS Wave 7 (2018) is about the bad effects of science in breaking down people's ideas of right and wrong, reflecting the fact that science and religion are sometimes pitted against each other. Chinese respondents are split in answering this question, as is evident from examining the

Table 7.8. Attitudes toward Science and Technology
(Mean scores on 10-point scale)

1. Science and technology are making our lives healthier, easier, and more comfortable.	8.63
2. Because of science and technology, there will be more opportunities for the next generation.	8.52
3. It is not important for me to know about science in my daily life.	2.63
4. One of the bad effects of science is that it breaks down people's ideas of right and wrong.	4.88
5. We depend too much on science and not enough on faith.	5.47

Table 7.9. Whenever Science and Religion Conflict, Religion Is Always Right (%)

	Disagree	Agree	No Answer/Don't Know
2012	72	5	23
2018	94	5	1

Note: Disagree includes both strongly disagree and disagree; Agree includes both agree and strongly agree.

Table 7.10. Crosstabulation between Belief in Religion and Attitude toward Science and Religion Conflict

	Religious		Not Religious	
	Agree*	Disagree**	Agree*	Disagree**
Whenever science and religion conflict, religion is always right.	85	388	66	2,444

*The category of "Agree" includes "strongly agree."
**The category of "Disagree" includes "strongly disagree."

mean scores in the responses to this question shown in Table 7.8. Another question concerns the relationship between science and faith. Findings in Table 7.8 indicate that significant numbers of Chinese people agree with the statement that we depend too much on science and not enough on faith. These findings reveal that a substantial portion of the Chinese people have ambivalent feelings about the impact and utility of science and technology. However, when science and religion are pitted against each other, an overwhelming majority of Chinese choose science over religion (see Table 7.9). Table 7.10 shows that even the majority of Chinese people who claim to be religious disagree with the statement that religion prevails over science when the two conflict with each other, even though a larger proportion among the self-identified religious people agree with the statement. A correlation analysis also confirms that the tendency of being religious to be associated with favoring religion over science when the two are in conflict is at a statistically significant level.

Attitudes toward Science and Technology in Comparative Perspective

How do mainland Chinese attitudes toward science and technology compare with those of the people of Hong Kong and Taiwan, who live in different political and social systems in which religion is much more important? Again we will also include the United States as a reference. When asked whether science and technology are making people's lives

Table 7.11. Attitudes toward Science and Technology in Comparative
Perspective (Part 1)
(Mean scores on 10-point scale)

	Science and technology are making our lives healthier, easier, and more comfortable.	Because of science and technology, there will be more opportunities for our next generation.
China (2018)	8.63	8.52
Hong Kong (2018)	7.35	7.06
Taiwan (2019)	7.32	6.92
U.S. (2017)	7.32	7.10

healthier, easier, and more comfortable on a scale of 1 (completely disagree) to 10 (completely agree), clearly more people in Hong Kong,
Taiwan, and the United States express doubt about this statement than
do the people of mainland China (see Table 7.11). In addition, more
people in Hong Kong, Taiwan, and the United States doubt that science
and technology will bring more opportunities to the next generation
(see Table 7.11). When people of these countries and regions are asked
whether it is *not* important for them to learn about science in their daily
life, the mean scores reported in Table 7.12 indicate that the people of
mainland China show more willingness to learn about science than their
counterparts in Hong Kong, Taiwan, and the United States.

When it comes to questions about whether we depend too much on
science and not enough on faith, and whether one of the bad effects
of science is that it breaks down people's idea of right and wrong, comparative findings from Table 7.12 show that there is surprisingly little difference between the people of mainland China, Hong Kong, Taiwan,
and the United States. A substantial number of people in Hong Kong,

Table 7.12. Attitudes toward Science and Technology in Comparative
Perspective (Part 2)
(Mean scores on 10-point scale)

	It is not important for me to know about science in my daily life.	We depend too much on science and not enough on faith.	One of the bad effects of science is that it breaks down people's ideas of right and wrong.
China (2018)	2.63	5.47	4.88
Hong Kong (2018)	4.42	5.91	5.37
Taiwan (2019)	4.00	5.48	5.42
U.S. (2017)	3.97	4.81	4.33

Table 7.13. Whenever Science and Religion Conflict, Religion Is Always Right (Comparative Perspective) (Percentage Disagreeing or Strongly Disagreeing)

China (2018)	94
Hong Kong (2018)	76
Taiwan (2019)	84
U.S. (2017)	64

Taiwan, and the United States have ambivalent feelings about the negative impact of science and technology—and so do many mainland Chinese respondents. But concerning the conflict between science and religion, substantially more people in Hong Kong (24 percent), Taiwan (16 percent), and the United States (36 percent) than in China (6 percent) believe that religion is always right when science and religion clash with each other (see Table 7.13).

Comparative survey data from mainland China, Hong Kong, Taiwan, and the United States show that mainland Chinese hold more positive views of science and technology and are more willing to learn about science than people of the other three societies. These findings may reflect two factors. First, the Chinese government in the reform era has intensively emphasized the role that science and technology play in national economic development and, to some extent, has indoctrinated the mainland Chinese population with the idea of scientific supremacy. The second reason may reflect the fact that highly religious people tend to downplay or dismiss the importance of science and technology, and far more people in Hong Kong, Taiwan, and the United States are religious than is true in mainland China.

Conclusion

This chapter examines mainland Chinese people's religious values and attitudes toward science and technology. The answers to questions about religion and science/technology are indispensable in gaining a full understanding of Chinese culture and values. Moreover, popular religious values and attitudes toward science/technology have significant political and social implications that bear on the possibility of China becoming a leading world model.

Findings from the WVS conducted in China from various years in the 1990s and 2000s indicate that by and large China is not a religious country and Chinese people lack strong religious beliefs. An overwhelming majority of Chinese people claim to be non-religious or atheist. However, the number of religious believers in mainland China has noticeably increased since 2000. The latest WVS, conducted in 2018, shows that 12.7 percent of the Chinese people hold religious beliefs, a substantial increase from 3.2 percent found in 1990. In the meantime, the number of people claiming to be atheists dropped from 42 percent in 1990 to 34 percent in 2018. A majority of Chinese religious believers are Buddhists. In comparison, people in the other two Chinese societies (Hong Kong and Taiwan) tend to be more religious overall. While only 17 percent of mainland Chinese believe in a god figure, 12 percent believe in life after death and heaven, and 14 percent believe in hell, roughly half of the people in both Hong Kong and Taiwan hold such beliefs. The mainland Chinese are much less religious than their compatriots in Taiwan and Hong Kong. Two major factors contribute to these divergent developments in mainland China versus Taiwan and Hong Kong. One is the atheist education that mainland Chinese citizens receive from childhood. Religious beliefs are equated with superstition in the mainland Chinese education system and official propaganda. Moreover, the official restrictions and limitations put on religious organizations in mainland China significantly constrain the growth of religion.

Our findings demonstrate that an overwhelming majority of the Chinese people are strong supporters of science and technology. They believe that science and technology make their lives healthier, easier, and more comfortable, and provide more opportunities for the next generation. In addition, most Chinese people feel it is important for them to know about science in their daily lives. However, a sizable portion of the Chinese population is worried that science may break down people's ideas of right and wrong and feel that we depend on too much on science and not enough on faith. But when facing a potential conflict between religion and science, the overwhelming majority of mainland Chinese choose science. In comparison, more culturally Chinese people in Hong Kong and Taiwan tend to be doubtful and critical of science and technology. More Taiwanese and Hong Kongers doubt that science and technology make their lives healthier, easier, and more comfortable, and provide more opportunities for the next generation. This difference is largely due to intensified Chinese official indoctrination and efforts in promoting science and technology as key to enabling China to become a stronger country and world power.

What are the implications of this chapter's findings for China becoming the leading power in the world? Chinese people's religiosity and their attitudes toward science and technology seem to positively contribute to making China an increasingly powerful country. The fact that China has a largely non-religious and secular culture means that China is unlikely to be divided by major religious conflicts such as those that currently polarize the United States. Some of the most destructive forces in the national development of many countries, such as India and Nigeria, are based on internal religious struggles. China has been fortunate in avoiding such religious conflicts due, partly, to the population's low level of religiosity. National cohesion is a necessary condition for any country's national development, particularly for one that aspires to become a world leader.

On the negative side, though, the lack of religiosity in Chinese society may lead to a lack of the moral ethos contributed to by religious teachings. Religions often regulate people's moral behavior more effectively than do official laws and regulations. Moreover, religious organizations are important parts of civil society and fulfill crucial societal functions. First of all, religious organizations can serve as training grounds for self-governing and civic leaders. For example, Chinese Christian house churches operate autonomously from the government. Church officials and parishioners alike gain civic experiences in running their church affairs cooperatively and independent of government intervention. A strong and healthy civil society can greatly enhance democratic rule in a democracy. Second, religious organizations provide charity assistance to the less fortunate in society. Buddhist organizations, such as Tzu Chi in Taiwan, are well-known for being extensive and effective charity providers for the poor not only in Taiwan but also in mainland China and other parts of the world. During the Sichuan Earthquake in 2008, a large number of Chinese Christians volunteered in the rescue missions and donated funds to the earthquake survivors. The Chinese government's restrictions and constraints on religions and religious organizations have prevented the healthy development of civil society and could harm the prospect of democracy in China.

The overwhelmingly positive attitudes toward science and technology among mainland Chinese people are no doubt beneficial factors in helping China become a world power. A major component in big power rivalry nowadays is technological competition. If China wishes to replace the United States as the number one power in the world, China must have a commanding lead in technological innovation and advancement. In fact, new technologies have no doubt played a significant role in rapidly developing the Chinese economy, and they have made China one of the world's foremost technological powerhouses in recent decades. Mainland Chinese people's popular view of science and technology and their willingness to learn about science provides the social support for technological advancement and innovation necessary for China's potential great power status in the world. It should also be noted that some have questioned how many ordinary Chinese people really grasp the true meaning and logic of science, which requires critical thinking. According to an editor of China's *Science Daily*, Chinese people still lack "science spirit" a century after the May Fourth Movement in 1919.[31] After all, China has failed to produce great scientists in modern times, and only one homegrown scientist (Tu Youyou) has won a Nobel prize in science. Nevertheless, in recent years the Chinese government has made progress in science and technology a top priority and has invested heavily in both. Given the popular support for this move, it seems likely that China will build itself into one of the world's leading scientific and technological powers.

Notes

1. Shenglai Zhou, "Tan Zongjiao Yici de Laiyuan ji Yanbian (On the Origin and Evolution of the Term of Zongjia)," *Shanghai Shifan Daxue Xuebao (Journal of Shanghai Normal University)* 40, no. 5 (2011): 116–17.

2. See David B. Wilson, "The Historiography of Science and Religion," in *The History of Science and Religion in the Western Tradition: An Encyclopaedia*, ed. Gary B. Ferngren (New York: Garland Publishing, Inc., 2000), 2–11.

3. John William Draper, *History of The Conflict between Religion and Science* (New York: Appleton and Company, 1916).

4. Wilson, "The Historiography of Science and Religion."

5. Edward J. Larson and Larry Witham, "Leading Scientists Still Reject God," *Nature* 394 (1998): 313; a survey of scientists who are members of the American Association for the Advancement of Science, conducted by the Pew Research Center in 2009, found that members of this group are much less religious than the general public: 33 percent of scientists said they believe in God, while 83 percent of the American public said they believe in God; David Masci, "Religion and Science in the United States," Pew Research Center, November 5, 2009, https://www. pewresearch.org/religion/2009/11/05/an-overview-of-religion-and-science-in-the-united-states/.

6. Pew Research Center, "Religion and Science," October 22, 2015, https:// www.pewresearch.org/science/2015/10/22/science-and-religion/.

7. See James Coleman, "Conclusion: The Political Systems of the Developing Areas," in *The Politics of the Developing Areas*, ed. Gabriel Almond and James Coleman (Princeton: Princeton University Press, 1960), 537.

8. Alex Inkeles and David Horton Smith, *Becoming Modern: Individual Change in Six Developing Countries* (Cambridge, MA: Harvard University Press, 1974).

9. Max Weber, *The Protestant Ethic and the Spirit of Capitalism* (Upper Saddle River: Prentice Hall, 1977).

10. Robert Bellah, *Tokugawa Religion* (Boston: Beacon, 1957).

11. Michio Morishima, *Why Has Japan Succeeded? Western Technology and the Japanese Ethos* (Cambridge: Cambridge University Press, 1982).

12. See Lars Peter Laamann, *Christian Heretics in Late Imperial China: Christian Inculturation and State Control, 1729–1850* (New York: Routledge, 2006).

13. See Wayne Flynt and Gerald W. Berkley, *Taking Christianity to China: Alabama Missionaries in the Middle Kingdom 1850–1950* (Tuscaloosa: The University of Alabama Press, 1997), 3.

14. For a more comprehensive description of development of Christianity in Communist China, see Philip L. Wickeri, *Reconstructing Christianity in China* (Maryknoll: Orbis Books, 2007).

15. Wickeri, *Reconstructing Christianity*, 2.

16. Brian J. Grim, "Religion in China on the Eve of the 2008 Beijing Olympics," Pew Research Center, May 1, 2008, https://www.pewforum.org/2008/05/01/religion-in-china-on-the-eve-of-the-2008-beijing-olympics/.

17. Pew Research Center, "Buddhists," December 18, 2012, https://www.pewforum.org/2012/12/18/global-religious-landscape-buddhist/.

18. Siqi Yang, "Life in Purgatory: Buddhism Is Growing in China, But Remains in Legal Limbo," *Time*, March 16, 2016, https://time.com/4260593/china-buddhism-religion-religious-freedom/.

19. See "An In-House Questionnaire Survey on Christianity in China," in *Annual Report on China's Religions*, ed. Jin Ze and Qiu Yonghui (Beijing: Social Sciences Academic Press, 2010), 191.

20. *Christian Today*, "Over 23 Million Christians in China, Official Survey Shows," August 12, 2010, https://www.christiantoday.com/article/over.23.million.christians.in.china.official.survey.shows/26488.htm.

21. Pew Research Center, "The Future of World Religions: Population Growth Projections, 2010–2050," April 2, 2015, https://www.pewforum.org/2015/04/02/religious-projections-2010-2050/.

22. Pierre-Yves Manguin, "Trading Ships of the South China Sea. Shipbuilding Techniques and Their Role in the History of the Development of Asian Trade Networks," *Journal of the Economic and Social History of the Orient* 36, no. 3 (1993): 253–80; Robert Finlay, "China, the West, and World History in Joseph Needham's Science and Civilization in China," *Journal of World History* 11 (2000): 265–303.

23. Shellen Wu, "How Science Saved China," *Nature* 574 (2019): 26.

24. Wu, "How Science Saved China," 27.

25. Deng Xiaoping, "Speech at the Opening Ceremony of the National Conference on Science, March 18, 1978" *China Daily*, accessed February 17, 2020, http://cpcchina.chinadaily.com.cn/2010-10/15/content_13918179.htm.

26. Reinhilde Veugelers, "China Is the World's New Science and Technology Powerhouse," *Bruegel*, August 30, 2017, https://www.bruegel.org/2017/08/china-is-the-worlds-new-science-and-technology-powerhouse/?utm_content=buffercd9dc&utm_medium=social&utm_source=twitter.com&utm_campaign=buffer+(bruegel).

27. Yanfei Li, "Understanding China's Technological Rise: The Three Factors Underlying China's Transformation into A Rising Technology Powerhouse," *The*

Diplomat, August 3, 2018, https://thediplomat.com/2018/08/understanding-chinas-technological-rise/.

28. Julian Baird Gewirtz, "China's Long March to Technological Supremacy: The Roots of Xi Jinping's Ambition to Catch Up and Surpass," *Foreign Affairs*, August 27, 2019, https://www.foreignaffairs.com/articles/china/2019-08-27/chinas-long-march-technological-supremacy.

29. Ronald Inglehart, "Giving Up on God: The Global Decline of Religion," *Foreign Affairs*, no. 5 (2020): 110–18.

30. Ronald Inglehart, *Culture Shift in Advanced Industrial Society* (Princeton: Princeton University Press, 1990).

31. https://zhuanlan.zhihu.com/p/42047416 (accessed June 7, 2020).

Bibliography

Bellah, Robert. *Tokugawa Religion*. Boston: Beacon, 1957.

Christian Today. "Over 23 Million Christians in China, Official Survey Shows." Agusut 12, 2010, https://www.christiantoday.com/article/over.23.million.christians.in.china.official.survey.shows/26488.htm.

Coleman, James. "Conclusion: The Political Systems of the Developing Areas." In *The Politics of the Developing* Areas, edited by Gabriel Almond and James Coleman, 537. Princeton: Princeton University Press, 1960.

Deng, Xiaoping. "Speech at the Opening Ceremony of the National Conference on Science." *China Daily*, 1978, http://cpcchina.chinadaily.com.cn/2010-10/15/content_13918179.htm.

Draper, John William. *History of The Conflict between Religion and Science*. New York: Appleton and Company, 1916.

Finlay, Robert. "China, the Wets, and World History in Joseph Needham's Science and Civilization in China." *Journal of World History*, no. 11 (Fall, 2000): 265–303.

Flynt, Wayne, and Gerald W. Berkley. *Taking Christianity to China: Alabama Missionaries in the Middle Kingdom 1850–1950*. Tuscaloosa: The University of Alabama Press, 1997.

Gewirtz, Julian Baird. "China's Long March to Technological Supremacy: The Roots of Xi Jinping's Ambition to 'Catch Up and Surpass.'" *Foreign Affairs*, August 27, 2019, https://www.foreignaffairs.com/articles/china/2019-08-27/chinas-long-march-technological-supremacy.

Inglehart, Ronald. *Culture Shift in Advanced Industrial Society*. Princeton: Princeton University Press, 1990.

Inglehart, Ronald. "Giving up on God: The Global Decline of Religion." *Foreign Affairs* 99, no. 5 (2000): 110–18.

Inkeles, Alex, and David Horton Smith. *Becoming Modern: Individual Change in Six Developing Countries*. Cambridge: Harvard University Press, 1974.

Laamann, Lars Peter. *Christian Heretics in Late Imperial China: Christian Inculturation and State Control, 1720–1850*. New York: Routledge, 2006.

Larson, Edward, and Larry Witham. "Leading Scientists Still Reject God." *Nature*, no. 394 (1998): 313.

Li, Yanfei. "Understanding China's Technological Rise: The Three Factors Underlying China's Transformation into A Rising Technology Powerhouse." *The Diplomat*, August 3, 2018. https://thediplomat.com/2018/08/understanding-chinas-technological-rise/.

Manguin, Pierre-Yves. "Trading Ships of the South China Sea. Shipbuilding Techniques and Their Role in the History of the Development of Asian Trade Networks." *Journal of the Economic and Social History of the Orient* 36, no. 3 (1993): 253–80.

Morishima, Michio. *Why Has Japan Succeeded? Western Technology and the Japanese Ethos*. Cambridge: Cambridge University Press, 1982.

Pew Research Center. "Buddhists." December 18, 2012, https://www.pewforum.org/2012/12/18/global-religious-landscape-buddhist/.

Pew Research Center. "Religion and Science." October 22, 2015, https://www.pewresearch.org/science/2015/10/22/science-and-religion/.

Pew Research Center. "Religion in China on the Eve of the 2008 Beijing Olympics." May 2, 2008, https://www.pewforum.org/2008/05/01/religion-in-china-on-the-eve-of-the-2008-beijing-olympics/.

Pew Research Center. "The Future of World Religions: Population Growth Projections, 2010–2050." April 2, 2015, https://www.pewforum.org/2015/04/02/religious-projections-2010-2050/.

Veugelers, Reinhilde. "China Is the World's New Science and Technology Powerhouse." *Bruegel*, August 30, 2017, https://www.bruegel.org/2017/08/china-is-the-worlds-new-science-and-technology-powerhouse/?utm_content=buffercd9dc&utm_medium=social&utm_source=twitter.com&utm_campaign=buffer+(bruegel).

Weber, Max. *The Protestant Ethic and the Spirit of Capitalism*. Upper Saddle River: Prentice Hall, 1977.

Wickeri, Philip L. *Reconstructing Christianity in China*. Maryknoll: Orbis Books, 2007.

Wilson, David B. "The Historiography of Science and Religion." In *The History of Science and Religion in the Western Tradition: An Encyclopaedia*, edited by Gary B. Ferngren, 2–11. New York: Garland Publishing, Inc., 2000.

Wu, Shellen. "How Science Saved China." *Nature* 574 (2019): 26.

Yang, Siqi. "Life in Purgatory: Buddhism Is Growing in China, But Remains in Legal Limbo." *Time*, March 16, 2016, https://time.com/4260593/china-buddhism-religion-religious-freedom/.

Ze, Jin, and Qiu Yonghui. *Annual Report on China's Religions*. Beijing: Social Sciences Academic Press, 2010.

Zhou, Shenglai. "*Tan Zongjiao Yici de Laiyuan ji Yanbian* (On the Origin and Evolution of the Term of Zongjia)." *Shanghai Shifan Daxue Xuebao (Journal of Shanghai Normal University)* 40, no. 5 (2011): 116–17.

EIGHT | Conclusions

YANG ZHONG AND RONALD F. INGLEHART

The authors of the preceding chapters have explored the political, economic, and social values of the Chinese people, how these values are changing, and how they differ from those of some other countries and regions. The evidence indicates that China is part of a group of Confucian-influenced societies that share relatively similar values. But these societies, in turn, fit into a broader global configuration in which economic development and rising economic and physical security tend to bring roughly predictable changes. These changes are not deterministic—they are also subject to the impact of major events, such as wars, and the influence of powerful leaders. But statistically, there is a fairly strong probability that rising existential security will bring such changes as declining religiosity and rising tolerance of diversity—and a move toward democratic institutions. In this respect, the Confucian-influenced societies have a wide range of diversity, with Hong Kong, Singapore, and Japan ranking among the world's most prosperous societies, and China as a whole still at a relatively early stage of development.

Does China have the soft power needed to support a position as the world's leading country? Already the world's leading manufacturing power, China's scientific, technological, and military capabilities are developing rapidly, but playing a leading role also requires soft power. Since the end of World War II, the United States has had superpower status not only because of its economic, technological, and military might, but also because of its democratic and liberal values—and the appeal of American pop culture.

On the whole, this book's findings suggest that the Chinese public does not hold drastically different social, political, and economic values from those of neighboring countries and even from countries in other parts of the world, provided that one controls for different levels of development. But the strongest claim that Chinese popular values—or even Asian popular values—are profoundly different from those prevailing in the West is the provocative argument put forward by Wenfang Tang in Chapter 2. We are convinced that it is useful to consider alternative viewpoints because quite often, one can learn from them. Tang argues that the Chinese public endorses democratic authoritarianism, an alternative that he considers to be at least as valid as the version of democracy measured by Freedom House, which he calls the Western Liberal Elite (WLE) version of democracy.

This book's editors have a different perspective, arguing that what evolved into liberal democracy did indeed originate in the West—as did the process of industrialization. But both democracy and industrialization have taken root in countries around the world. It would be hard to argue that industrialization is only appropriate to Western countries at a time when it is growing most rapidly in Asia and China has emerged as the world's largest industrial power. And it would be equally misleading to claim that liberal democracy only exists in Western countries. The most recent Freedom House ratings give Finland, Norway, Sweden, Canada, and the Netherlands the five highest ranks—but Japan, Chile, Cyprus, Slovenia, Taiwan, Costa Rica, and Mauritius all rank higher than the United States.[1] The Varieties of Democracy (V-Dem) project based at the University of Gothenburg has recruited over 3,000 country experts from almost every country in the world to evaluate key features of democracy in 170 countries.[2] Though using different methodologies, V-Dem's expert ratings are closely correlated with those from Freedom House. At the expert level, there is broad consensus about what constitutes democracy.

In fact, if put in comparative perspective, the Chinese support and understanding of democracy may not be that unique and different from that of other countries. Table 8.1 presents descriptive data comparing mainland Chinese support for democracy with three other Chinese societies, some of China's Asian neighbors, and selected countries from the Middle East, Latin America, Eastern Europe, Africa, and the Western world. The majority of Chinese respondents (57.2 percent) in WVS Wave 7 agree that it is a bad thing to have a leader who does not have to bother with parliament and elections. This percentage is higher than those found in Taiwan, South Korea, and most other developing countries in the table. Similarly, a majority of Chinese people, as do people in most of the other countries compared, oppose authoritarian military rule. More people in China (as high as 90.3 percent) than in the United States (83.5. percent) believe it is a good thing to have a democratic rule. The percentage of people favoring democracy is among the highest in the selected countries and regions in Table 8.1.

Table 8.1. Support for Democracy: Comparison of China with Selected Countries and Regions*
(% in Agreement with the Statements)

Countries/Regions	It is a bad thing to have a leader who does not have to bother with parliament and elections.	It is a bad thing to have the army rule.	It is a good thing to have a democratic rule.
China	57.2	57.1	90.3
Hong Kong	64.7	85.6	79.4
Macau	59.4	78.2	76.3
Taiwan	31.5	85.2	91.3
South Korea	33.6	82.7	70.4
Thailand	8.6	37.4	85.7
Indonesia	38.8	34.6	88.9
Kazakhstan	19.2	49.0	71.3
Egypt	50.6		82.3
Jordan	42.0	53.3	63.5
Lebanon	61.1	33.9	75.6
Tunisia	75.5	67.3	71.2
Brazil	30.3	46.4	75.4
Argentina	31.9	79.3	88.7
Bolivia	31.4	77.6	84.0
Mexico	27.6	52.9	74.2
Russia	37.1	69.2	66.9
Romania	16.4	54.3	81.6
Serbia	42.4	49.7	63.9
Ethiopia	53.7	63.5	90.2
Zimbabwe	59.5	71.6	90.3
Nigeria	39.4	59.0	87.9
Australia	71.3	89.4	89.4
Germany	70.3	96.7	96.0
Greece	88.8	92.8	97.4
The U.S.	66.0	80.8	83.5

*Data are from World Values Survey Wave 7.

As for the understanding of democracy or what democracy does, Chinese people are on par with people of most other countries (see Table 8.2). It seems that Chinese people share the feeling of "all good things go together" with people in most other countries when thinking about democracy. The majority of Chinese respondents (56.6 percent and 85.1 percent respectively) believe that in a democracy the rich

Table 8.2. What Democracy Does? Comparative Understanding of Democracy (% of 6–10 on a 10-point scale)

Countries/ Regions	People receive aid for unemployment	Taxing the rich and subsidizing the poor	Civil rights protect people's liberty against oppression	People choose their leaders in free election
China	85.5	56.6	87.6	78.2
Hong Kong	64.0	57.3	68.0	83.2
Macau	65.2	53.5	78.2	77.2
Taiwan	77.5	68.7	84.3	92.0
South Korea	77.1	81.5	85.5	89.7
Thailand	49.1	30.2	58.2	59.5
Indonesia	40.8	76.6	82.5	79.3
Kazakhstan	72.1	61.9	64.2	66.0
Egypt	52.2	74.2	60.5	82.5
Jordan	59.2	69.5	63.3	76.2
Lebanon	74.8	74.8	70.2	80.1
Tunisia	78.2	75.9	74.5	76.4
Brazil	66.7	26.3	62.1	73.1
Argentina	78.3	62.4	79.8	87.9
Bolivia	51.8	88.3	60.6	76.3
Mexico	46.9	43.3	49.6	62.6
Russia	77.1	75.6	79.0	80.7
Romania	72.7	56.5	79.0	80.7
Serbia	61.3	44.5	54.8	69.9
Ethiopia	71.1	63.2	79.1	88.4
Zimbabwe	75.3	59.6	80.2	85.7
Nigeria	66.4	57.5	75.8	80.0
Australia	57.6	57.8	72.1	85.9
Germany	88.2	76.3	85.3	95.1
Greece	88.6	65.5	81.7	96.0
The U.S.	47.9	48.9	75.6	81.9

*Data are from World Values Survey Wave 7.

should be taxed to subsidize the poor and the government should provide aid to the unemployed, as do people in most other compared countries in Table 8.2. Therefore, Chinese people are not alone in having an economic approach toward the concept of democracy. Like most people in other countries, the majority of Chinese people also believe that democracy is also about civil rights protecting people's liberty against oppression, and that people should be able to choose their leaders in free election. Comparative survey data show that Chinese people do not seem to have separate and different views on the worthiness of democracy and the essence of democracy.

However, Tang has a valid point in arguing against a one-size-fits-all theory of democracy. It has long been noted that democracy is most likely to emerge and flourish in prosperous countries.[3] Both industrialization and democracy have spread around the world because industrialization tends to bring prosperity, which is conducive to democracy, which tends to increase free choice—and both prosperity and democracy are linked with higher levels of human happiness, which is arguably the ultimate goal of government. But they do so over a long time scale, and the relationship between democracy and happiness varies at different stages of development.

Escaping from starvation-level scarcity brings a dramatic increase in subjective well-being. But there is a threshold at which economic growth no longer increases subjective well-being significantly. At this level, starvation is no longer a real concern for most people, and survival begins to be taken for granted. As increasingly postmaterialist cultures emerge, further economic gains no longer produce substantial increases in subjective well-being. If people and societies behaved rationally, one would expect this to bring a shift in survival strategies, and it does.

At low levels of economic development, even modest economic gains bring a high return in terms of caloric intake, clothing, shelter, medical care, and life expectancy itself. But eventually, one reaches a point at which further economic growth brings only minimal gains in life expectancy and subjective well-being. There is still a good deal of cross-national variation, but from this point on non-economic aspects of life become increasingly important influences on how long and how well people live. Beyond this point, a rational strategy is to place increasing emphasis on non-economic goals such as freedom of choice, rather than to continue giving top priority to economic growth as if it were the ultimate goal itself.

This strategy actually seems to work. Economic development tends to bring a cultural shift toward rising gender equality, growing tolerance of homosexuality and other outgroups, and democratization—all of which tend to increase a society's levels of happiness and life satisfaction.[4] Both economic development and democratization increase free choice, and the feeling that one has free choice and control over one's life is closely linked with happiness.[5] This seems to be universal: Happiness is linked with one's sense of freedom in all cultural zones.[6] People who live in democracies tend to be happier than those who live in autocracies.[7] This reflects the fact that democracy provides a relatively wide range of free choice, which is conducive to subjective well-being.[8] High levels of existential security also are conducive to growing social tolerance, which is also linked with happiness—not just because tolerant people are happier, but because living in a tolerant society makes life less stressful for everyone.[9]

Figure 8.1 shows the relationship between life satisfaction and per capita GDP in the ninety-five countries containing 90 percent of the

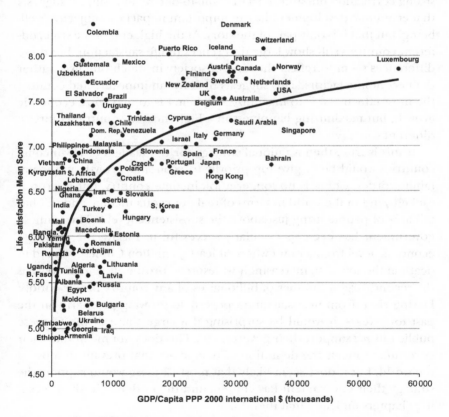

Figure 8.1. Life Satisfaction by Economic Development
Mean Life Satisfaction scores on all available WVS/EVS surveys from given country, 1981-2014, by World Bank 2000 GDP/capita purchasing power parity estimates. Logarithmic curve plotted (r =.60).
Source: Inglehart, 2018: 108.

world's population.[10] To maximize reliability, this figure is based on data from all of the WVS waves carried out from 1981 to 2014. These countries' mean life satisfaction scores are plotted against per capita GDP in 2000. The curve on this figure shows the logarithmic regression line for the relationship between per capita GDP and life satisfaction. If each society's life satisfaction level were wholly determined by its level of economic development, every country would fall on this line. Most countries are fairly close to the line, but the figure shows a curve of diminishing returns. At the low end of the scale, even small economic gains bring relatively large gains in subjective well-being—but the curve then levels off among rich countries, and at the high end of the scale, further economic gains bring little or no further gains in subjective well-being. A country's GDP and its life satisfaction level correlate at $r = .60$, a fairly strong correlation but well short of a one-to-one relationship. It suggests that economic development has an important impact on subjective well-being, but that it is only part of the story. At the high end of the scale, different countries still show large differences in life satisfaction, but these differences seem to reflect the kind of society in which one lives rather than economic factors. This suggests that, for an impoverished country, the most effective way to maximize well-being is to maximize economic growth, but maximizing happiness in a high-income country requires a different strategy.

If this is true, then a rational strategy for the leaders of low-income countries would be to give top priority to economic growth and maintaining order. China is no longer a low-income country, but in 2019 it ranked 72nd in the world in terms of real per capita income and still has millions of people living just above the subsistence level.[11] The Chinese government has been spectacularly successful in raising the country's economic level from a point where at least 30 million Chinese starved to death in the 1960s, to increasingly widespread prosperity. China now has the second largest number of billionaires of any country in the world.[12] Having risen from near-starvation poverty to growing prosperity in the past forty years, it would be surprising if a large share of the Chinese public did *not* support their government. This does not mean that their government meets the definition of democracy that prevails in most of the world, but it does seem likely that most Chinese would support the strategy their government has chosen, and the evidence in the preceding chapters indicates that they do.

China's chances of continued success as a knowledge society are enhanced by the facts that the Chinese show high levels of interpersonal trust and trust in government, as we saw in Chapter 6, and strong trust in science, as Chapter 7 demonstrated—both of which are linked with a deep-rooted Confucian cultural tradition that held out the possibility of social mobility through education. Apart from this, the book's findings suggest that the basic values of the Chinese people are not fundamentally different from those found in the rest of the world—provided that we take into account how recently China has reached its current economic level. Compared with other East Asian societies, China is still at a relatively early stage of a trajectory that moves from giving top priority to economic and physical security, to placing increasing emphasis on personal autonomy and free choice in all aspects of life.

Tang's chapter demonstrates that a majority of the Chinese public views a democratic political system as highly desirable. At this stage, their concept of what constitutes democracy emphasizes order and economic security far more strongly than elections, political rights, and freedom, though these elements are not completely absent. Tang further finds that people with more education have a stronger desire for democracy, and urban residents are less satisfied with the Chinese political system as a whole. Tang argues that the authoritarian aspect of China's "democratic authoritarian political culture" is embodied in the fact that many Chinese favor the idea of having a strong leader. In fact, support for having a strong leader is not unique to China: The percentage of people who endorse having a strong leader who does not have to bother with elections and parliament is even higher in most low-income countries, but relatively weak in most high-income countries (as demonstrated in Table 8.1). Like democracy itself, support for rule by a strong leader varies with a country's level of economic development.

Evolutionary modernization theory implies that as an increasing share of the Chinese public grows up with high levels of economic and physical security, their values and motivations will evolve in a roughly predictable direction, although other historical factors, including the country's leadership, also influence the process. For example, as we saw in Chapter 4, although the Chinese are less postmaterialist than the people of such high-income Western countries as Germany, Sweden, and the United States, and less postmaterialist than their more prosperous Confucian-influenced neighbors in South Korea, Taiwan, and Japan, China as a whole is moving toward more postmaterialist values. Moreover, as Chapter 5 demonstrates, a growing share of the Chinese people are coming to hold such liberal values as acceptance of homosexuality, divorce, and gender equality, although they are not yet as far advanced in this respect as the people of South Korea, Japan, Taiwan, and Hong Kong. However, if China continues to become increasingly industrialized and urbanized, and living standards continue to rise, it seems likely that the Chinese people's political, social, and economic values will come closer to those found in rich neighboring East Asian countries and developed Western countries. Chapter 6 finds that urbanization in China increases interpersonal trust among the population, providing further evidence in support of modernization theory.

Another consistent finding in the preceding chapters is that, as in many other countries, educational level, income, and age are strong predictors of value shifts among the Chinese people. Those with higher education and income tend to have a more participant political culture; similarly, the more educated and higher-income respondents have more liberal values than their less educated and less prosperous compatriots; and less educated people are likelier to hold religious beliefs. Moreover, younger people tend to hold more liberal social values than their elders, and the young are more likely to hold postmaterialist and self-expression values and place more emphasis on ideas than money. Thus, the findings reported in the preceding chapters seem to indicate that China has been moving on a long-term trajectory rather similar to that of other modernizing countries. The fact that Taiwan adopted democratic institutions when it reached an advanced level of development, and the fact that the people of China's most prosperous region, Hong Kong, show a strong desire for autonomy and freedom of expression, suggest that democratic institutions are perfectly compatible with Confucian-influenced societies when they attain high levels of education and prosperity.

What are the implications of our findings for China potentially becoming the number one power in the world? A slightly different question is: To what extent do the values of the Chinese people have the potential to make China an attractive role model for other countries? We do not intend to exaggerate the implications of our findings, however we do believe they have implications for the Chinese government's efforts in building up China's soft power.

Joseph Nye coined the term "soft power" and developed this concept in his article "Soft Power," published in *Foreign Policy* in 1990.[13] Nye recognizes that the traditional conceptualization of power is no longer sufficient for the post–Cold War world, and he believes that we have to add another dimension, the so-called "soft power," to conventional power sources such as military force and economic might. Soft power is about co-optation and persuasion rather than coercion and force. When Nye first introduced the concept of "soft power," he had two goals. The first was an academic one: enriching the concept of power. The second goal was related to the policy issue of responding to the decline of American power.[14] Nye specifies three elements in his definition of soft power: culture, ideology (or political values), and institutions (or foreign policy).[15] The dominance of American power worldwide owes much to its attractive culture, its liberal ideology (emphasizing freedom and democracy), and its partially morally based foreign policy. What makes American soft power strong is the high level of consistency and unification among its liberal popular culture, its liberal ideology at both the official and unofficial levels, and its liberal-oriented foreign policy, all of which reinforce one another.

To replace the United States as the number one power in the world, China has to become a more comprehensive or multidimensional power, including crucial elements of soft power. At the official level, China has yet to articulate and espouse an alternative attractive ideology, different from Western liberalism, to the rest of the world. China is certainly not preaching Marxism abroad. Even though the Chinese Communist Party declares that China is a socialist democracy, it has not actively pushed the Chinese version of democracy overseas. China has financed hundreds of Confucius Institutes around the world. Even though it is suspected that the Chinese government intends to use these organizations to promote China's soft power, most of them are by and large Chinese language schools, not to mention that Confucianism is hardly an ideology suitable for the twenty-first century. In contrast, Chairman Mao was arguably more successful in spreading revolutionary ideology around the world in the 1960s and 1970s, resulting in increased Chinese soft power overseas.

According to Nye, much of a country's soft power is projected by civil society or private actors, not by the government.[16] American soft power influence around the world is due, in large part, to Hollywood movies, American pop culture, and civilian organizations spreading democratic and liberal ideas overseas. Political and social values in China tapped by the WVS are part of popular culture, a source of soft power contributed to by Nye. WVS findings in China over the past two decades show that the majority of Chinese people do support democratic ideals and favor freedom, even though there are also some anti-democratic elements in the Chinese society that are also found in many other countries, including Western democracies. As mentioned earlier in this chapter, majority of Chinese people think it is a bad thing to have a ruler who does not have bother with parliament and elections, and most oppose military rule. About 90 percent of the Chinese public believe it is a good thing to have democratic rule. Finally, the majority of the mainland Chinese people do regard protecting people's civil liberties against oppression and electing leaders in free election as essential elements of democracy.

Moreover, liberal social values are emerging in China, especially among the young and educated population, even though many Chinese people still remain conservative in their attitudes toward issues such as homosexuality, gender equality, and divorce when compared to their neighboring Asian societies. WVS data also confirm that there is a rising trend of postmaterialist values emphasizing individual autonomy, self-expression, and quality of life among Chinese people. Analyses show again that young people tend to hold more of these postmaterialist values than do older people. The trajectory of these value shifts is not different from China's Confucian neighbors and countries in other parts of the world. Since the popular political values and social value trends in China are not unique or much different from those found in other countries, they cannot be projected as an alternative set of values enabling Chinese soft power to challenge Western democratic and liberal values.

According to *The Soft Power 30*, a reputable soft power ranking index based upon Nye's elements of the soft power concept and published by Portland Communications and the USC Center on Public Diplomacy, Chinese soft power was ranked near the bottom of the thirty countries selected for ranking, and the United States was consistently ranked among top five countries between 2015 (the first year the index was published) and 2019 (see Table 8.3). The rank indexing combines both objective and subjective data. Objective measures of a country's international influence include digital, enterprise, education, culture, engagement, and government; subjective data come from international polling. In fact, Chinese soft power ranked below even that of countries such as

Table 8.3. *The Soft Power 30* Ranking of the United States and China (2015–2019)

Year	Ranking of U.S.	Ranking of China
2015	3	30
2016	1	28
2017	3	25
2018	4	27
2019	5	27

Source: The Soft Power 30 (https://softpower30.com/).

Portugal, Poland, and the Czech Republic. However, it is worth noting that China's rankings improved three spots, from 30th to 27th, while the ranking of the United States slipped two spots, from 3rd to 5th, between 2015 and 2019.

Another piece of evidence showing that China still has some way to go to replace the United States as the leading power in the world comes from a Eurasia Group Foundation survey conducted between April 27 and May 16, 2021, spanning nine big countries and covering close to 5,000 adults from four continents.[17] Table 8.4 shows the percentages of people in these nine countries saying having the United States or China as the leading power in the world is better for their country. Vast majorities of people from Japan, Poland, India, Brazil, Germany, Nigeria, Mexico, and Egypt prefer the United States as the leading world power over China. The survey also found that "huge majorities in Nigeria, India, Poland, Brazil and Egypt view U.S. democracy favorably and want their governing system to become more like America's."[18] Furthermore, vast majorities in eight countries (including China and excluding Egypt) believe that U.S. movies, music, and TV programs have had a positive impact upon their country, indicating American soft power still remains strong in the world.[19]

Africa is an important testing ground for the effectiveness of China's soft power promotion overseas. In the past two decades, China has made significant inroads across the African continent economically, politically, and culturally. Research by Maria Repnikova, a specialist in China's soft power expansion in Africa, shows mixed results of the Chinese government's efforts to increase China's soft power presence in Africa. China

Table 8.4. Percentages of People Saying Whether They Prefer the United States or China as the Leading Power in the World

	U.S.	China
Japan	98	2
Poland	92	8
India	88	12
Brazil	87	13
Germany	84	16
Nigeria	82	18
Mexico	69	31
Egypt	65	35
China	7	93

Source: Eurasia Group Foundation.

spends a billion U.S. dollars a year in public diplomacy in Africa, covering areas such as media, education, and culture; China hosts about 80,000 African students (compared to 40,000 in the United States); and China has established sixty-two Confucian Institutes in African countries.[20] China's efforts have certainly produced great influence at the elite level and led to African countries' diplomatic support of Chinese positions on the world stage. However, China's soft power influence has yet to reach the societal level in Africa. The U.S. development model is still more preferable to the Chinese development model among ordinary Africans, although the gap is narrowing. Even though Africans who have participated in training trips organized by the Chinese government are very impressed with China's economic development, they still have doubt about the applicability of the Chinese political system in the African context.

Liberal democracy emerged relatively recently—not because people were not intelligent enough to adopt it earlier, but because it is unlikely to survive in a subsistence-level society populated mainly by illiterate peasants. Liberal democracy evolved along with industrialization, urbanization, mass literacy, and growing prosperity, and it spread because it is a relatively good way to govern modern societies. One of its key advantages is that it is based on merit recruitment for limited terms. The fact that Deng Xiaoping was able to adapt this component of democracy to the Chinese setting played a key role in China's success under his guidance, and his economic reforms were implemented by competent leaders who shared power for limited terms. China's economic performance over the last forty years has been so impressive that, especially for leaders of low-income countries, it presents a credible alternative to the Western economic development model. However, whether and how China can develop and project its soft power based on an alternative set of ideological, political, and social values that replace Western democratic and liberal values remains to be seen. The success of that endeavor determines, in large part, whether China will replace the United States as the number one power in the world in the years to come.

Notes

1. Freedom House, *Freedom in the World: A Leaderless Struggle for Democracy*, (Washington, DC: Freedom House, 2020),16.

2. V-Dem Institute, *Democracy Facing Global Challenges: V-Dem Annual Democracy Report 2019* (Gothenburg, Sweden, 2019), 7–9.

3. Seymour M. Lipset, "Some Social Requisites of Democracy: Economic Development and Political Legitimacy," *The American Political Science Review* 53, no. 1 (1959): 69–105; Ronald Inglehart and Christian Welzel, *Modernization, Cultural Change, and Democracy: The Human Development Sequence* (New York: Cambridge University Press, 2005).

4. Ronald Inglehart, *Cultural Evolution: People's Motivations Are Changing, and Reshaping the World* (Cambridge: Cambridge University Press, 2018), 143–46.

5. Wendy Johnson and Robert F. Krueger, "How Money Buys Happiness: Genetic and Environmental Processes Linking Finances and Life Satisfaction," *Journal of Personality and Social Psychology* 90, no. 4 (2006): 680–91.

6. Inglehart and Welzel, *Modernization, Cultural Change, and Democracy,* 140; Amartya Sen, *Development as Freedom* (New York: Anchor Books, 2001).

7. Ronald Inglehart, *Culture Shift in Advanced Industrial Society* (Princeton: Princeton University Press, 1990); Robert J. Barro, "Determinants of Democracy," *Journal of Political Economy* 107, no. S6 (1999): 158–83; Bruno S. Frey and Alois Stutzer, "Happiness Prospers in Democracy," *Journal of Happiness Studies* 1, no. 1 (2000): 79–102; Ronald Inglehart and Hans-Dieter Klingemann, "Genes, Culture, Democracy, and Happiness," in *Culture and Subjective Well-Being,* ed. Ed Diener and Eunkook M. Suh (Cambridge: MIT Press, 2003), 165–83.

8. Max Haller and Markus Hadler, "Happiness as an Expression of Freedom and Self-Determination: A Comparative Multilevel Analysis," in *Challenges for Quality of Life in the Contemporary World,* ed. Wolfgang Glatzer, Susanne Von Below, and Matthias Stoffregen (Dordrecht: Kluwer Academic Publishers, 2004), 207–31; Inglehart and Welzel, *Modernization, Cultural Change, and Democracy*; Jan Ott, "Did the Market Depress Happiness in the US?" *Journal of Happiness Studies* 2, no. 4 (2001): 433–43; Ruut Veenhoven, "Freedom and Happiness: A Comparative Study in Forty-Four Nations in the Early 1990s," in *Culture and Subjective Well-Being,* ed. Ed Diener and Eunkook M. Suh (Cambridge: MIT Press, 2003), 257–88; Heinz Welsch, "Freedom and Rationality as Predictors of Cross-National Happiness Patterns: The Role of Income as a Mediating Value," *Journal of Happiness Studies* 4, no. 3 (2003): 295–321.

9. Inglehart and Welzel, *Modernization, Cultural Change, and Democracy*; Peggy Schyns, "Crossnational Differences in Happiness: Economic and Cultural Factors Explored," *Social Indicators Research* 43 (1998): 3–26.

10. Life satisfaction was assessed by asking respondents how satisfied they were with their lives as a whole, using a scale ranging from 1 (not at all satisfied) to 10 (very satisfied). The economic data are from the World Bank.

11. *Statistical Times,* "Comparing United States and China by Economy," May 15, 2021, http://statisticstimes.com/economy/united-states-vs-china-economy.php#:~:text=Per%20capita%20income%20of%20United,China%20comes%20at%2072th%20rank.

12. Jie Zhang, "China Has Second-Most Billionaires in the World," *China Daily,* May 10, 2019, https://www.chinadaily.com.cn/a/201905/10/WS5cd513b3a310484226obafd4.html.

13. Joseph S. Nye, Jr., "Soft Power," *Foreign Policy* 80 (1990): 153–71.

14. See Joseph S. Nye, Jr., "Soft Power: The Evolution of a Concept," *Journal of Political Power* 14, no. 1 (2021): 196–208.

15. Nye, "Soft Power: The Evolution of a Concept,"
16. Nye, "Soft Power."
17. Dave Lawler, "Countries Prefer U.S. to China as Leading Superpower, Poll Finds," *Axios*, June 16, 2022, https://www.axios.com/2022/06/16/countries-prefer-us-china-superpower-poll.
18. Lawler, "Countries Prefer U.S. to China."
19. Lawler, "Countries Prefer U.S. to China."
20. See Maria Repnikova's presentation, "China's Soft Power Projection in Africa," at Woodrow Wilson Center on May 12, 2021, https://www.wilsoncenter.org/event/chinas-soft-power-projection-africa.

Bibliography

Barro, Robert J. "Determinants of Democracy." *Journal of Political Economy* 107, no. S6 (December 1999): 158–83.
Freedom House. *Freedom in the World: A Leaderless Struggle for Democracy*. Washington, DC: Freedom House, 2019.
Frey, Bruno S., and Alois Stutzer (2000). "Happiness Prospers in Democracy." *Journal of Happiness Studies* 1, no. 1 (2000): 79–102.
Haller, Max, and Markus Hadler. "Happiness as an Expression of Freedom and Self-Determination: A Comparative Multilevel Analysis." In *Challenges for Quality of Life in the Contemporary World*, edited by Wolfgang Glatzer, Susanne Von Below, and Matthias Stoffregen, 207–31. Dordrecht, The Netherlands: Kluwer Academic Publishers, 2004.
Inglehart, Ronald. *Cultural Evolution: People's Motivations Are Changing, and Reshaping the World*. Cambridge: Cambridge University Press, 2018.
Inglehart, Ronald. *Culture Shift in Advanced Industrial Society*. Princeton: Princeton University Press, 1990.
Inglehart, Ronald, and Christian Welzel. *Modernization, Cultural Change, and Democracy: The Human Development Sequence*. New York: Cambridge University Press, 2005.
Inglehart, Ronald, and Hans-Dieter Klingemann. "Genes, Culture, Democracy, and Happiness." In *Culture and Subjective Well-Being*, edited by Ed Diener and Eunkook M. Suh, 165–83. Cambridge: MIT Press, 2003.
Johnson, Wendy, and Robert F Krueger. "How Money Buys Happiness: Genetic and Environmental Processes Linking Finances and Life Satisfaction." *Journal of Personality and Social Psychology* 90, no. 4 (2006): 680–91.
Lipset, Seymour M. "Some Social Requisites of Democracy: Economic Development and Political Legitimacy." *The American Political Science Review* 53, no. 1 (1959): 69–105.
Nye, Joseph S. Jr. "Soft Power." *Foreign Policy* 80 (1990): 153–71.
Nye, Joseph S. Jr. "Soft Power: The Evolution of a Concept." *Journal of Political Power* 14, no. 1 (2021): 196–208.
Ott, Jan. "Did the Market Depress Happiness in the US?" *Journal of Happiness Studies* 2, no. 4 (2001): 433–43.

Repnikova, Maria. "China's Soft Power Projection in Africa." Presentation at Woodrow Wilson Center, May 12, 2021. https://www.wilsoncenter.org/event/chinas-soft-power-projection-africa.

Schyns, Peggy. "Crossnational Differences in Happiness: Economic and Cultural Factors Explored." *Social Indicators Research* 43 (1998): 3–26.

Sen, Amartya. *Development as Freedom.* New York: Anchor Books, 2001.

Statistical Times. "Comparing United States and China by Economy." May 15, 2021, http://statisticstimes.com/economy/united-states-vs-china-economy.php#:~:text=Per%20capita%20income%20of%20United,China%20comes%20at%2072th%20rank.

V-Dem Institute. *Democracy Facing Global Challenges: V-Dem Annual Democracy Report 2019.* Gothenburg, Sweden, 2019.

Veenhoven, Ruut. "Freedom and Happiness: A Comparative Study in Forty-Four Nations in the Early 1990s." In *Culture and Subjective Well-Being*, edited by Ed Diener and Eunkook M. Suh, 257–88. Cambridge: MIT Press, 2003.

Welsch, Heinz. "Freedom and Rationality as Predictors of Cross-National Happiness Patterns: The Role of Income as a Mediating Value." *Journal of Happiness Studies* 4, no. 3 (February 2003): 295–321.

Zhang, Jie. "China Has Second-Most Billionaires in the World." *China Daily*, May 10, 2019, https://www.chinadaily.com.cn/a/201905/10/WS5cd513b3a3104842260bafd4.html.

Contributors

Eduardo Araral is Associate Professor and Co-Director of the Institute for Water Policy at Lee Kuan Yew School of Public Policy, National University of Singapore. His articles have been published in *World Development, Environmental Science and Policy, Policy Sciences,* and *Policy and Society,* among other journals.

Lingnan He is a doctoral student in the Department of Political Science at the University of Chicago.

Biao Huang is Assistant Professor at the School of Public Affairs, Zhejiang University. His articles have been published in *Policy & Politics, Public Administration Review, Public Performance & Management Review,* and *Journal of Chinese Political Science.*

Ronald F. Inglehart (1934–2021) was the Amy and Alan Loewenstein Professor of Democracy, Democratization and Human Rights, and Research Professor at the Institute for Social Research at the University of Michigan. He also was the founding director of the Ronald F. Inglehart Laboratory for Comparative Social Research at the Higher School of Economics in St. Petersburg, Russia. He helped to found the Euro-Barometer surveys, and was the founding president and directed the World Values Survey (WVS). In addition to his groundbreaking mono-graph *The Silent Revolution: Changing Values and Political Styles among Western Publics* in 1977 and his last books in 2018 (*Cultural Evolution: Peoples' Motivations are Changing, and Transforming the World*) and 2021 (*Religion's Sudden Decline: What's Causing it, and What Comes Next?*), he authored and co-authored twelve other books and published over 400 peer-reviewed articles. His books have been translated into many languages including Chinese, and his theories have been analyzed and studied in most global and regional contexts.

John James Kennedy is Professor of Political Science at the University of Kansas, and he has also been the Director of the Center for East Asian Studies since 2018. He has published articles in *The China Quarterly*, *Journal of Contemporary China*, *Asian Survey*, the *Journal of Chinese Political Science*, the *Journal of Peasant Studies*, *Asian Politics and Policy*, *Journal of Diplomacy and International Relations*, and *Political Studies*.

Wenfang Tang is Dean and Presidential Chair Professor of School of Humanities and Social Science at the Chinese University of Hong Kong, Shenzhen. His current research focuses on political culture, comparative public opinion, and mass politics.

Alfred M. Wu is Assistant Dean (Research) and Associate Professor in Lee Kuan Yew School of Public Policy at National University of Singapore. He is the author of *Governing Civil Service Pay in China* (Nordic Institute of Asian Studies, 2014). His articles have been published in *International Tax and Public Finance*, *Social Policy & Administration*, *Ageing and Society*, *Journal of Contemporary China*, and *China: An International Journal*, among others.

Yu Yan is Assistant Professor in the School of Government at Beijing Normal University. He received his doctoral degree in political science from University of Tennessee (Knoxville) and conducted his postdoctoral research at Tsinghua University in Beijing. His research covers political participation, government responsiveness, and digital governance in China. He has published in *China: An International Journal* and other English and Chinese journals.

Dali L. Yang is the William C. Reavis Professor of Political Science at the University of Chicago. He is the author of *Remaking the Chinese Leviathan: Market Transition and the Politics of Governance in China* (Stanford, 2004); *Beyond Beijing: Liberalization and the Regions in China* (Routledge, 1997); and *Calamity and Reform in China: State, Rural Society, and Institutional Change since the Great Leap Famine* (Stanford, 1996). He is editor of *Discontented Miracle: Growth, Conflict, and Institutional Adaptations in China* (World Scientific, 2007) and co-editor and a contributor to *Holding China Together: Diversity and National Integration in Post-Deng China* (Cambridge, 2004).

Yang Zhong is Professor of Political Science at University of Tennessee, Knoxville. He is the author of *Political Culture and Participation in Urban China* (Palgrave Macmillan, 2017), *Political Culture and Participation in Rural China* (Routledge, 2012), and *Local Government and Politics in China: Challenges from Below* (M. E. Sharpe, 2003). His articles have appeared in journals including *The Journal of Politics, Political Research Quarterly,* and *Comparative Political Studies.*

Index

same-sex relationships, tolerance/
acceptance of, 114, 121, 124
SARS pandemic, handling of by
Confucian-influenced societies
of, 12–13
science: attitudes toward (in China),
184–85, 184*t*, 185*t*, 186*t*, 187*t*, 201;
attitudes toward, in comparative
perspective, 185–87; in contemporary
China, 175–77; crosstabulation
between belief in religion and
attitude toward science and religion
conflict, 185*t*; relationship of with
religion, 171–72
Science Daily, on Chinese People
lacking "science spirit," 190
self-expression, as postmaterialist
value, 84, 86, 204
Shi, Tianjian, 54
Singapore: average GNI per capita
and growth rate (1995–2018),
97*t*; distribution of materialist
and postmaterialist values in, 99*t*;
gross national income per capita
in, 97*f*, 98; postmaterialism across
generations in, 100*t*
social acceptance/social tolerance, as
emancipative value, 113
social media, rise of, 103–4
social tolerance: influence of
education and age on tolerance
of homosexuality in, 134–35, 135*f*;
of persons with AIDS, 132–33,
134; would NOT like to have as
neighbors, 133*t*; would not like to
have homosexual neighbors, 132*t*;
would not like to have neighbors
with different religion, 132*t*; WVS
2018 and tolerance: the people
respondents would not want for a
neighbor, 130–31, 131*t*
socioeconomic variables, summary
statistics for, 56*t*
soft power: origin of term, 22;
rankings on, 204–5, 205*t*; use of
term, 202–3
"Soft Power" (*Foreign Policy*), 202

The Soft Power 30, 204, 204*t*
South Korea: acceptance of divorce
in, 122, 123*t*, 126*t*; acceptance
of homosexuality in, 124*t*, 127*t*;
average GNI per capita and
growth rate (1995–2018), 97, 97*t*;
distribution of materialist and
postmaterialist values in, 99*t*; gross
national income per capita in, 98;
online participation in, 70*f*; other
types of political participation
in, 70*f*; political interest in, 69*f*;
postmaterialism across generations
in, 100*t*; respect for authority
in, 120, 120*t*, 121*t*; support for
democracy in, 196*t*; on what
democracy does, 197*t*
Southwest University of Finance and
Economics (China), on China's
Gini coefficient, 103
strong leader, support for having a
strong leader who does not have
to bother with parliament and
elections, 44*f*
Supreme People's Court, on divorces
in China, 121
survival vs. self-expression values, on
global cultural map, 14*f*, 15
Sweden: average GNI per capita
and growth rate (1995–2018), 97,
97*t*; distribution of materialist
and postmaterialist values in, 101*f*;
gross national income per capita
in, 98, 98*f*; postmaterialism across
generations in, 101*f*

Taiwan: acceptance of divorce in,
122, 123*t*, 125–26, 126*t*; acceptance
of homosexuality in, 124*t*, 125–26,
127*t*; attitudes toward science
and technology, 185–87, 186*t*,
187*t*; average GNI per capita and
growth rate (1995–2018), 97*t*;
distribution of materialist and
postmaterialist values in, 99*t*;
general interpersonal trust in,
155*f*; gross national income per